Dr. Ka

M000316448

WRONGLY BLAMED

The real facts behind 9/11
and the London bombings

KNOWLEDGE HOUSE PUBLISHERS
Buffalo Grove, Illinois

For information contact:
Knowledge House Publishers
P.O. Box 855
Buffalo Grove, IL 60089.

Printed in the United States of America

First Edition

ISBN 1-931078-20-3

To order this or additional Knowledge House books call: 1-866-618-2503

For book information visit:
www.knowledgehousepublishers.com

Table of Contents

Dedication

For those who seek the truth

Introduction

Islam, or as spelled here *Islaam*, where the second syllable is pronounced with the same vowel sound as the word lamb, has much to offer the human race. Rather than a religion it is a system of life. This system is based upon divine revelation. This revelation was received in the seventh century by the Prophet Muhammad. Islaam represents a wealth of knowledge. It is based upon generosity and love. Its grand principles soothe human hearts. What's more, this system provides guidance directly for human benefit. Furthermore, it has modern applications.

This is not the Arabs' religion. The Arabs originally worshiped idols if anything. This is the religion of God sent to this world. The pagan Arabs were the original recipients. However, now they form a minority. It was brought to them by one of their own, the Prophet Muhammad. This man was part of a chain of Middle Eastern prophets which included Abraham, Jacob, Moses, and Jesus among others. All practiced the same religion: submission of the entire self to the will of God, literally Islaam. This is because Islaam means "to submit." A Muslim is merely a person who gives the whole self to God. He does so in peaceful submission. Islaam also means security as well as peace.

The Qur'an is the essence of this faith. Like the original contents of the Bible this is divine revelation. It is a vast text with much-needed guidance for the human soul. Then, there is the rich history, as well as sayings, of the Prophet, a great and merciful guide. This man left humanity with guidance and wisdom—a gracious legacy, which is truly beneficial.

This must be so. People are turning to Islaam in droves. They are interested in its benefits. There are elements within this system which are highly attractive and which people are unable to find elsewhere. People are attracted to it because it is based upon obvious truth. This is the truth of unaltered divine revelation. The fact that it is unaltered and purely from almighty God gives people the confidence to commit to it.

Islaam is highly sophisticated. It has a rich history. This includes a phenomenal contribution: the creation of the modern sciences. Despite all its challenges and any negativity directed against it Islaam remains brilliantly divine. Its purpose is to guide humans. This will be evident to anyone who investigates it, because it is obvious that no human created it. The fact is any careful assessment of the contents of the Qur'an leads to one conclusion: that it is obviously from God.

Deep probing reveals that it is, in fact, the ultimate truth. There is nothing that can compare to it. This is a mercy from God through the sophisticated Qur'an and the vital teachings of its Prophet. This is the intact Islaam, which deeply impacts people and which brings them to a deeper sense of purpose.

The basis is the giving of all authority to almighty God. This is because He is the exclusive Lord. This is why it is called Islaam, because it truly means to submit. This submission is of the heart and soul to God. Abraham, Moses, Jesus, and Muhammad were all of this nature.

People serve other powers besides God. These powers include the lust for wealth, self-importance, family pride, and even power itself. This is the opposite of Islaam. In this respect it is simple. Only God is to be served. Humans and other powers cannot be the masters. No man can have God-like powers, nor should any other power or entity be served. Humans are incapable of creating even a being. For instance no one can create even a single living cell let alone an entire creature. Rather, this earth and its contents have been created for humans. This is why all submission is to Him. The fact is this is the only sensible approach to take. This submission is the basis of this religion.

In the Qur'an God warns people not to serve other masters besides Him. He reminds them that He alone is all-powerful, the source of all might, the true and only God. In fact, from the Qur'anic point of view this giving of power to others besides God, making them as if divine, is unforgivable.

The worship of God creates peace. It does so within human hearts. It also creates peace in society. Islaam is derived from the word *salima,* which means according to Penrose in *Dictionary and Glossary of the Koran* to be "safe and sound." This is the opposite of the West's portrayal.

The Qur'an urges people of all faiths to gather together in peace: for the worship of the one and only God. It makes it clear that there is only One universal God: the God of all peoples. Regardless of denomination people are urged to join in the worship of this mighty being—to eliminate all forms of tyranny, oppression, and barbarism. The Qur'an calls for all people to create this peace. Humans, it says, must obey the rules of decency by bowing in unison to their Lord in worship. What's more, a person need not change his religion to do so, although Islaam is the most sophisticated form of the divine systems. The consequences of this submission are monumental. It is success both in this life and the next.

The media says Islaam is the enemy

The media is controlled by big business. Government is also influenced directly by business interests. In Western media Islaam is portrayed negatively, as if it supports terrorism. Yet, the inflicting of terror is the opposite of its meaning. This negative emphasis is constant. There have even been claims that most Muslims 'secretly' support terror, as if Westerners must always be on guard against them.

In contrast, the very purpose of Islaam is to prevent terror. Thus, there is no justification in this religion for terrorizing anyone. Even bullying a person is prohibited. Yet, there is a simple explanation for this dichotomy. There are major business interests which are threatened by it. Examples include the alcohol industry, the pornography industry, the illicit drug trade, the oil cartel, and the armaments industry.

Lobbyists from these industries actively spread disinformation about Islaam. They attack it and disseminate vast lies regarding it. Such individuals/organizations also actively promote agendas which target Muslims, including the creation of wars against Muslim countries. The fact is certain of these industries vastly profit from such wars, rather, their very existence is dependent upon them.

Consider the political efforts of the CEO of General Electric, Jack Welch. With its vast military division, this company enormously profits from war. To keep the company viable a war agenda was promoted. The fact is this company makes every effort to continue the war agenda in order to advance profits. Welch specifically harassed the authorities at NBC and Fox News to proclaim George Bush as President.

This was even before the latter was legally confirmed. This GE mass media connection also explains the unrelenting emphasis on supposed Islaamic terror. It was and is strictly to perpetuate the war agenda. Welch was well aware that Bush would immediately wage war, which, of course, benefits GE immensely. This is due to billions of dollars in government contracts. What's more, there were no global enemies, and, thus, an enemy had to be created. That enemy, while fabricated, is Islaam. This dependence upon war was a great incentive for a frightening proposition: a self-imposed terror act. This, it was known, would neutralize any internal opposition to war and would, in fact, create the desired indignation. To do so a massive strike was necessary: thus, the destruction of the World Trade Center. Now, America had a perceived enemy. Now, it could justify the attack.

People speak incessantly about the Muslim desire for jihad (pronounced *jihaad*). The fact is it is the superpowers who desire wars to feed this war-mongering industry. If the Muslims wage a jihaad, it is to defend themselves from this vicious attack. People will feel hatred at this observation and even act threateningly. Yet, the question is can anyone disprove it?

The alcohol industry promotes the war agenda. A good example is the Coors Beer group. This group funds the Free Congress Foundation, an organization which unabashedly promotes racism. This group has actively opposed integration and calls for a virtually exclusive Anglo-Saxon, that is "Judeo-Christian," society. It is a Masonic order that has as its goal the driving out from the United States of all other peoples. Yet, the origin of Americans was never Anglo-Saxon. Rather, the original inhabitants were of unique races, that is the Native Americans, and they were not Christians.

The hate campaign advanced by Coors is based upon a financial focus. One of its members, Robert Spencer, has written numerous books that aggressively target Islaam. Funded by the Coors Group he writes, as well as speaks, vast falsehoods. What's more, he does so strictly for personal gain. As proven by the Foundation's charter its purpose is to drive people of other religions and cultures from the West. Thus, his message is entirely racist. It is also aimed at creating international warfare. For race supremacy he calls for violent action to be taken against people of non-Judeo-Christian heritage, a true goal of the Free Congress Foundation.

The hate campaign waged by Coors is based upon money. Islaam prohibits the consumption of alcohol. Coors finds this threatening, so it attacks this faith. War is also good for this company, since it drives the sales of its goods. The fact is Coors will commit any conceivable deed to gain market control. Thus, money funneled from Coors directly funds espionage efforts to topple foreign governments, for instance, in the Middle East and Central America. For Coors and similar corporations Muslims, as well as traditional ethnic populations, are a poor source of income. Thus, these corporations fear the growth of Islaam and do all that they can to attack it.

The media tells the opposite: rather than corrupt 'Western' politics, Islaam, it says, is the issue. After all, 9/11, Madrid, Bali, the London bombings, as well as the more recent Jordanian bombings, were all supposedly Islaamic attacks.

Yet, consider how this image is created. Terror events occur. Immediately, the Muslims are accused of it. All the news wires carry the supposed evidence, statements by organizations such as the Secret Organization of Al-Qaeda in Europe, 'al-Qaeda,' Abu Hafs Brigade, and Islaamic Jihaad. These are broadcast as if true. Yet, incredibly, there is not even a single person who claims to be a member of any such group. The only known members are those recruited by Western espionage agencies. What's more, in the media the only identified members who are actual Muslims are deceased, or forced into admission under torture. Without even the slightest proof of the existence of such organizations all is broadcasted as truth. Yet, this arises from a highly controlled media. The fact is this media is controlled largely by Jews. So, the major goal of these media is the support of the Israeli entity. What's more, this is done through "any means necessary." This includes deceit. To implicate the Muslims as the global terrorists keeps the pressure off the Israelis. This allows the latter to proceed aggressively with their violent agenda. Since the recent disasters—9/11 and the London bombings—the Israelis have freely pursued a vast criminal agenda, an apartheid, along with countless murders. Yet, due to the distraction resulting from these terror acts there has been no global scrutiny of their crimes.

Yet, incredibly, regarding these supposed Islaamic terror groups all the aforementioned 'organizations' are largely creations of the Israelis, a fact which will be clearly demonstrated throughout this book. Thus, the Israelis are the global experts in disinformation as well as terror.

After 9/11 the Muslims were immediately blamed. Americans are largely trusting people. If the authorities say it is so, they believe it. "Why would the government lie to us?" people say "surely, government officials would only speak the truth." Yet, how incredible: in a matter of hours ideas are planted in people's minds, and without even the slightest scrutiny it is accepted as truth. With constant repetition on the news and in newspapers this is a type of brainwashing.

To a degree this is understandable. Images are repeatedly shown and insinuations constantly made that the culprits are supposedly 'Arabs' or Muslims. In other words, they are dark-skinned. In contrast, no Anglo-Saxons are portrayed as international terrorists. In any major terror act, promptly, Muslims are generally accused. Yet, how could anyone know so quickly? How can anyone know among such chaos the exact facts, all within a few hours? The fact is this makes no sense.

Among other issues the weapons of mass destruction in Iraq was a lie. This led the American people into a brutal war. So, why should anyone believe anything else said by the government? Regarding 9/11 and the London bombings the official stories are suspect. That in both instances government exercises occurred virtually simultaneously is proof of a plot. There is no possibility that this is a coincidence. These exercises were being conducted at the same places as the bombings. If the exercises would have occurred in another part of the city or on a different day, perhaps a coincidence is plausible, but not in these cases.

The odds for such exercises to occur simultaneously with the actual events are billions to one. This reveals a dire issue: there was foreknowledge. Rather, it tells of a wicked plot. In case anything went awry the government could readily use the exercises as a cover. Yet, no one suspected this. The events moved too quickly. A few isolated individuals supposedly randomly attacked the public. Then, abruptly there are international wars? The fact is these terror attacks directly bolstered the war agenda. As a result, billions of dollars were poured into specific companies. These are companies whose finances are dependent upon war and which founder financially during times of peace.

The timing of the terror acts was ideal for a financially crippled so-called defense industry. For instance, prior to the war Boeing was on the verge of bankruptcy. Now, it is financially revived. The terror acts were also ideal to neutralize any public opposition to the war. Without these acts the opposition would have been massive. Thus, the perpetrators acted maliciously. They knew that the public was resistant to war, so they neutralized this through premeditated terror acts blamed on a fabricated enemy. Government involvement in both 9/11 and the London bombings is obvious. This is confirmed by the government exercises occurring just prior to or on the day of the events. The likelihood that in both instances terror acts would occur simultaneously with government exercises is nil. The plot is supported by the timing. The latter favors military involvement. This incriminates the military industry. This industry is in constant need of creating wars to support it. A major terror attack would vastly benefit it.

These military powers can only create a market for their wares through chicanery. Only the military-related businesses profited from this war. Thus, much evidence points to the primary role of these powers in such fabrications, including the well-planned 9/11 and London bombing acts. In contrast, for these an Islaamic role is non-existent. The fact is rather than being the beneficiaries all that the Muslims have experienced is loss. Thus, it makes sense that there are other forces behind these acts, which directly benefit from their perpetration. What follows is a scientific analysis of the possibilities.

It will be shown that, incredibly, the official stories are based upon lies. It will also be demonstrated that they are impossible to confirm by independent inquiry. It is necessary to clarify the evidence, so people can have an unadulterated view. This is so the truth can be revealed in order to determine the true culprits of these atrocities.

Remember, history repeats itself. The Reichstag and Gulf of Tonkin, which were used to justify war, were fabricated. So was 9/11.

CHAPTER 1
Official Conspiracy

The London and World Trade Center bombings were government operations. In other words, rather than foreign or Islaamic attacks these were self-attacks by the governments. This is made obvious by a careful analysis of the facts. Another possibility is attacks by a secret or supposedly allied government. Regardless, the attacks were plotted and perpetrated by non-Muslims, who needed a rallying point for their corrupt policies. This backing could only be achieved through violence.

Essentially, without incident Muslims have lived as citizens in the West. What's more, they have done so for hundreds of years. Muslims were blamed for these attacks, which justifies, then, their slaughter. It justifies invasions of their lands. This is precisely the opposite of what the Muslims strive to achieve.

Even before 9/11 the U.S. had planned invasions of several Muslim countries. Covert operations in Iraq and Afghanistan were already in place. To attack such countries overtly the government needed a provocation. Thus, the terror attacks could hardly be a coincidence. 9/11 led to immediate warfare, which is precisely the goal of Western powers.

It is a proven fact that prior to these attacks war had already been initiated by the West, with U.S. and British special forces teams being operational in Afghanistan. So, rather than the catalyst 9/11 was the disguise for a deliberate war plot. In London prior to the bombings immense pressure was placed by the authorities for a British withdrawal from Iraq. Then, suddenly, there occurred the tube and bus bombings: the pressure was eased.

Yet, despite obvious plotting by the American government the fact is the Israelis are also directly involved. At a minimum the Israeli rulers knew about it and took numerous precautions. What's more, fake terror acts are an Israeli specialty. In fact, according to Christopher Sykes in his book *Crossroads to Israel* rather than the Muslims, who have no such history, public terror was invented instead by the Israelis. To gain their political goals, notes Sykes, Zionists are dependent upon terror. These terror acts are used as a distraction. Even though the Israelis are the sources, they effectively blame others. The fabricated terror they commit is an assault on peoples' intelligence. Thus, people are being purposely misled about the real source of these crimes.

The Israelis are constantly doing this. Their attempts to create fabricated "al-Qaeda cells" demonstrates the degree of aggression. This was even done in Palestine. It began with statements by the former Israeli 'Head of State,' Ariel Sharon, who according to the BBC said that al-Qaeda militants were using the occupied territories as a staging ground and that "We know that they are there. We know that they are in Lebanon, working closely with Hezbollah (note the use of absolutes, like 'we know')." Conveniently, Hezbollah is Sharon's adversary, which defeated his forces in South Lebanon after a prolonged war.

Michele Steinberg and Hussein Askary write in their intelligence article *Mossad Exposed in Phony 'Palestinian Al-Qaeda Caper* that the United States government has proof that Israel creates al-Qaeda cells. Evidence of Israeli fabrications surfaced in December 2002, when Palestinian police held a press conference in the Gaza Strip to reveal the details. These revelations discounted the lies told by Sharon to justify murderous attacks on Palestinian towns. Through indisputable evidence plus captured Israeli agents the Palestinians have proven that the al-Qaeda mentioned by Sharon was precisely his creation.

The authors note that the Israelis had previously made dubious claims regarding a terrorist attack in Kenya in which several Israelis died, attributing it to al-Qaeda. "Sharon's…ministers went on an immediate propaganda rampage announcing worldwide revenge (even though) *authorities in Kenya denied the al-Qaeda link*."

Incredibly, note the authors, Foreign Minister Binyamin Netanyahu called the Kenya attacks a "golden opportunity," that is to conjoin the American so-called fight against terror with the 'war' against the Palestinians. Yet, this was a mere diversion. In fact, this is a deliberate attempt to confuse people. This is so that any atrocities committed by the Israelis are viewed as "justifiable." It is as if to say, "We are just responding to terror—thus, any invasion or killing we do is justified. They are merely terrorists."

They have created this false picture, and the majority of people accept it. What's more, this is precisely what the Israelis did. They brutally attacked entire populations, killing and maiming countless thousands of civilians, while destroying peoples' homes and property. They were "responding only to terror," they claimed, but this was mere lies. Thus, just as the Zionists planned through this strategy there was no world outcry. In other words, in advance they neutralized any opposition.

The Israeli presence in East Africa is well known. Kenya and Uganda are major destinations for Israeli tourists. Thus, there is an enormous presence in these countries of Israeli agents. It would be difficult for Islaamic fighters to operate readily in these regions. Thus, it is unlikely that any plot for a terror event would occur without the Israelis' foreknowledge. This means that rather than the Muslims it is the Zionists who are the likely culprits of this attack. It was easy for them to plant the evidence and, then, alert the media—"a golden opportunity"—capitalizing on the deaths of the innocent: how vile. What's more, there is no strategic purpose for Palestinians to attack and kill Jews vacationing in Kenya.

Here is what occurred: An attack on a hotel in Mombassa led to the deaths of three Israelis. Shortly thereafter, there was a "failed" rocket attack against an Israeli charter jet leaving the Mombassa airport. People may recall the news reports, complete with police showing the abandoned rocket launcher. This was conveniently left behind, with no attempt to disguise it. There was no evidence of the identity of the bombers, but, immediately, and without evidence Palestinians and other Muslims were blamed.

In early December 2002 Sharon and his minions launched a propaganda campaign on the basis of that 'aggression.' Then, as mentioned previously on December 7 Reuters reported the uncovering of a Zionist espionage cell: an attempt to 'synthesize' an al-Qaeda of Palestine. According to the head of Palestinian security, Colonel Rashid Abu Shbak, on December 6th his forces "identified a number of Palestinian collaborators who had been ordered by Israeli security agencies to work in the Gaza Strip *under the name of al-Qaeda*." This was done to justify massive attacks against the Palestinians planned by the—as coined by British scholars—"Zionist terrorists." The Palestinians provided absolute proof of the Israeli connection in the form of cell phone transmissions and messages, all of which came from Israel. The potential recruits—actual Palestinians—were given weapons and cash directly by the Israelis, who were under disguise as Muslims. However, most of the weapons were defective. The money was transferred directly from Jerusalem and Israel. This is absolute evidence of the Israeli source for this terror.

The Zionists planned this entire process. This was to make it appear that the Palestinians are anti-Western and that they are terrorists. It is also to create the impression that Palestinians harbor anti-American terrorists. This is to justify invasions, in fact, atrocities. Yet, they created these images purely through deceit. Apparently, Muslims do not cause sufficient terror to foster the Western agenda. Western powers must murder and terrorize people on their own behalf, while blaming it on Muslims in order to gain the desired result.

This is how it developed. Through advertisements Israelis recruited Muslims on the basis of the latter "doing their Islaamic duty" and fighting a "holy war." They did not look for particularly religious Muslims—any dark-skinned/Arab-appearing persons would do. Often, they would prey on the poor, even drug addicts, that is the ignorant. For instance, they recruited a Palestinian named 'Ibrahim' by asking him to send his photo and a mobile phone number to a specific Jerusalem address, as found, apparently, in a magazine. A man bearing an Arabic name then contacted him. After developing a relationship with the Palestinian and telling him how much he resembled his son, who, he said, had been killed, the Arabic-appearing Israeli spy, whose name appeared Islaamic, then sent $2,000, a virtual fortune in Gaza. Then, he instructed the man to become a more devout Muslim.

After a five-month "indoctrination campaign" the undercover Israeli agent told the Palestinian, essentially, "You are a good candidate to work for us in the company of Osama bin Laden and the al-Qaeda group." He added, 'We are the internal al-Qaeda of Israel, and we can carry out significant terrorist acts here.' Suspicious, the Palestinian approached the Gaza authorities, and the espionage cell was uncovered.

Wisely, the authorities told him to maintain the communication, when the Israeli told him the true purpose: they wanted him to take credit, *directly from Gaza*, for bombing attacks inside Israel. In other words, they wanted Ibrahim to confirm the existence of a definite anti-Western al-Qaeda group within Palestine. The Israeli, who said his name was Youssef, the Arabic word for Joseph, a common Jewish name, emphasized that his group was fully capable of carrying out bombing operations inside Israel, but that "*the al-Qaeda group of Gaza should claim responsibility* (italics mine)." In other words, as soon as the Palestinian heard about the attacks described to him as "mega military operations," he was to take all the credit, being sure to keep the Israeli connection disguised.

Credit was to be claimed exclusively on behalf of this new group: the al-Qaeda Society of Gaza. He was to send a communique to the press similar to the ones posted on the Internet, falsely claiming responsibility for previous terror acts. Incredibly, rather than the Muslims it was the Israelis who were attempting to synthesize terror. They were the ones responsible for this incitement.

The Palestinians have proven this case. All the documents—all phone calls and money trails—connect to Israel. This was an Israeli attempt to blame Muslims for the deaths of innocent people, primarily Jews. In other words, these Jews or, perhaps, Israeli Arabs were to be sacrificed, all to further the aims of the vile Zionists. Thus, as a political tool the Israelis had planned to inflict terror acts upon fellow Israelis. This type of aggression is nothing new. It is mentioned in the Old Testament and, particularly, the Qur'an, that is that the Jews would kill their own people and even drive them into exile to achieve a specific end. Here, the victims include Semitic Jews, who the Zionists find dispensable.

Since the role of any Islaamic terror is now in doubt it is necessary to determine the true culprits of global terror. Several major terrorist acts will be reviewed. The following describes the true origins of international terror.

Attack against the British—Islaamic or Zionist?

Only the Israelis and their terrorist gangs have a history of attacking British interests. It is true that over the past 200 years the British have invaded numerous Muslim countries, including, Palestine, Iraq, and Iran. Yet, in contrast to the Zionists reprisals by Muslims are rare. In this regard the Muslims have been docile. What's more, within England they have clearly been a law-abiding community. So, the question is was Britain attacked by the Muslims or by Western elements, notably the Israelis? The British secret service is also capable of committing self-inflicted wounds. However, it is the Israelis who have the most flagrant history of civilian terror. They alone are the global experts in the bombing of civilian structures, including buses and trains.

It was exclusively the Israelis, specifically Menachem Begin's Irgun gang, which in 1948 blew up the British Headquarters of Palestine. The headquarters was in Jerusalem's King David Hotel, which was utterly destroyed by terrorist bombs. An entire section of the building was obliterated, and people were buried alive under the rubble. The bombs were planted in the basement by Irgun terrorists *dressed like Arabs*. This resulted in the deaths of over 80 British soldiers, diplomats, and civilians. This terrorist act led to Britain's withdrawal from the region.

Again, the Zionists have the prior history of the destruction of public buildings. Thus, in any modern civilian bombing they alone would be the first consideration.

Previously, Jewish thugs from various gangs assassinated British diplomats, including in 1944 Lord Moyne, a close friend of Churchill. Thus, during World War II Zionist terror squads were freely active. Yet, Churchill was himself the main force behind the creation of the Jewish entity. Churchill was half Jewish.

Regarding terror acts Winston Churchill had a sordid history. Frequently, to achieve so-called political goals he placed his fellow man at risk. He leaked intelligence to German agents that the passenger ship Lusitania carried weapons. This was a lie. As it neared the British coast it entered a U-boat infested region and was, apparently, sunk by the Germans. This forced the formerly reticent United States president into action: America joined the war.

Because he himself was part Jewish Churchill vigorously pursued the Zionist agenda. Like other Zionists he committed crimes against humanity to achieve his goals. His greatest crime was incitement to war. He did this largely with one goal in mind: the creation of a Jewish exodus. This was to forcibly populate Palestine. In this regard it is important to remember a simple fact: it takes a monumental effort to forcibly displace a sovereign people, those who have existed in a region for countless centuries. Thus, the creation of the Israeli entity was truly a vast international crime, all achieved through a deliberate, malicious plan. In this the dedicated Zionist Churchill played a predominant role.

Again, in contrast to the Muslims there is a history of the Zionists attacking British interests. This is particularly true if the British refuse to submit to their demands. This is surely the case now, since the British have legislated a gradual withdrawal from Iraq. This withdrawal was announced just prior to the London bombings. True, God-fearing Muslims are frustrated by the West's oppressive policies. Even so, the recent terrorist bombings in the United States and London severely damaged the Muslims' goodwill. In fact, the only beneficiaries of these attacks have been Western, as well as Israeli, elements. Thus, again, it is Islaam's enemies who are the culprits.

Is it possible that Western powers could cause terror acts on their own soil? For most people this is unfathomable. One revelation is an article by an American journalist, which proves the extent of the Israeli connections in London. According to the source and as reported on *Israeli National News* an Israeli firm, Verint Systems, now heads security for London's Underground train network. Thus, the entire video network for the Underground is Israeli operated. This means the Israelis are directly involved in all security aspects of the Underground as well as buses and in tunnels.

They have full access to these sites, without monitoring. They control the video operations. They can do with them whatever they will. They are there, while the Muslims have no access nor any power.

The Israelis have a vast history of bombing vehicles and buildings. They are experts in explosive devices and the setting of charges, plus, they control all security. Their expertise is demonstrated by the fact that in occupied Palestine in the midst of major British security they, incredibly, destroyed the British headquarters.

The Zionists have a history of creating fake terror acts, while blaming them on others. What's more, if exposed, they know how to cover any evidence. Thus, only the Israelis could easily plant bombs and/or evidence without detection. What's more, they have the motive to do so.

In any crime the motive must always be considered. Again, it is the Israeli entity which benefits enormously from these crimes, while the Muslims, as well as various dark-skinned look-alikes, endure only torment, vicious torture—even death.

The fact is throughout America and England virtually all the major security firms are Israeli-owned. No such firms are owned by Muslims. This conveniently gives the Zionists access to strategic sites, so they can perpetrate their wicked deeds. In this manner they can create terror acts at low risk, and virtually eliminating the possibility of being caught.

Equally telling is this fact: the Zionists are supposedly the experts. Yet, in London under their 'scrutiny,' people are to believe, two groups of bombers placed and set bombs. Yet, none of this expertise could prevent it? Then, of what benefit is this Israeli security? Furthermore, in 9/11, where, again, the Zionists controlled security, any Israeli security agents at the World Trade Center had long before abandoned their posts. Normally teeming with armed or undercover Israelis in these buildings not a single Israeli guard or espionage agent was killed. Furthermore, the Israeli, agencies knew that the destruction of the buildings was imminent but issued no public warning. Instead, only Israeli nationals were warned. None of these individuals came to work that day. What's more, only Israeli-operated companies took precautions—such as the massive Zim Moving—which long before evacuated the premises, forfeiting all deposits. Thus, it is the Israelis who are the exclusive beneficiaries of global terror. Americans don't benefit, nor do the Muslims. Plus, there is virtually no international scrutiny of their acts. For them the Iraq war is a necessary crime, so they can perpetrate further horror: the vile act of driving entire populations from their homes, wantonly killing of the innocent. This is to create Greater Israel. Thus, the war itself is an Israeli one, fully orchestrated and coordinated by Israeli agents. Thus, regarding heinous acts committed globally it is they who are the ultimate culprits. The degree of their terror is demonstrated by the countless tens of thousands of Muslims in Iraq, Iran, and Palestine, who have been killed and maimed as a result of Israeli aggression.

In 9/11 it was mainly Christians who were slaughtered, along with a significant number of Muslims. A number of Jews and Hindus were also killed. Thus, this was a heinous crime, which afflicted all realms of humanity.

Regarding the Muslims these victims were mainly foreign nationals, people from, for instance, Turkey, India, Pakistan, the Middle East, and Bangladesh. In addition, there were a number of American Muslims who died. Yet, of the nearly 4000 Israeli nationals who normally work in the building none showed up to work that day. Only one Israeli died: a janitor.

CHAPTER 2

Conspiracy to Murder: Crimes Against Humanity

Islaam has been portrayed as a sponsor of terror. Media outlets proclaim it as the source of global instability. These are all lies sponsored by antagonistic elements, which seek to undermine it. This has led people to make wild claims such as calling for the "killing of all 'fundamentalist' Muslims." Some have even promoted the extermination of all Muslims. Yet, would such people propose the same if they determined that instead of the Muslims it was the Jews who were responsible? Such individuals are ready to condemn Islaam or at least question its veracity as a true religion. Yet, they base this on mere lies. Again, despite their vast history of committing terror will people call for the extermination of all Zionists or for the destruction of Judaism?

The Mexican Congress: absolute evidence

The attempted bombing of the Mexican Congress is an example of blatant Zionist tyranny. It proves that rather than Islaam it is Zionism which is the source of international terror. Zionism is exclusively political. It was originated by wealthy and prominent European Jews. This was to create a

Jewish empire. Its purpose is the creation of vast wealth and power. It has nothing to do with religion. Its avowed methods are to achieve wealth and power through any means possible, including the use of terror.

In October 2001 in Mexico City, less than a month after the terror attacks in New York City, a group of Israelis—in fact, illegal immigrants—were caught attempting to commit a terror act. The operatives, which included a former Israeli 'defense' colonel and presumed spy, were caught after penetrating security. These men had sufficient weapons to destroy the government offices. They possessed some nine grenades, various explosives, detonators, and 9 mm automatic pistols, firepower which was aimed at government officials as well as civilians.

Authorities said that the Israeli terrorists took advantage of a situation where a large group of industry workers were attempting to go through security. The Israelis followed the workers to *the office of the President of the Mexican Congress, Beatriz Pardes*. At first they pretended to be press photographers, but their agitated behavior alerted the suspicion of the workers. They were confronted, and it was discovered that they had guns as well as explosives. The workers held the Israelis until security personnel took them into custody. The head of security confirmed that they possessed *weapons of mass injury*, including, incredibly, sticks of dynamite, rapid-fire handguns, wiring, and hand grenades. Due to only the alertness of the locals an impending catastrophe was avoided.

There was only one purpose for the dynamite and grenades. It was to blow the Mexican Congress into oblivion, while slaughtering the innocent. Surely, the Israelis had a concomitant plan where other faux agents dressed as Muslims would make a scene, creating the false image of Islaamic terror. However, the plan was foiled. Only one month after 9/11 the Israelis were caught in the act. A disaster with global implications was averted. There is no doubt that this was an attempted Israeli terror act. The purpose: to punish the Mexicans for failing to support Israel's global tyranny. It was also to simultaneously implicate Islaam as a sponsor of terror.

Despite their obvious attempt to commit mass crimes the Israelis were ultimately released. Unlike numerous innocent Muslims they were never tortured. Rather, they were returned to the terrorist entity: Israel.

What if these deviants would have been Muslims? The fact is the type of punishment they would have endured can only be imagined. Surely, under no circumstances would they have been let go. The fact is they would have been punished severely, perhaps executed.

While heavily reported in Mexico there was no U.S. coverage of this event. Again, if Muslims would have attempted this the consequences would have been dire. The fact is the Zionist-controlled press completely suppressed this event. In contrast, had Muslims been caught doing so, it would have been broadcast to the entire world.

The reasons for this act are explained by Ernesto Cienfuegos of La Voz de Aztlan. According to Cienfuegos:

> What were the Israelis up to? We think we know. The Vicente Fox government has been very careful of involving Mexico in a war against Islaam. The Mexican population, as well as the two major opposition parties, the PRI and the PRD, will not allow it. President Bush and the U.S. Zionists want Mexico fully involved in the war, principally because if things get tough in the Middle East and the oil-rich Arabs leave the coalition, the U.S. military

machine is going to need alternative sources of oil and PEMEX is just across the border. We believe that the two Zionist terrorists were going to blow up the Mexican Congress (complete with massive loss of life). The second phase was to mobilize both the Mexican and US press to blame Osama bin Laden. Most likely, then, Mexico would declare war on Afghanistan as well, commit troops and all the oil it could spare to combat Islaamic terrorism.

After being imprisoned the Mossad agents were relieved of prosecution. They were merely deported. This proves the great hostility against Islaam. For instance, Muslims who have committed no crimes are wrongfully imprisoned, for instance, in Gauntanamo and Abu Ghraib, as well as various so-called secret prisons. Then, how can it be that Zionists who were caught with the means and the intension of destroying a critical Mexican landmark, creating vast carnage, killing and maiming untold hundreds of people—these are released?

The Israelis placed great pressure on the Mexican government to release these spies. Thus, Jews, proven terrorists, were set free. In all likelihood using the American public's money the Israelis bought the Mexican government off, in other words, they bribed them. They made it worth their while to release these criminals.

Types of terror acts invented by the Zionists

The Zionists have employed every conceivable method of terror to achieve their goals. Previously, the actual European Jews committed the terror acts. This was a time when they committed clear acts of terror using obvious Zionists, that is light-skinned or European people. This proved scandalous and failed to serve their objectives. Then, they created Arab-

and/or Muslim-appearing individuals or groups, for instance, Abu Nidal, Islaamic Jihad, even al-Qaeda, to carry out their attacks. These names were used to maintain the image of Middle Easterners as 'Muslim' terrorists. These groups are Western fabrications. No Muslim belongs to any of them. The Israelis are ruthless. For instance, Yitzak Shamir, a European Jew, mastered the science of letter bombs. In the 1960s he used them to kill German scientists working in Egypt. Yet, Shamir's main targets were Semites, that is Middle Easterners. A partial list of the Zionist tools of terror include:

- Car bombs
- Truck bombs
- Roadside bombs
- Railroad bombs
- Bus bombs
- Bombings of refugee or civilian ships
- Bombings of high rises by placing bombs in the basements
- Micro-nukes (the so-called suit-case or 'dirty' nuke is, essentially, an Israeli invention; which is broadcast to create a derogatory image of Muslims)
- The injection into vulnerable regions of the body nerve agents, strychnine, and similar immediate killers
- Subterranean bombs
- The bombing of industrial sites
- Poison gas
- The injection of cancer-causing pathogens or biogerms

These terror devices were largely invented by the Zionists. Many were originally used in Palestine against the Muslim inhabitants as well as the British.

Large scale terror acts: global shock

On September 11, 2001, war was waged on America. Quickly, Islaam was blamed. This is now being disputed, even by top government officials. Family members of the 9/11 victims also have reservations, that is regarding the accuracy of government claims and are, therefore, suing for damages. It is now believed that the U.S. rulership, along with the Israeli government, were the culprits. People can appreciate the potential conspiracy through using their common sense. Then, it becomes evident that the official story is a lie.

The attack on the Pentagon is the most glaring example of a possible false front. This building, a vast edifice, is the largest office building in the world. On 9/11 it was supposedly struck by an American Airlines jetliner. A 757, this monstrous plane would have weighed with fuel some 80 to 100 tons. It would have caused massive damage to the building. Plus, there would have been a vast amount of wreckage, that is vast sheets of metal, chunks of vinyl, food service containers, engines, landing gear, body parts, seat cushions, clothes, and luggage. As in all previous crashes there would be materials strewn all over the region for hundreds of yards. There was no such wreckage. Thus, the official story was fabricated.

The government says that this massive plane struck the Pentagon, leaving essentially no wreckage. Then, say official sources, the wreckage, bodies, and luggage somehow all entered the Pentagon and were "consumed." This is ludicrous.

People must give this thought: how could a 757 strike such an important building, and no one saw it? Then, how could it do so without leaving a trail of vast amounts of obvious wreckage? The fact is this is impossible. What's more, curiously, while the World Trade Center airplane strikes received extensive coverage, there was essentially no coverage regarding the Pentagon once the official story was presented. This was because people, including numerous reporters on the scene, disputed the claim that it was struck by such a large plane. There are no eyewitnesses confirming a huge plane strike. For instance, no common citizens on the highways which surround the Pentagon saw it. Again, the news broadcasts carefully neglected to cover the Pentagon disaster. The crash site was never investigated. There was a sudden ending of coverage with an emphasis instead on the World Trade Center attack. Yet, for many Americans the Pentagon is more symbolic of national pride than the World Trade Center. This lack of coverage alone is highly suspect. Obviously, this minimization of coverage was ordered at the highest levels.

Regarding the crashing into the Pentagon of such a huge plane the majority of eyewitnesses state otherwise, saying, instead, it was at best a small plane, like a jet fighter. The first reports were of a missile or possibly a small jet. A key Pentagon official, Donald Rumsfeld, also witnessed to this. Incredibly, he made mention that the damage at the Pentagon was, in fact, due to a "missile." Other eyewitnesses said the following: "there was no plane, no wings, nothing." Another said, "I heard what sounded like a missile (a whoosh sound)." Yet another said "There was no plane." Someone else said he was sure a bomb went off, that it was an explosive and that he could smell bomb residue—cordite—which he was familiar with. The latter could also mean that rather than a jetliner it was definitely a missile or a bomb. There is no cordite on jetliners. However, the exit blast on the opposite side of the Pentagon would justify the missile theory.

In airliner crashes there is always strewn wreckage. What's more, there are vast quantities of it. It cannot just evaporate. However, somehow, miraculously, at the Pentagon there was virtually none? Not one piece of the commonly expected airline items from a crash was found: no 757 jet engines, no cockpit devices, no wing or fuselage parts, no luggage, and no black box.

The engines and wings are huge: where were they? This was confirmed by CNN's Jamie McIntyre, live on the scene, who said, categorically, that no plane crashed into the Pentagon. What's more, since McIntyre's accurate eyewitness coverage countered the standard story CNN stopped broadcasting it.

Rescue workers said, while working in the building, there were no plane parts. Yet, anyone could observe this. The pictures are available. At the crash site outside the building, that is on the Pentagon lawn, there would have to be a wide range of items: luggage, clothing, body parts, plastic/vinyl, doors, seats, cushions, massive amounts of twisted metal, parts of the wings/fuselage, beverage containers, lavatories, and much more. There were no such items.

A small piece of aluminum, with blue, red, and white paint, was found. This evidence was planted (see Operation Northwoods, pages 151-160). This process is known in espionage agencies as "strewn wreckage." The temporary black-out mentioned previously would have been conducive to the planting of such evidence. The metal was freshly painted, and it was without wear or air-staining. So, it could never have been from an active plane. What's more, it was free of any charring.

No wonder the post-9/11 coverage on the Pentagon was halted. People would see the images and wonder where were the plane parts. Experts would take notice and begin raising questions. So, these images were not shown. What's more, when such planes crash so low to the ground, they always severely damage the grounds near or along the crash site. Such planes would rip the ground to shreds. About the Pentagon there was no such damage. The lawn was perfect. For the crash of a huge jetliner this is impossible. No one can argue this. It means that the official story is a lie.

Incredibly, within the building, where the plane, somehow, according to the official story, miraculously blended or 'folded' into it, no parts of a 757 were found. Talk show commentator Bill Boshears of WLW 700 has repeatedly analyzed this, demonstrating that it was impossible for a 757 to have struck this building. The hole in the building was only 16 feet across. The airplane, wing-tip to wing-tip, is some 130 feet. Everyone who has seen the video of the World Trade Center (south tower) crash knows that such a crash would always cause an indentation for the length of the plane. In addition, the wing span of a 727 is approximately 73 feet. This proves that the hole was created through another source. So, rather than a 757 the Pentagon was most likely struck by an explosive payload, a specialized missile, remote controlled small jet, or perhaps a bomb. There were numerous reports by experienced military people of the smell of cordite, a military explosive. Thus, something other than a massive passenger jet struck this building. This would have been fired or set-off deliberately.

Again, there is no way that it could have been struck by a large jetliner; the hole was too small. This is obvious to anyone with even the slightest common sense. Thus, there was no Islaamic attack against the Pentagon. What's more, someone is attempting to disguise the most crucial fact: that this was a tactical strike against an American building using a powerful military-grade explosive. The region reeked of the smell of cordite, exclusively a military-grade explosive. No Muslim in this country has access to such devices or explosives.

The bizarre issue is that of all possible sites of the Pentagon to strike—and there are many such sites—it was only the site under construction which was hit. No Muslim group knew that the Pentagon was under construction. Only insiders knew this. Thus, an attack by a "secret" government is the only possibility. This is supported by the fact that the Pentagon strike occurred at the wing whose military experts had recently implicated the Mossad as a possible culprit, "a cunning, ruthless wild card…" The fact is experts in this now stricken Army command center had stated categorically that the Mossad was capable of creating in the United States bogus terror acts, while blaming it on Muslims. This assessment was released by the U. S. Army on September 10th, *one day prior to the strike*. This is no coincidence. Obviously, the Mossad demonstrated to these U.S. advisors how truly cunning, rather, ruthless, it is. Thus, this strike, which was directed at their adversaries—within the U.S. military, is absolute proof of a direct Israeli role in these catastrophes.

A Pentagon security camera confirmed that this was no 757. Rather, it was a relatively small object. All that the camera definitively showed is an explosion occurring within the outer part of the building. There is no absolute proof of the source. However, what is certain is that it was not a huge jetliner. Much of this scenario is covered in detail in the video documentary *In Plane Site* by Dave Van Kliest (available on DVD from ThePowerHour.com). In addition, there are numerous other documentaries, which dispute the official story. Here is the point: all this doubt and analysis is because the official story is so baseless. If this story were obviously true, that is that a 757 struck this building, there would be no need for investigation.

A Dulles airport flight controller confirms the lack in Pentagon airspace of such a big plane, saying that, instead, it was probably a fighter plane. Certainly, a flight controller knows the difference between a large and small object.

This exact nature of the Pentagon strike could have been confirmed by the numerous video cameras which were found in businesses about the Pentagon. However, virtually immediately after the blast in a systematic effort the FBI confiscated them. They have since refused to release them. This is proof of a conspiracy. What's more, in a proven act by Muslims, surely, the government would relish publicizing it. Yet, even under court order the government refused to release these videos. This is contempt of court, a criminal act.

The FBI immediately confiscated all videos. This is evidence that rather than a group of suicidal Muslims the government is entirely culpable for this act.

Again, there is only one explanation for the fact that the videos were so rapidly confiscated. It is that the information would implicate the government. Obviously, the FBI knew in advance about the attack and, in fact, was a perpetrator. In the chaos of this event without foreplanning there is no way government agents could have so rapidly moved against these video systems. Unless it was preplanned no such action would have been taken. The government is obstructing evidence. Thus, rather than the Muslims it is the evil agents of global powers—the secretive and/or powerful ones in the governments—which are the perpetrators of these acts. The Muslims had nothing to do with it.

Usama bin Laden

The Zionists aggressively target bin Laden. They claim he is the arch-terrorist. They blame him for terror acts against civilians. Repeatedly and without evidence they attribute to him great terror acts: the embassy bombings in Kenya and Tanzania, 9/11, Bali, and the London tube/bus bombings. No proof is provided regarding any role: he is merely accused.

Not a single shred of evidence links this man to these acts. Yet, millions of people seemingly hate him for what they believe he represents: the force behind the 9/11 bombings and other attacks against Americans.

Again, there is no evidence linking bin Laden to these bombings. Rather than in any court of law he is tried merely in the media. He is implicated exclusively by the White House and its Zionist agents. It is true that he sent troops to fight against U. S. soldiers in Somalia. This is represented in the book/movie *Black Hawk Down*. Yet, ultimately, he is demonized to support a global agenda. It is the portrayal of Islaam as the source of terror. It is also the creation of an "us against them" mentality.

Regarding 9/11 bin Laden has never claimed responsibility. Nor has he claimed responsibility for the U.S. Embassy bombings. In the only truly accurate interviews of him by people who know him and who personally talked to him, for instance, Hamid Gul, former head of the ISI, Pakistan's secret service organization, he denied it. Said bin Laden when asked about a possible role in 9/11 (*Ummat* Magazine, Karachi):

> I have already said that I am not involved in the September 11 attacks…As a Muslim, I try my best to avoid telling a lie. I had no knowledge of these attacks, nor do I consider the killing of innocent women, children, and

other humans an appreciable act. Islam strictly forbids causing harm to innocent women, children, and other people. Such a practice is forbidden, even in the course of a battle. It is the United States, which is perpetrating every maltreatment on women, children, and the common people...

Shortly after being accused he released a video in which, again, he denied responsibility. A later video claiming responsibility has been proven by Swiss authorities as bogus. If he clearly denied any responsibility or knowledge of these terror acts, why rely only on the media representations? Thus, virtually all claims of Islaamic terror based upon bin Laden are bogus. What's more, since he had nothing to do with 9/11 the point is he is wrongly targeted. Furthermore, the perpetrators needed a scapegoat, and they had planned in advance to use bin Laden, much like Lee Harvey Oswald and Sirhan Sirhan were used as decoys in the Kennedy murders. Sirhan Sirhan, a mere bus boy, was set up to portray Palestinians as murderers. This was exclusively to distract attention from the real culprits. What's more, Bobby Kennedy was no friend of the Israelis. The fact is the bogus video of bin Laden plus the use of patsies proves that there are major powers which have manipulated the news to create a certain image. This is the image of an 'Islaamic' enemy.

Yet, of all who have been wrongly blamed Usama bin Laden has undergone the greatest degree of slander. His image has been manipulated completely to serve the agenda of massive global powers. The fact is he had nothing to do with any civilian bombings. Statements against him of bombing and maiming the innocent are lies.

There is much proof of the false nature of these statements. The postings claiming credit are easy to disprove, as are the suicide notes and wills used to incriminate Muslims. These were created instead by non-Muslims. There is no Islaamic language in these notes or postings. Then, obviously, the Muslims are being framed. There is also the continuous attempt to tarnish their religion. The primary source: the Israelis.

The hijacking statements are also baseless. Large jets are enormously complicated. The statement that untrained men could overpower the crew and, then, successfully fly these jets is ludicrous. Then, people are to believe that these men, who had never before piloted even a prop plane, successfully commandeered massive jets and successfully struck their targets? This is implausible if not impossible.

It was reported that they prepared for this by performing weight training. This has recently been proven false, since it was only men *posing as the hijackers* who did so. What's more, the gym in Maryland which they supposedly joined is near the CIA headquarters. Eyewitnesses said the men merely gathered as if having meetings and never truly worked out. What's more, airline pilots universally agree: there is no possibility that amateurs practicing merely in flight simulators could have effectuated the 9/11 events.

This could only have been accomplished by experienced pilots, or, more likely, remote control. The statement that groups of various Muslims who have no experience in flying massive jets or even small planes could perfectly or even imperfectly do so is ludicrous.

These jets are far too complicated. Anyone knows this by merely looking into a cockpit: it is intimidating, all those lights, dials, and gadgets. The fact is it is overwhelmingly complex, that is for the novice, and there is no means for an amateur to singlehandedly achieve a successful flight. It has never been done in the past: why now? The fact is it takes a long time to be qualified to legally fly even a tiny single-engine plane let alone the most sophisticated jet airliners in the world. Thus, the basis for an Islaamic attack is now refuted. Yet, on patriotic Web sites and government postings, as well as in the orthodox media, the accusations remain that these were bin Laden's men and that, what's more, he ordered and orchestrated 9/11. This is bogus.

Even the video where bin Laden purportedly claims responsibility has been proven fraudulent. This was confirmed by top Swiss investigators, who have demonstrated that the man in this video was not bin Laden. Nor was this his voice. This fake video is the only evidence thus far presented against this man.

People need to use their common sense. How could bin Laden achieve a perfect attack on the United States from the remote regions of Afghanistan? He doesn't even use a cell phone. How could he from such a vast distance perfectly coordinate this act? How could systematically any foreign invader evade all America's elite defense systems: NORAD, the Air Force, espionage agencies, and military surveillance, to strike successfully at its heart? Is this anything other than a fable? The fact is this makes no sense. Only a truly uninformed, rather, ignorant person could believe so. Bin Laden is targeted, because he fought against the American system, that is American imperialism. Plus, he was pre-selected as the scapegoat. Thus, the American military powers sought to crush him.

Rather than the destruction of civilians and/or their property bin Laden's fight was against colonial powers. The fact is due to his beliefs he was exiled, a true political refugee. What's more, he is undeserving of the hate registered against him. There is no similar hate registered against truly sinister elements, such as the Saudi puppet princes and the so-called Saudi kings, who usurp the peoples' assets—who imprison, torture, and kill any dissidents. So, obviously, rather than any legitimate basis the hate against bin Laden is for a diabolical purpose: to portray Islaam in a negative light and, what's more, to distract attention from the true sources of terror: the Israeli Zionist cabal.

With bin Laden there was no trial: only accusations. Even with the worst criminals, proven to commit violent crimes, there is always a trial, that is before guilt is established. Not so with many Muslims. The fact is they are convicted in the media, without a trial and, what's more, this media is largely controlled by their enemies. Even Saddam Hussein, a known and proven mass murderer, is allowed a trial.

There is no evidence that bin Laden authorized the killing of civilians. If anyone has such evidence, let him produce it. What's more, incredibly, bin Laden has been universally blamed for terror acts for which he had culpability. Regarding 9/11 the U. S. government now confirms that there is no evidence of his involvement.

To confuse people bin Laden is described as a CIA operative. However, there is no evidence to support this. What's more, the ludicrous nature of this statement is proven by the fact that his entire purpose is the opposite of the CIA's: to replace the corrupt Saudi leadership with an Islaamic government. The CIA strives to uphold that government. The fact is the CIA's avowed purpose is to prevent the collapse of this regime. Rather than bin Ladin it is the Saudi kings who are the Western operatives, essentially, CIA officers in disguise. Yet, if bin Laden were truly a U.S. government operative, why would there be such a vast effort to kill or capture him?

Regarding the London attack it also was an inside job. Here too scapegoats would be necessary. Certainly, there would be published video images of the supposed bombers. Surely, these supposed culprits would be dark-skinned, without doubt, Muslim. That is the methodology of those in power today. This is whom they want people to focus on. This is whom they wish to create hate as well as war.

Yet, even so, people might say, "The London bombings had to be Islaamic." People need to use their common sense. It makes no sense that highly educated Pakistani youth, that is Muslims of such origin, would do this. If they truly intended to fight, that is the "British perpetrators," why would they attack the common people? These are the very people who oppose the war. Surely, they would have more sense than that.

Why would they ruin any chance for positive public relations—which the Muslim community has so diligently worked for—for instance, to foster a positive understanding of the nature of Islaam: all for naught? Why would a 22-year-old sports enthusiast suddenly kill himself, along with dozens of innocents? Rather, it makes sense that the culprits are enemies of Islaam, for instance, secretive British or even American elements and, particularly, the bloodthirsty Zionists. Regardless, the Pakistani Muslim community played no role in this attack.

In England the common person has no argument with the Muslims. In fact, Muslims and other British people are often the dearest of friends. What's more, regardless, there is no "Secret Organization of al-Qaeda" created to torment the people, at least none that the Muslims have produced. This is a mere publicity stunt, clearly orchestrated by Islaam's enemies. The Web site which posted this name is traceable to the United States, that is Maryland. This is where the CIA offices are located. Mossad also operates from this region. The latter has been proven to fabricate terror acts, all for mere financial gain. This would indicate that the various spy agencies: the Mossad, CIA, and MI6, all played a role in the London bombings.

The fact is terror is a Western specialty. No one should be surprised at that, for instance, American or British agencies have brutalized the masses. The CIA routinely trains foreign government officials in the use of terror. It trained Iranians to use terror and torture against their own people. Admitted in the *New York Times*, June 11, 1979, the article was entitled "Torture Teachers." The author, A. J. Langguth, quoted an American spy in Iran, who revealed, "the CIA (trained) the Shah's secret police…in torture." The article continues with a most gruesome revelation, a kind of proof of the terror caused by the American system, which is hypocritically proclaimed, to be the leader of freedom. For nearly forty years the Shah's torture apparatus, a true division of the American government, engaged in the systematic "torture and execution of political prisoners, suppression of dissent, and alienation of the religious masses."

All this was paid for by U.S. citizens. The fact is it is only Western civilization which specializes in profiting from exporting terror. For instance, in Iran during the 1970s while people were brutalized, special interest groups along with the Shah reaped tens of billions of dollars. People enriched themselves on human blood and limbs. This is the dire nature of godlessness, the evil of wanton imperialism.

Only Western cultures profit from torture. No Islaamic society does so. The techniques used against the Iranians were adopted from those used by the Nazis. Yet, Americans spewed hatred towards Khomeini, who despite media vilification rescued his people from this brutality. Americans only find hate for him, the opposite view of his people. This torture and murder of the innocent by the West is the reason for the Iranian chant: "Death to America."

Khomeini too was a victim of imperialism. He was chased into exile, driven from his home. This was all due to U.S. interference. His son and a number of his associates, all God-fearing men, were brutally murdered by U.S. or U.S-financed espionage agents.

The hatred against Khomeini is truly bizarre. There are Christian monks with 'beards and robes:' nobody hates them. This man liberated his people from some 50 years of oppression, brutal crimes of torture, imprisonment, murder, and genocide. Regardless of whatever the media proclaims Iran is more democratic today than it was under the Shah's or, rather, U.S.'s rule. Do not forget: the torture endured for decades by the Iranians was U. S.-orchestrated. The fact is during the revolution five million of his people went to the streets to acknowledge him as their savior. He was the peoples' choice as leader, and that is truly democracy. In contrast to U.S.-installed rulers he ordered the torture of no one. Nor did he, as did the U.S.-sponsored Shah, attack and kill the common people with tanks, machine guns, and helicopter gunships.

Even so, he is mainly attacked by the world Jewry. Any attack by the Shah's family members is also a Zionist one. Actually, this is because the Shah was Jewish. Of Russian origin this Zionist was installed into power by the U.S. government. Khomeini, identified him as a Zionist. This is confirmed by the recent monograph, Pollack's *The Jewish Shah*. She verifies that this imposter was an Israeli agent. This is also proven by the fact that as described by William Shawcross in his book the *Shah's Last Ride* the Shah's top agents, who helped install him in power, were the arch-Zionists Henry Kissinger and David Rockefeller.

In fact, Khomeini purged a barbaric institution: the torture of the innocent. He relieved his people of the dire hate crimes based upon religion as well as race. In Iran indigenous Jews and Christians are safe; Khomeini mandated their protection. Thus, regardless of denomination for the common Iranian people he was their protector. What's more, he conquered colonialism, for which he is hated by the American power-brokers. Furthermore, since his revolution Iran has been under siege by the Americans, as well as Zionists. This constant pressure has much to do with Iran's economic woes. It is constantly attacked and boycotted by the world's greatest superpower, which only leads to further despair and difficulty. Remember, the Iranian Muslims have been tormented by both Americans and Zionists, while they have never oppressed the American people.

The Shah oppressed the Muslims, torturing and murdering them. He usurped their wealth. In contrast, he fully supported the Israelis. Thus, the Shah was a Zionist agent.

In Iran the Israelis seek to regenerate Zionist control. For nearly forty years in this country the Muslims suffered direly. This was directly due to the brutality of American/Israeli authority. To the U.S. the previous Iran under the rule of the arch Zionist and Muslim imposter, the Jewish Shah, was "acceptable." In contrast, there is no accepting an Islaamic Iran. This demonstrates the raw hypocrisy of the American government. Yet, this government is merely serving its Zionist masters. Similar Zionist agents are now in power in numerous other Muslim countries, including Egypt and Jordan.

The West deems any Islaamic rule in Iran, as well as Iraq, essentially, as evil. Western powers use the word Axis to create a derogatory image, almost Nazi-like. Yet, all this is merely a ruse to support a financial agenda. This is the agenda of constant militarism. In contrast, Western mercenaries, as well as soldiers, admittedly rape and torture, even sodomize, Iraqis. Then, the Iraqi people, forced from their homes, emigrate to neighboring countries, including Iran, adding to these countries' burdens. The fact is by such comments—this statement of the so-called Axis of Evil—Western powers are essentially deeming Islaam evil. Thus, rather than the Muslims they are the ones who have initiated hostilities. This is because, for instance, regarding the Iranian Revolution it was exclusively Islaam which created it. This confirms that there is a war of American and Israeli powers against this faith. So, too, there is a war from Islaam's position against Western interference. Yet, all this is due to the aggression of Western powers, which, globally, are continuously stealing the wealth and rights of the Muslim people as well as people of other cultures.

So, America is responsible for much of this country's agony. Even so, if Iran is so hated, why invade it? Why spend the public's money, as was done in 1956 when the CIA toppled the elected Iranian president, creating coups? Why constantly interfere in this country's affairs? Obviously, rather than the Iranians the evil arises mainly from the West. This evil includes the devastating Iran-Iraq War, which was strictly an American, as well as Israeli, creation.

Regarding the Iranian people there is great blood on the hands of the Americans as well as the Israelis. Now these powers are clamoring for additional blood. What's more, they are willing to sacrifice their own blood—the blood of America's youth—in the process.

Again, why hate Khomeini? Did he ever harm any American? On the contrary due to U.S. policies *he* suffered vast harm. His son was assassinated by SAVAK, the secret police installed by the U.S. Thus, essentially, his son was murdered by the U.S. government. Then, did Khomeini tyrannize, pillage, and/or torture Americans? He was exiled and tormented, three times driven from his home. Even with hostage taking, which, in fact, Khomeini disputed the validity of, the fact is all these hostages survived, while Khomeini's son and tens of thousands of other Iranians were killed. Then, how can even these be compared?

In contrast, no Iranian has ever tortured an American and, surely, has never fomented terror acts against U.S. residents. U.S. soil is safe from the Muslims. They have lived here in peace for hundreds of years. In contrast, it is the Zionists who have bombed U.S. facilities and murdered U.S. citizens, and who, in fact, continuously plot to do so—on a vast scale.

Like other immigrants Muslims born in the West have added to its wealth. Many Muslims are among the West's greatest citizens. There is no reason to fear them. For example, there is virtually no evidence that they are terrorizing the British or American people. This is despite the fact that their fellows in various countries endure torture, torment, even rape and murder, due to precisely U.S. policies, Abu Ghraib is a prominent example. It is also despite the fact that certain American Muslims have been wrongfully imprisoned, some even beaten and tortured, while completely innocent of any crimes.

Obviously, instead of Western countries it is Islaam which is under attack. In fact, globally, it is the Muslims who are the true victims of terror. Again, consider the issue of Iran. After nearly 30 years of berating this country as a terrorist state has it ever even once attacked the West? Rather, Iran has been victimized by terror acts such as the Western-created Iran-Iraq war and the shooting down of an Iranian civilian airliner by a U.S. warship. The culprits: the United States, Britain, and Israel. This is terrorism in the extreme.

The Iranians are constantly under siege. They are the ones subjected to mass crimes. They are being constantly targeted by the Zionists and the various hostile Christian fundamentalists. Again, it was a Christian nation which attacked and destroyed an Iranian commercial jetliner, killing all 290 on-board. Over one-third of the victims were children. In contrast an Islaamic nation has never been responsible for any such atrocity. The U.S. serviceman who fired this murderous missile, a 'Christian,' was given a commendation for it. This is anything but a Christian act? Surely, it is terror of the most grotesque degree.

Yet, the atrocities are even more vast than this. In the Kissinger-orchestrated Iran-Iraq War, or, rather, the American-Israeli-instigated war, over two million people were slaughtered and maimed. All were Muslims. This was genocide, a holocaust perpetrated strictly by Jews and fundamentalist Christians. All were victims of greedy Zionist and Christian war-mongers. Thus, while arms dealers made billions of dollars the Muslims were slaughtered en masse. This was an invasion of Iran by the United States and Israel using Iraq as a client state. Saddam Hussein was given billions of dollars to do so. The evidence for this was in Saddam's Iraq but is also found in Italian bank records. This was one reason for the invasion—to purge Iraq of all evidence. So, Hussein had threatened to blackmail his former allies with the evidence. This is why the U.S. government unseated him. What's more, for some 40 years they had maintained his brutal regime to the detriment of tens of millions of people. No wonder the Iranians call those entities the Great Satans. The fact is, today, the Iranians are merely defending themselves, against their constant aggressors.

It is worth reiterating. The Iran-Iraq war was initiated exclusively by Kissinger and his Israeli masters. This was a vast Western crime, true terrorism. In its entire history there is no Islaamic act which is comparable. This was strictly a

U.S. and Zionist orchestrated war, and Kissinger, along with Rumsfeld and their superiors, were the primary perpetrators. Such individuals are directly responsible for the murder of the innocent. They organized the funds for paying off Hussein. This was to initiate hostilities. In contrast, Islaam had nothing to do with it. For his dutiful act Hussein was paid handsomely by the United States: billions of dollars. This was, again, money from the American public, which is used to subsidize a bloodthirsty tyrant. The goal: to maintain the balance of power in favor of Israel. Then, after nearly two million dead—men, women, and children— at the hands of powerful Israeli and U.S. perpetrators why should anyone give even the slightest credence to so-called Islaamic terror?

When Hussein was at risk of losing the war, he was encouraged by the West to use any means possible, even poison gas. This poison gas was supplied by Western companies. Thus, on what basis can anyone proclaim Islaamic terror?

All terror is horrifying. Yet, only Islaam is attacked as the terror source. In some arenas the media even insinuates that it is a form of terrorism. This is done purposely to foment hate.

The mega-wealthy are responsible for this agenda. Then, what would anyone call the men who perform the crimes of Abu Ghraib, which include beating people to death and homosexual acts against children? Is this the "Christian duty?"

This is a mere fabrication, this hate directed against a people. It is to deflect attention from the true terrorists. How can supposed Islaamic terror compare to the slaughter of 7 million Iraqis and Iranians directly due to Western policies? **This means that approximately 700 people were murdered every single day for thirty years.** This fails to include the countless millions who were/are maimed, tortured, and disfigured. Then, too, there are tens of millions, both Eastern and Western, whose lives are being ruined by depleted uranium. Thus, it is the powerful ones behind these acts who are the true global terrorists, these Western powers and their greedy Israeli cohorts—who are the spreaders of the uranium toxins and biological poisons, who are the criminals guilty of mass atrocities of the most unfathomable degree—the true and fulminant terrorists of this earth.

Now in Iraq the leukemia rate has increased ten-fold: a dreadful testimony to the future of these souls. All this blood, rather, terror, is on the American's, as well as Israeli's, hands. Yet, while Islaam is condemned this is conveniently ignored. The fact is Islaam is the creator of peace, while the Western system is the fomenter of global horrors.

Islaam has no World Wars, Vietnam War, Pol Pot, Khmer Rouge, Agent Orange, "depleted" uranium, land mine amputees, corporate-generated wars, Abu Ghraib, Gauntanamo, Bosnia, African genocide, Central American slaughter, Israeli apartheid, continuous coups, and Fallujah. These are "Western" and/or "European" crimes. Then, who are the real criminals, the ultimate terrorists?

Regarding the constant effort to berate Islaam by Christian and Jewish authorities, again, how, regardless of the degree of any supposed Islaamic terror, how can it be likened to the death and despair resulting from the colonization of the entire Muslim world, that is by Western powers? How can it compare to the daily horror experienced by Muslims, who are arrested, imprisoned, tortured, and brutally beaten—even sodomized, even forced to recant their faith—only due to their beliefs? Too, how can it compare to the dire agony experienced by the Palestinians, who are victims of the merciless oppression of Western powers? Here, by supporting the Israeli entity the United States has again committed genocide. A portion of every 'tax-dollar' which is collected by the U.S. government is used to repress the people overseas. Like the horrors of 9/11 and the London bombings, these are true crimes against humanity.

The true anti-Semites

Zionism is anti-Semitic. It is a political movement. Its purpose is to create an economically and militarily powerful state as stated by its founding members, including Theodor Herzl. Thus, it has nothing to do with 'religion.'

This vile system originated in eastern Europe, that is countries such as Poland and Rumania as well as parts of Russia and Germany. Men from these countries conceived of this as a political movement. None of such people are Semites. Yet, today, it is these people who rule over the Semites, tormenting, torturing, and murdering them. What's more, to attack such people is never anti-Semitic, because, incredibly, they are non-Semites.

Think about it. People who are non-Semites, the European Israelis, are proclaiming they are victims of anti-Semitism. This is impossible. The fact is the Zionists routinely brutalize the Semites in every conceivable way. Thus, those in power who promote Israel are vicious anti-Semites, who perpetrate the torture, imprisonment, rape, and murder of various Semitic people, particularly Muslims. Yet, Christians, for instance, various Christian Lebanese and Palestinians, are also tormented. Consider also the various Christian peace-keepers, who while working in Palestine were/are treated brutally. Some were/are even brutally murdered. The fact is the Israelis continuously commit gross crimes, brutally tormenting, torturing, and murdering the innocent. Thus, the Israeli entity is a Western crime syndicate.

This entity is controlled primarily by eastern European and to a lesser degree American Jews. These are exclusively non-Semites. They have not even a drop of Semitic blood. Thus, any attack against them could never be deemed anti-Semitic.

The rulers of this entity lack even a remote degree of Mediterranean blood. Thus, the entire argument for the Muslims as anti-Semitic is debunked. In fact, to be against Israel is, in fact, to be pro-Semitic, that is pro-Palestinian. This is because the Palestinians are the only major group of Semites in the region. These Middle Eastern Muslims, as well as Christians, are pure Semites. These are the victims of anti-Semitism. This is again confirmed by the fact that, incredibly, their tormenters—the Israelis and their American cohorts—are non-Semites.

The Iraqi Jew and former Zionist Naem Giladi has documented the racist nature of Zionism. He has shown that even the Semitic Jews are treated inferiorly. Thus, the fact is it is the Zionist cabal, exclusively European, which is the true source of anti-Semitism. This is because the Zionists treat anyone of Semitic ancestry as second class citizens.

The Israelis are the primary fomenters of terror. The word terrorist was invented by the British to describe them. They kill and maim countless people, while blaming others. Thus, they are the primary perpetrators of civilian terror. In many of the infamous terror acts the bombs were made by Israeli agents and/or planted by such agents while they were falsely disguised as Muslims. Thus, vast death and devastation was at the hands of the Israelis, yet, as an example, only the Muslims are beaten to death in vigilante killings.

When the World Trade Center collapsed, the Zionists— actual Israelis—were jesting and celebrating. In contrast, the Muslims were cowering in fear, their businesses fire-bombed, their mosques set on fire, and their people murdered. In the United States in the aftermath of 9/11 as a result of vigilante acts at least ten Middle-Eastern-appearing people were murdered. What's more, while the Israelis escaped unscathed some 500 Muslims, nearly one sixth the total, perished in the World Trade Center. In contrast, there were essentially no Israeli deaths in this disaster. However, a number of American Jews also perished.

The Israelis bomb embassies and blame Palestinians, 'Arabs,' and Iranians. They destroy high rise buildings and hotels and blame the Muslims. They create the exclusive image of dark-skinned Arab-appearing terrorists. Then, they repeatedly create terror acts, while making them appear as if 'Islaamic.' Thus, they make it appear that terrorism is primarily associated with this faith. This is despite the fact that the British invented the word terror to describe only Zionist acts.

Wherever the Muslims attempt to gain their rights there are the Israelis. They are there to prevent any Islaamic revival. They fight the Muslims in their own countries by undermining them and by attempting to create sectarian strife. They use cash and weapons to create sub-groups. Then, they instigate these gangsters to fight against any peoples' movement. This results in the deaths yearly of tens of thousands of innocent Muslims as well as numerous Muslim freedom fighters. What's more, untold thousands of Muslims have been slaughtered merely for attempting to defend their countries against Israeli aggressors.

From the Zionist machinations no region of this earth is exempt. The fact is as a routine Zionists kill Muslims. They hunt and murder them throughout the world. They create entire military campaigns against them, perpetrating atrocities, while setting up the Muslims for blame. What's more, they do so globally.

Christians are also victims of Zionist brutality, Rachel Corrie and the family of Casey Sheehan being prominent examples. In contrast, Islaam has no history of tormenting Christians and, rather, fully honors the Christian faith. Yet, if the news wires are to be believed, there is much bloodletting by Muslims against Christians, for instance, in Nigeria, Pakistan, and, particularly, Sudan.

The latter is a case in point. In order to alienate the Christian peoples against Islaam a major disinformation campaign has been created. Here, it is reported, the Muslims have displaced and killed millions of indigenous Christians. Yet, these are all malicious lies.

Henry Kyemba in his book *A State of Blood* proves the opposite. Clearly, he demonstrated that rather than the Muslims it was the Israelis who created the crisis in southern Sudan. This was by supplying ignorant tribesmen with money and weapons. The purpose was to fight and conquer the Muslim-leaning north. This is because the avowed objective of the Israeli entity is to prevent the rise of Islaam. Regarding East Africa the Israelis are invaders and thieves. They have no history nor any right to this region. This crisis is discussed in greater detail on pages 137 through 141.

The fact is the Israelis invented international terror. Thus, the Zionist entity is the primary source of global aggression. Any terror from Islaam if any is comparatively insignificant. International terror has its roots exclusively in Zionism. In comparison there is no Islaamic organization which plots terror. Thus, when highly coordinated terror acts occur, the Israelis are the likely culprits, perhaps followed by their associates, the CIA and the MI6.

The Jews have marked Palestinians as terrorists, while they freely terrorize the entire world. Like all conquerors, they write history their way. What's more, they control the major media. People are well aware that if they speak out against Zionist policies they will at a minimum lose their jobs or be viciously attacked. These are the tactics of the Zionists, all to prevent the revelation of their vile deeds.

This is no minor issue. The Zionists are fully positioned to control how people think. What's more, they use every conceivable means to do so. Consider the so-called State of Israel. Due to its aggression legions of peoples have been expelled and isolated. Refugees have been trapped in the entity itself, cut off from their land and relatives. The Israelis have forced untold millions into squalid refugee camps. They have also driven other countless millions into refugee status throughout the world, creating entire generations of homeless people. This is the greatest terror conceivable. The fact is this entity has created only tyranny on this earth. There is no Islaamic equivalent, not even remotely so. Rather, the entire purpose of Islaam is to halt, as well as reverse, such tyranny. Thus, the entire claim of Islaamic terror is now disproved, because the Israelis are the ultimate terrorists.

The official stories of numerous terror acts are suspect. To determine the truth the first few moments in any disaster are the most telling, that is before government spin takes over. In the case of the London bombings nearly immediately afterwards experts described a critical finding: the explosives were exclusively military-grade. This is not something that a few private citizens could procure. Three days after the bombings the *Chicago Tribune* reported that only sophisticated explosives were used, described by Scotland Yard's Brian Paddick as "high explosive." This means they were exclusively military-grade. What's more, regarding comments made by the Israelis there were numerous contradictions.

As always, the Israelis were in the midst of it. Furthermore, globally, it must also always be asked, who benefits? It certainly isn't the Muslims. They only endure pain, false imprisonment, financial loss, torment, and even death. The fact is only Western governments, particularly the governments of Israel, Britain, France, and the United States, benefit from these acts. All that Muslims endure is slaughter. Regarding financial beneficiaries the English pound was shortened. Someone knew about the crisis in advance. The same was true of 9/11. Yet, it wasn't the accused Muslims or their families. People earned much wealth on the blood of their brethren. Other beneficiaries of the bombings in New York City and London include security agencies, law enforcement, and, particularly, the oil and arms industries. In contrast, no Muslims benefitted. This is because these bombings portray them in a direly negative light and encourage the continued wars against them.

Regarding the London bombings the Israeli entity is the primary beneficiary. All focus is distracted from its extreme atrocities. What's more, immediately after the bombing its agents sought an additional 2.2 billion dollars in gifts from the U.S. government. This could hardly be a coincidence. The fact is the Israeli entity is directly supported by the United States. So, the latter is also responsible for these crimes. The two are inseparable.

Genocide in Iraq: a Western crime

Iraq is a former British and, now, U.S. colony. The name of the country itself is Western and was invented by Winston Churchill.

The media concentrates on the supposed brutality of the Iraqi insurgents. In contrast, there is no mention of their vast suffering. They are portrayed as killers of the innocent. Yet, no one explains the cause for any rebellion.

Any rebellion in this country is due exclusively to the policies of the United States as well as the Israeli entity. Powerful American rulers and business-people, supported to some degree by an ignorant and patriotic public, are directly responsible for this atrocity. Under U.S. hegemony over a period of some 50 years countless Iraqis have been slaughtered. Saddam is no more to blame than his Western associates, since the fact is, originally, he was put in power by the American government. What's more, it was U.S. support which kept him there. Surely, many of the weapons came from Russia, however, the money to buy them was American. This is why the blood of each of these humans is on the hands of the American rulership. In contrast, millions of peace-loving American citizens marched against the war. The American people are a good people. It is their leadership which is corrupt.

The so-called sanctions were another cause of genocide. Through these sanctions former president Bill Clinton, as well as his co-architect, Hilary Clinton, caused the slaughter of some one million Iraqi children—Muslims as well as Christians. George Bush, Jr. is directly responsible for the deaths of several thousand additional Iraqi children as well as some three thousand of America's sons and daughters. These sons and daughters are being lost for no good cause. These murderous presidents even ignored pleas by starving children, who begged them to halt this tyranny. Yet, these rulers in their hearts showed no mercy. Then, how could they be true Christians?

This desperate warning by the children was through hand-written post-cards. When read, as found in the book *Challenge to Genocide*, the post cards break a person's heart. Regardless of religion or race children are the same: they all have the same needs and desires. In contrast, while this tyranny was perpetrated by the West bin Laden was giving his millions away to feed the poor. Meanwhile, the United States spends billions of dollars attempting to kill this man, while allowing the Iraqi children to starve to death: how cruel. This is a vile crime against humanity. Then, who are the real terrorists? The fact is, obviously, the attack on bin Laden is baseless. Bin Laden has no intent on harming the American public, nor, unlike Western powers, does he perpetrate mass harm on the innocent.

Officially, the attack on bin Laden is based exclusively upon one issue: his supposed involvement in 9/11. Yet, he denies any involvement. The oft-quoted video demonstrated as proof has been proven a fraud. Thus, bin Laden is being used as a scapegoat. Then, what was the basis of bombing him?

Consider the deaths of Middle Easterners from leukemia. This disease was formerly rare in the area. Since the early 1990s these deaths have risen 10- to 20-fold. The cause: the barbaric and illegal use by the United States of uranium-based munitions. Even on a conservative talk show—the Oprah Winfrey Show—it was admitted, January 23, 2006, that thousands of Iraqi children languish in hospitals due to previously unheard of spinal deformities. Thus, again, who are the true terrorists who are brutalizing the masses? The fact is for certain this isn't bin Laden. Yet, as many U.S. 'dignitaries' say, "We don't care anything about those (expletive deleted) 'Arabs:' all we want is their oil." The key is the use of the word *their*. Bin Laden knew this. That is why he was fighting them.

Due to Western interference the Iraqi people received a triple punishment: the imposition by the United States government of the brutal tyrant Saddam Hussein, the wicked sanctions, which truly caused the deaths of untold hundreds of thousands of people, and the theft by Western powers of their oil. Incredibly, now, the oil is merely stolen from their country: the people have no control over it. This is perpetrated by U.S. warriors, as well as mercenaries, an imperialistic army. It is an army which has no productive agenda. Rather, the only agenda is to control and brutalize. The victims are the common people.

The U. S. military never went to Iraq to help the people. Any such claim is a mere PR stunt. The fact is during the first Gulf War New York City PR firms were hired by the Pentagon to demonize the Iraqi people—to make them appear as if animals—all so they all could be grotesquely slaughtered.

The crimes committed by the U.S. government are so vast that their scope cannot be quantified. Based upon lies entire countries, Iraq and Afghanistan, have been invaded and corrupted. The devastation is beyond measure. How horrifying it is to realize its vast crimes, this government which portrays itself as the leader of freedom. Yet, how wicked, how truly hypocritical, it is, while its 'authorities' even order the slaughter of their own civilians: David Koresh and his followers, which included dozens of innocent children.

The policies of the U.S. government cause the slaughter of the innocent globally. This is seemingly well planned. There is no discrimination, rather, all people are subject to it. Michelle Kimball in her article *Let the Children Live* detailed the horrors. In Iraq, she discovered, the policies of the U.S. government are killing even fellow Christians. In response to her visit Basra's catholic Archbishop, Gabriel Kassab, Christmas, 1997, wrote:

> We appeal to all Catholics and to all Christians (and people of conscience) in America and the world. The sanctions are killing our people, our children, the ones (God) has given us to protect. They are killing our

beloved Muslim brothers and sisters. They strike at our poor and our sick most of all. In the name of God's people, we ask you: Tell your government to end the sanctions against the Iraqi people. End the seven years of war against Iraq.

Now, Iraq is a mere Western colony. Western countries have no interest in the welfare of the Iraqi people. They are there strictly because of the oil. If there were no oil, there would be no war. What's more, if there were no Israeli entity, there would also be no war. This means that American people are dying for the sake of money as well as to serve the Zionists. Yet, rather than such imperialists the oil belongs to the residents. Thus, rather than the protection of any supposed freedoms the war is purely strategic: to gain control of this region, to own the oil reserves, and, more importantly, to attack and control the Muslim peoples. Yet, the ultimate goal is to target—and conquer—the Islaamic nation of Iran.

This agenda was enacted by U.S.-based Zionists. In other words, the Zionists use the powers of the United States for their own wicked gains. This is to prevent Iraq from becoming Islaamic. This is also the agenda of Wall Street. This is the primary reason for the invasion.

Diplomat or Zionist spy?

Rather than for their country or supposed 'freedom' Americans are fighting for only one cause: the desires of the world Jewry. This is obvious. No prominent Jews are sending their sons to die in this quagmire. America's youth are being 'used and abused.' The Iran-Iraq war was also a Zionist creation. This war was started purely through espionage, led by the arch-Zionist, Henry Kissinger.

The fact is Kissinger is no diplomat. As documented by F. Prouty, retired United States Air Force colonel, in his book *The Secret Team* Kissinger is a mere spy—a front man for global Zionism. He also served U.S. colonial interests. In other words, he was a 'top level' CIA, as well as Mossad, agent, who reported directly to the President.

What's more, all the former supposed shuttle diplomacy missions that gained this man fame were mere espionage operatives. The purpose: to prevent the rise of Islaam. The fact is Islaam is a direct threat against the colonial theft committed by the Zionists and other Western powers. This alone is the reason they fight it.

This war has nothing to do with any supposed terror that Islaamic civilizations may cause. The fact is, historically, Islaamic civilization has proven to be a wedge against tyranny. An excellent example is the saving by the Islaamic Ottomans during the Inquisition of Spanish Jews from genocide.

Zionists murder their own people to gain political advantage. Then, they blame others to further their goals. During the 1940s they blew up their own refugee ships to gain world sympathy. In destroying the King David Hotel they killed fellow Jews. In contrast, there is no such history of the Muslims doing this. Their killing of their own people proves that it is the Zionist Jews alone who are the true international terrorists. The fact is they are the only known group which routinely slaughters its own people to achieve worldly goals.

It was Henry Kissinger who said U.S. service people are/were pawns, fully expendable to suit the globalists' desires. Now it is known that this man is an international war criminal. Said Kissinger as reported by Leuren Moret, quoting the book *Kiss the Boys Goodbye: How the United*

States Betrayed its Own POWs in Vietnam, "Military men are just dumb stupid animals to be used as pawns in foreign policy."

When Kissinger was selected to head the 9/11 investigation committee, people raised issues. Commentators and politicians demanded that he reveal any business connections, that is any conflicts of interest. He refused to do so. This is because his entire purpose in the Middle East is self-serving. Through his so-called step-by-step diplomacy he became a multimillionaire. This is through the sale of weapons and other corporate goods. Thus, rather than the American nation he served only himself. He was a mere private contractor, pursuing his own financial agenda. That is why he resigned, refusing to release information.

Why would he release it? The information would have incriminated him as not only a fraud but also a mass murderer.

Through the slaughter of the innocent Kissinger enriched himself, earning untold millions. Yet, again, it is bin Laden, the wealthy man living a simple life, that the West pulverizes, while allowing the likes of Kissinger and other Israeli oppressors to run amok: how brutal.

Kissinger is a European Jew. He is responsible for the mass slaughter of people of color: South Americans, Central Americans, Southeast Asians, Sudanese, Egyptians, Iraqis, Iranians, Saudis, Philippinos, Vietnamese, Cambodians, and Palestinians. He has personally instituted policies that have led to the imprisonment, torture, rape, and deaths of thousands of Palestinians, pure Semites. Thus, Kissinger, who has no Middle Eastern blood, is the most murderous of all anti-Semites. What's more, on his hands is the blood of, incredibly, hundreds of millions of people from every conceivable race and culture. His financial supporter is the arch-Zionist Nelson Rockefeller, another anti-Semite. These are the architects of the modern Israeli entity. This is the very entity which has perpetrated the mass displacement, torture, imprisonment, murder, and destruction of the Palestinian people as well as the people of dozens of other Muslim, as well as Christian, countries. The fact is Israel and the various Western powers are true allies: against Islaam. What's more, the Israeli entity is an espionage base for the commission of vast crimes against the various peoples, particularly the Muslims but also Middle Eastern Christians, who resist tyranny: any such people may be attacked by this entity.

Do not forget: the U.S. soldiers in Iraq have died in vain. There is no patriotic reason to be there. No Iraqi attacked the United States. The ultimate architects for this war are the Israelis. Thus, rather than the protection of their sovereign land, which is far removed from Iraq, American service-people are dying exclusively for the Israeli entity. Surely, this war is about oil, but it is also about the imperialism of Israel. This is why the American people are dying. Yet, they are also dying financially. The fact is the American people are paying for this war and the enrichment of an imperious few.

CHAPTER 3
Western Crimes

In Iraq or any other Muslim country the U.S. military serves no purpose. What's more, the claim for rebuilding or protecting Iraq is fraudulent. The fact is the U.S., as well as Britain, destroyed Iraq's infrastructure. These countries were merely attempting to regain their age-old colony, which was first established after World War I. Saddam Hussein no longer suited their purposes. Thus, they deposed him.

Why should anyone give credit for any rebuilding? Regarding schools the entire Iraqi infrastructure has been decimated. If there are people in the streets demonstrating or resisting violently, this is strictly the U.S.'s doing. Any blame on the Muslims is specious.

Do not forget: prior to the invasion of Muslim lands in the Middle East by the powerful Zionists and American elements there were no so-called suicide bombs of any kind. To blame Islaam for the rash of violence now afflicting these regions is particularly cruel, since if there is any such violence, it is in response to the heavy handed tactics of the Zionist entity and the U.S. government.

This is never mentioned—these murderous acts of the West—in the media circles: only Islaam is blamed. Yet, the basis of Islaam is divine; the surrendering of the person's will to the will of God. This is God's method, as prescribed in all scriptures, as taught by the prophets. It is nothing new. However, this is a massive threat to the establishment.

In this attack against Islaam there is another significant issue. The people attacking it, the power-brokers of the United States, as well as the hierarchy of the Israeli entity; these are the very perpetrators of mass atrocities. Corporations also make it their agenda to attack Islaam, particularly those involved in the alcohol, pork, pornography, movie, drug, and weapons industries. What's more, there are billionaires, for instance, Rupert Murdock, who are Zionists and who make every effort to diminish it. The fact is their avowed purpose is to attack and destabilize Islaam. Thus, this religion is under siege.

Yet, rather than Islaamic it is exclusively Western powers which are genocidal. The West is directly responsible for a number of mass crimes. This includes the destruction of entire races, that is the black African, the native Mexican, the native Caribbean, the peoples of Iraq, the Palestinian, and the Native American. These are undeniable acts of genocide. Thus, the West is surely no reliable judge of what is terror. Nothing proclaimed by Western powers can be trusted. This is because such powers are the inventers of terror. There can be no credible information coming from Western powers, particularly the media. Yet, how can anyone believe in the validity of Islaamic terror when the gross atrocities committed by the global, that is Western, rulership are never mentioned?

The oil belongs to the Muslims. It is their land. They have lived there for over a thousand years. The powerful ones of the West are a pack of thieves who wickedly steal the peoples' resources. Then, when the common man resists, when he fights with all his might against this tyranny, he is deemed a militant and/or insurgent: how vile. Yet, the invasions of the Muslim lands are themselves based purely on fraud. For instance, the invasion of Iraq and Afghanistan was based upon 9/11. Even so, the Muslims had no involvement in this atrocity. Thus, could there be a greater fraud than this?

Regarding terror most people associate this with Islaam. Yet, Islaam has never been responsible for such acts, that is as have been committed by Western governments. Evaluate all modern history as evidence. Are there any Muslim-orchestrated world wars or even wars against specific countries? Is there even a single Islaamic Saddam Hussein, Shah of Iran, Henry Kissinger, Paul Wolfowitz, Richard Perle, George Bush, Dick Cheney, Dov Zakheim, Douglas Feith, or Donald Rumsfeld? Are there any Islaamic corporate chiefs, such as GE's Jack Welch, who promote war agendas, merely to boost profits? All such men have perpetrated the mass murder of the common persons, particularly Muslims. What's more, let them prove that they are not responsible for the murder of the innocent.

Is there an Islaamic Mossad or CIA? Is there a Muslim-orchestrated invasion/destruction of a sovereign land: Chechnya, Bosnia, Vietnam, Cambodia, South Africa, and/or Palestine? What's more, are there any Islaamic apartheids? Only the West perpetrates these. So, if the Muslims are truly the source, again, where is the evidence? Where are the Islaamic tyrants who are brutalizing the people at large? Where are the Muslim societies, which bomb the common people into oblivion, even striking them with poison gas, that is when they resist oppressive rule? Where are the Muslims who create clandestine wars to brutalize the masses and undermine their strength? Where are the Muslim governments, which create genocidal policies to reduce global population? Where are the Muslim clandestine groups, which expel the rulers of other countries, all for material gain? Name a single example, if anyone can. There are no such examples.

Where are the examples of Muslims causing people to starve to death through brutal international sanctions? Where are the examples of Muslims sitting in judgement over the peoples of entire countries—entire races and cultures—deeming them less than human, determining whether they shall survive or die? There are no such examples. On the contrary, all such deeds were/are committed by the West.

Surely, all deaths of the innocent are atrocious. Yet, there are vast atrocities perpetrated against Muslims, as well as various Christians, particularly in the Middle East, which are never reported. Consider the Israeli assassination squads in Iraq. These squads have murdered in cold blood some 500 Iraqi scientists, supposedly because of the latter's knowledge of weapons manufacturing. These are hit teams, which murder civilians, in fact, intellectuals. The same is being perpetrated against both Muslims and Christians of Palestinian origin. Thus, rather than Islaam it is the West which is forcing Iraq into the 'dark ages.'

Americans surely would never tolerate this on their soil. Then, how could it be acceptable against another people? These scientists posed no threat to Americans. Yet, since the U.S. invasion no Iraqi intellectuals are safe. All are fair game. These men and women were/are hunted down like animals and murdered in cold blood, all by Western espionage agents. None of these Iraqi civilians has harmed even a single American nor any other Westerner. Yet, due to the evil agenda of the criminal Zionists these highly educated and socially valuable people are being wantonly slaughtered. This is a war crime beyond comprehension.

Americans must be leery of who they support, even with their hearts. This is particularly true of those who fear God. Yet, it is also true of non-believers. The fact is why support someone who fails to reciprocate? It was the brute Ariel Sharon who said that the U.S. doesn't determine any policies. Rather, he said, *Israel determines them* and the U.S. must submit to it. Even so, the U.S. government is also responsible, that is along with the Israelis, for the slaughter. Despite this people feel it is their "duty" to support these crimes, such as, the Iraq war. This is despite the fact that by supporting George Bush and "the troops" each American is, actually, supporting the illegal Israeli regime as well as a war that violates all decency. They are also supporting the needless deaths of American youth. Yet, even if it was truly a well-intended policy, even if, somehow, it was believed that invading Iraq was for the good of the 'homeland,' still, would anyone knowingly support a man such as this:

> God told me to strike at al-Qaida and I struck them: and then He instructed me to strike at Saddam, which I did: and now I am determined to solve the problem in the Middle East. If you help me, I will act, and if not, the elections will come and I will have to focus on them (an exact quote of George Bush as reported by the Israeli newspaper *Haaretz*).

Is he really talking to God? Or, is this merely human delusions? What's more, of which al-Qaeda does he speak, the Israeli one or the CIA's? Is there anything about what he said that is God-like? Or, is he merely attempting to secure the so-called Jewish vote? When has God ordered anyone to bomb a country, wantonly killing the innocent—all based upon lies? There is another name for this: Satan. As reported in the prestigious English medical journal the *Lancet* the vast number of innocent Iraqi civilians slaughtered through

Bush's war numbers at least 100,000. Will Bush now attribute to God the deaths of these pitiful souls? Is Abu Ghraib, with its attempts at forced conversions, part of that rite? If he does claim this as a divine right, that is the torture and attempted forced conversions of the innocent, then, will Americans continue to tie ribbons in support of his deeds?

If George Bush truly worships God, the same God that the common person bows to in worship, then, he must realize a simple fact. It is that rather than authorizing any slaughter almighty God condemns the killing of the innocent and, what's more, has established specific rules against this. It is the same One who says "You shall not spread corruption nor steal or torment anyone." However, according to Somia al-Zubeid, a Baghdad housewife:

> Seven U.S. soldiers stormed into my house at night and ordered us to lie prone with their weapons pointing at our necks as if we were sheep, four of them scoured the house for more than one hour they were heedless to the fact that we were women at home alone. They turned the house upside down and stole (the equivalent of $2500, a fortune in poverty-stricken Iraq) in addition to some of my daughters' jewels.

These are the soldiers of the same George Bush, who, supposedly, talks to God? The fact is Bush is violating the divine law, per the Qur'an, "Do not spread corruption on the earth" and "Do not steal" and, what's more, "do not spread tyranny."

Yet, people are largely apathetic. This is because they have fully accepted the official stories. The New York City and London bombings are examples of a kind of mind control. Truly, these acts demonstrate how easy it is to control peoples' thinking. In London Muslims are being subjected to mass arrests and numerous other abuses. Yet, no Jews are harassed, even though the second group of London bombers included a known Jewish spy.

False terror: the Israeli connection

In the United States and England Muslim communities are united in one critical area: they condemn all terrorist acts. However, will all churches and ministries also condemn the gross terror which is inflicted upon the Muslims such as the horrors of the Iraqi invasion and the Israeli apartheid? The fact is numerous ministers fully support the war, even if it results in the deaths of the innocent, including American youths. What's more, if a Christian commits a violent crime, like a mass killing, no churches or Christian neighborhoods are raided. This latter response is reserved exclusively for Muslims. They are even punished for acts they never committed, even bombed into oblivion. Incredibly, this is for acts committed in their names by their enemies.

Surely, in England the Queen and her minions have an agenda against the Muslims. With the violent and arbitrary raids in that country she has proven her hatred towards Islaam.

Yet, regarding the London bombings no religious Muslims were involved. This was a government operation, timed perfectly to suit the agenda of global powers. There is no evidence of an Islaamic act. Consider the second London bombing. The four who apparently committed this are not religious. They are not members of the recognized Muslim community. What's more, curiously, they were all relatively recent immigrants, from Ethiopia and Eritrea. These are war-torn and poverty-stricken regions. These men were paid to commit these crimes on the basis that they would be protected. Only a fool would commit such deeds in full view of hundreds of surveillance cameras and under the vast degree of scrutiny at the time. What's more, the Muslim community had already condemned such acts. If they were Muslims, they were surely outcasts.

Even the *New York Times*, July 26, reported that the original story is faulty. Here, interviews with British police make it clear that the original claim of suicide bombers, who intended to harm the common people, is false. British investigators concluded that there was no evidence of a so-called Islaamic suicidal act.

There is even much doubt that these bombs were built or set by Muslims. Regarding the seeking of revenge 'against the West' there is no evidence for this. Rather, it would appear, the vengeance was against Islaam. This is because one of these bombers is a Zionist agent. This individual was fully hired and payed for by the Israelis. He disguised himself as a Muslim. He used the alias Osman Hussain. However, his real name is Hamdi Isaac or Hamdi Ishaq. Rather than a Muslim he is an Ethiopian Jew. Part of his disguise was the fact that he wore 'Islaamic' clothes and had a wife who was 'veiled.'

For Eritrean/Ethiopian Jews Isaac and Ishaq are highly common Jewish names. Another spelling of this bomber's name, Issac, is exclusively Jewish. What's more, there is an extensive Israeli/Mossad presence in these countries.

After the bombing he made a daring escape to Rome. According to Italian police Isaac boasted a sophisticated 'network' of agents, which covered his escape. The police repeatedly emphasized the scope of this network, describing it as "dense." In other words, they had difficulty penetrating it. Thus, rather than a dutiful Muslim—Isaac, a confessed bomber, was an agent of terror "on retainer."

It is no surprise that Eritreans and Ethiopians would be paid by the Mossad. The Israelis have a heavy presence in Eritrea and Ethiopia. The fact is they are the main architects of the Eritrean/Ethiopian war. What's more, they used this war as a means to create a Sudanese element, the so-called southern Sudanese resistance. This was in order to topple any potential Islaamic government there. Regarding the Eritrean and Ethiopian conflict they created it for multiple purposes: to destabilize the Muslim country of Somalia, to sell masses of weapons, to greatly destabilize Ethiopia, and, ultimately, to invade Sudan. Regarding this they were highly successful. In Ethiopia their efforts led to the mass emigration of this country's Jews, some 90,000 or more. These wars were perpetrated to create international strife, all to orchestrate a refugee crisis. This was in order to forcibly settle the Palestinian territories with Ethiopian Jews.

This influx of the poor and disadvantaged greatly serves the Zionist agenda. This chaos of Jewish mass migration is a mainstay of Zionism. The Zionists did the same in Iraq, fabricating terror events against fellow Jews. This was again to force the emigration of Iraqi Jews to Israel. The greater purpose is the complete colonization of the entire Middle East, making it one vast Jewish empire. This is what is, in fact, happening. Essentially, the Muslims, as well as Christians, are being pushed into the sea.

The New Zealand connection

The Mossad is the most ruthless terror organization known. Its reach is extensive. Recently, New Zealand officials uncovered a Mossad cell responsible for numerous crimes. These agents were captured and imprisoned. Definitely proving they were Mossad agents, they also discovered an identity theft ring. They even determined that the agents killed people to steal their identities. The agents kept their distance from the murders by hiring criminal Asian gangs, who they payed for the killings. The identities were then forwarded to Mossad agents for use in espionage. This was obviously a 'clean' way to gain false identities.

One of these agents, Ev Barkam, now on the run, attempted to create al-Qaeda cells in Thailand. This was so that terror acts could be created which would, then, be blamed on the Muslims, who are already under siege in this country. In this high profile case, known as Passport Theft Ring, two Mossad agents were caught and jailed, while the ringleader remains at large. What's more, reported Thai police, Israeli terrorists are "posing as Muslim terrorists," who, then, attempt to recruit disgruntled Muslims. Then, they provoke these Muslims to perpetrate terror acts. They urge them on the basis that it is their 'Islaamic duty' to 'fight the oppressors.' Thus, these Israelis are predators, who target the innocent. If the Muslims fail to do so, they perform the acts themselves. Then, once the terror act is completed they issue a claim of responsibility for a supposed Islaamic terror organization.

They often attempt to recruit people via email, one such email supposedly being signed by bin Laden. It has now been determined that the email was false. Perhaps this capturing of Australian identities was part of the process leading to the Bali bombing, which was, again, erroneously blamed on Muslims.

Using stolen Canadian identity documents, Barkam is thought to be hiding in North Korea. He is originally from New York City, his family name being Zev Bruckenstein. The New Zealand government identified the two Mossad agents, who were captured and imprisoned, as Eli Cara and Uriel Kelman.

The investigation revealed phone calls to the recruits purporting to be from Pakistan, Lebanon, and Germany. However, deeper probing by New Zealand police determined that all the calls came "from Israel." Then, once the Mossad agents determined that the Muslims or other Muslim-appearing recruits were suitable, they gave them money, weapons, and documents. These documents were mainly Australian passports. The money was transferred directly from Israel, as well as Jerusalem, said the New Zealand official. In other words, the Zionist conspiracy is proven. The use of real Muslims would help confirm any terror as Islaamic.

There are those who would attempt to dispute such findings. Yet, why would this surprise anyone? These are the same perpetrators who drove 4 million people from their homes through every conceivable terrorist act, a fact fully documented by British historians. Through these vile atrocities countless thousands have been killed. Why would a few Australian tourists be exempt?

The London bomber is Jewish

It bears repeating. He used a Muslim name and lived as if a Muslim, although he maintained a double life. Apparently, he maintained a fully covered 'Muslim' wife. Yet, he partied frequently, keeping in Rome an Italian girlfriend. He maintained contacts with his girlfriend continuously, visiting her as often as possible. Yet, this is who the media promotes as an "Islaamic" bomber?

The reason this is crucial is because people use these events to justify the contempt directed towards Islaam. Rather than a Muslim, Hamdi Isaac is a Jew. This revelation was apparently so threatening that after the bombing a "hit" was ordered on him. Thus, the murder of the Brazilian

Charles de Menezes was due to mistaken identity: the killers thought he was Isaac. Once again, the enemies of Islaam prove their wickedness.

Isaac said his sole purpose was to "sow terror." Zionist operatives, as well as the Israeli high command, are the only ones who use such terminology. What is certain is that Muslims never say this. This is because the incitement of terror is prohibited in this faith. Furthermore, he had a thorough 'cover' network, aiding in his escape from London all the way to Rome.

The proof of the Zionist connection is compelling. According to Italian investigators Isaac "counted on an extensive network from the Horn of Africa (that is the Israeli enclave of Ethiopia) in Italy to protect him in his flight from London, through Paris to Rome." Thus, there is no possibility that this was an Islaamic bombing. Rather, this was an espionage act conducted by 'professionals.'

Ethiopia is an Israeli protectorate. Its weapons are from Israel. There are hundreds of Israeli military advisors there. According to Moshe Fergie, Mossad agent and expert on African affairs, the Israelis specifically train both Ethiopian and Eritrean Jews in espionage. This is a focus, because these Eritreans and Ethiopians are Islaamic-appearing. They begin the indoctrination at a young age, therefore, the origin of Adus Isaac.

Many of these trainees become global Mossad agents. The entire unit which attempted to ensure Isaac's protection was Ethiopian. Only Israel has displaced and, then, re-established nearly 100,000 Ethiopians. Hamdi Isaac is one of these.

During the investigation a false document center was discovered. This was similar to the one uncovered by New Zealand police. In the creation of forged documents only the Mossad is the international expert.

In Ethiopia there is no al-Qaeda network. However, the Mossad operates there. In fact, it has extensive offices in this country. Rather, it largely runs the Ethiopian government. The same is true of Eritrea. In fact, this country is one of the largest importers of Israeli arms. Thus, the Eritrean-Ethiopian connection points to Israel. What's more, in contrast to the Muslims only the Israelis have an extensive history of bombing British and Australian establishments. They have previously killed hundreds of innocent British. What's more, the Israelis have the motive: just prior to the bombings the British had proclaimed a plan to reduce troops in Iraq by 50%. Likewise, when Mexico refused to support the Iraq war the Israelis attempted to destroy the Mexican equivalent of the U. S. Senate, just as when the Australians marked their position against the war, Bali was bombed. The pattern is confirmed. Thus, the proposed British withdrawal greatly angered the Israelis, so they chose to attack. This is also why they maintained the claim that the bombings were due to "Muslim anger over the atrocities in Iraq." In other words, the Mossad wanted the bombings to be centered on an Islaamic or Middle Eastern theme. Yet, incredibly, rather than Muslim anger it was Israeli rage which was the source.

Even so, regarding the captured bomber he is a minor player. The only foreign authority in power in his country of origin is the Israelis. This is absolute proof of an Israeli attack on London, that is through the African-Italian conduit. In contrast, there is no Islaamic presence in Ethiopia or Eritrea. What's more, no Islaamic organization supported these bombers. Rather, the fact is an Islaamic group had long before reported these aggressors to the police for the expressed purpose of preventing such an attack. Thus, the London bombings, as well as 9/11, were

Israeli plots. What's more, rather than the Muslims the blood is on the hands of the Zionists.

Here is a revealing fact. Of all the accused bombers, the nineteen of 9/11 and the eight of the London attacks, only one has confessed to involvement. In other words, only one has *admitted to committing terror*. This is the Zionist Jew Adus Isaac. This man masqueraded as a Muslim in an attempt to diminish Islaam and to create international indignation against it, a subject which will be covered in more detail later.

CHAPTER 4
Israeli Terror

It is obvious that the Muslims are being framed. This is perpetrated mainly by various Israeli elements, which seek the destruction of this religion. The Israelis have been caught in the midst of committing terror, for instance, in Mexico City, India, and England, impersonating Muslims. In contrast, no Muslims have been caught impersonating Jews. The recent bombing of a nightclub in Indonesia demonstrates the degree of Israeli venom. Rather than any plot by angry or 'extremist' Muslims the bombing was industrial or, rather, military. What's more, it was directly related to the war agenda. From these wars the Israelis have earned untold billions of dollars. In contrast, the Muslims have lost countless billions of dollars, along with millions of lives. Plus, in some regions the entire future of the Muslims has been ruined, all at the hands of Zionist perpetrators.

The Bali bombing

This was engineered to place blame on the Muslims. Yet, there is no evidence of Islaamic involvement in this crime.

The fact is the Muslims are incapable of causing such a disaster. Then, the source of this act becomes obvious.

The timing of the incident is also suspect. The explosion occurred at the same time as vast resistance in Australia against the Iraq war. Hundreds of thousands of Australians protested, marching in the streets, resisting any effort to send Australian troops. Shortly thereafter this bombing occurred, which ended the resistance.

Again, the timing belies an Islaamic act. True, the victims were mainly Westerners, that is Australians. However, this was a professional job. They were brutally murdered by a wicked fireball, a bomb of great power and sophistication. These Australians were precisely the people who massively protested against the war. Then, are people to believe that one or two lone Muslims, who supposedly wanted to root out corruption, were the culprits? This is ludicrous. Regardless, the bombing was a professional job, and the types of explosives used were military-grade. There is no possibility that this was a suicide bomb. What's more, whoever did this made a deliberate effort to kill Australians.

Would the Muslims be so imbecilic to alienate a great anti-war movement, in other words, to feed directly into the Zionist agenda? Would they be so unaware that such heinous acts would aid the coalition, forcing the hand of the Australian Prime Minister, encouraging him to send troops? The fact is rather than any Muslim cause it was the war agenda which benefitted. The bombing damaged the Islaamic cause globally, increasing aggression against it. Thus, rather than angry or crazed Muslims the culprits were obviously Islaam's enemies.

An investigative report by an American Citizen group, Physics 911, resulted in the following analysis, much of it based upon work by now late former government insider Joe Vialls.

Late at night, on October 12, 2003, a busy nightclub in Bali, Indonesia was blown to shreds, killing 187 people. The bomb was placed *under a nearby road*. It excavated a vast crater. The force of the blast set some 27 buildings in the neighborhood on fire. The night club was completely destroyed. Said Vialls:

> No known conventional explosive is powerful enough to have the destructive effect of this one, yet still fit inside a localized section of drain. However, micronuclear devices are small enough to fit most public drains and can be fished into place from the nearest maintenance port.

Australian physicians were puzzled at 'flash burns' on victims. Other victims vanished 'without a trace.' The media claimed that a fuel-air explosive packed into a van was the source of the blast. Yet, the media has no expertise in the nature of such a bombing. Says Vialls the official claim is baseless. "It is absolutely impossible for a passive explosive…to dig a five foot crater." Moreover, a fuel-air explosive could not account for the vast damage found for hundreds of yards.

Micronuclear devices readily fit in a suitcase. These devices are capable of pulverizing entire buildings, rather, city blocks. What's more, they are capable of turning living beings, as well as metal and concrete, into mere dust. Furthermore, Muslims have no access to them. The fact is they are made by the Israelis, who have dozens of them.

Victims of the blast were dying weeks later for no apparent reason, unless it was from inhaling deadly plutonium released into the local atmosphere. This is a progressively lethal poison, which explains the persistent deaths seen in the Bali debacle. Because of their adamant resistance to the war the Australians were sent a message. Obviously, this was not from the Muslims. Regardless, again, the Muslims do not have the capabilities or funds to build such bombs.

Today, in Iraq and Afghanistan they are being attacked with nuclear munitions. Then, if they had such weapons, why do they not use them, that is in actual battle?

Yet, the blast was blamed on them. A lone Muslim, Abu Bakar Bashir, was held liable. However, he immediately accused Israel and the United States of the crime. Ultimately, he was released as innocent.

The effort to pin this on locals was continuous. Under pressure from Western governments the Indonesians found a supposed culprit. An auto mechanic named Amorzi confessed to it. However, it was determined that prior to the confession the man had been drugged and tortured; he was subjected to brutal electroshock therapy with 220-volt electrodes. He also supposedly confessed to links with al-Qaeda and Islaamic 'terror' groups. Yet, a top Indonesian official and parliamentary speaker, the highly respected Amien Rais, stated publicly that he "doubted that Amorzi was responsible for the bombing."

In a repeat of the 9/11 debacle all material, as well as soil, from the blast site was removed and dumped far out to sea. Obviously, this was a government coverup. Bribes were exchanged in order to achieve it. Incredibly, of some 30 people who were at the blast site not a trace, not even a fingerprint, was ever found. Anyone too near the center of the initial wave of intense heat, approximately 400,000 degrees Celsius, was vaporized. Obviously, this was a professional job, which, again, implicates a government or military power.

The destruction at Bali was politically motivated. The Muslims had nothing to do with it. The source of the bomb, most likely a micronuke, was almost assuredly Israel.

The Madrid bombing

There is no possibility that this was the work of Muslims. Like Bali, this was exclusively a professional job. Highly sophisticated, these bombs were detonated simultaneously by remote control. It was surely a kind of Zionist punishment—for the withdrawal by the Spanish from the war. This would serve the Zionists vastly: to punish the Spanish and remind them who is really in control as well as to lay blame against the Muslims.

The people responsible had access to the trains prior to their departures. In other words, the bombs were planted. As usual Muslims were blamed but, conveniently, there were no witnesses. Nor is there any video footage showing Muslim bombers. What's more, as confirmed by Spanish officials none of the bombs were caused by suicide bombers. The fact is like Bali: this was punishment for the Spaniard's withdrawal from the war.

The bombing materials used to rip the Madrid trains apart were military-grade. This has led authorities to regard this as a "professional job." The bombs were also sequential, indicating a *high degree of sophistication.* Yet, the key is that in order to bomb these trains access was required. As demonstrated by Vialls all the trains were at first initial runs which had been serviced the night before. Thus, there was ample time for bombs to be planted and for any suspicion to be avoided. The Muslims, already under extensive scrutiny, had no such access. Rather, only non-Muslim agents, including Israelis, had such access.

Globally, people are told that this was an Islaamic act. Yet, remember this: the information arises from the Zionist-controlled media. Clearly, the bombings were caused by military-grade explosives. What's more, this was a highly sophisticated attack caused by bombs strategically placed, which were simultaneously exploded. No amateur bomber could achieve this. In order to do so, again, the bombs had to be planted. Does anyone believe that obvious Muslims would have even a remote degree of such access? The fact is such a claim is ludicrous.

Prior to the attack there was massive pressure by the Spanish public to exit Iraq. This was the same pressure which developed in Australian. Then, both the Spanish and Australians were slaughtered. This was dubiously blamed on Muslims. The fact is this makes no sense. Why would the Muslims bomb the very countries which resisted the war effort? Rather, only the war perpetrators would logically do so.

Yet, only professional grade explosives could have caused such carnage. This degree of damage, Vialls notes, would require some "40 pounds of high-yield explosive." A number of Middle Eastern appearing men carrying such heavy loads would surely have aroused suspicion; surely, there would be pictorial proof of this. Yet, there is no such proof.

Despite media hype the blasts "could not have originated from inside the cars. Rather than downward blast holes, the floors were obviously *bent upwards*. Shrapnel from the floors of the cars was found *embedded in the ceilings*." The fact that metal from underneath the train was imbedded in the ceiling eliminates the possibility of a human-carried bomb.

Vialls also observed that while the media reported that the supposed bombers had boarded trains that were "passing through" the Acala de Henares station "in fact all four trains originated from the nearby rail yards, starting their day's run from that location." Obviously, the explosives were planted by "security" the night before and, then, were exploded simultaneously by remote control. Only experienced espionage agencies, notably the Mossad and Haganah, perhaps the CIA, have such capacities. Note also that both the Spanish and the Australians—the latter being the main victims of Bali—were bombed. Both had violently protested the Israeli-mandated Iraq war. There is no possibility Muslims would have deliberately targeted civilians from the very countries which were against the war. Rather, it is the war mongers of the West who would have done so. The Israelis hold their supposed nation as all-high, as if a divinity. Thus, any act which sustains it is warranted. This includes the wanton slaughter of the innocent.

When the attack occurred, there was massive pressure by the public upon the Spanish government to exit Iraq. What's more, incredibly, this attack had the opposite effect of the globalists' plan.

For Muslims the timing of the bombings could not have been worse. Globally, indignation against their cause was the result. For the Muslims to strike at that time would have been a public relations disaster. Yet, it was the now deceased Vialls who wisely noted that the purpose of the attack was to "enrage the Spanish public who, up to that time, were more than 90% against this war." Thus, who was it that sought to enrage them? Surely, it wasn't the Muslims.

Yet, a person can demonstrate all the proof in the world. Arguments can be made. Points can be emphasized. Common beliefs can be disproved. However, it will make no difference in many peoples' minds. People believe what they wish to believe. After decades of proclamations the emphatic claims by the media that Islaam supports terrorism, even though there is no firm evidence regarding this, even though, historically, the reverse is true, still, people hold firmly to these beliefs. The fact is it is Western powers which are the obvious perpetrators of terror: World War I, World War II, the Vietnam War, Waco, the Iran-Iraq War, and Ruby Ridge being only a modicum of the examples. Then, there are, more recently, 9/11, the London bombings, Bali, Madrid, and more.

Even so, the purpose here is never to 'convince' anyone. People can only convince themselves. Rather, it is to warn the population regarding the obvious lies, which are perpetrated for wicked gains. In this regard Islaam is the major victim as well as the target. For anyone who gives it thought this is obvious.

Previous terrorist acts: history is revealing

The King David Hotel

According to top U.S. Army officials Zionists routinely target Western assets, including civilian buildings. Then, when they commit any carnage, they blame the Muslims as culprits.

The Zionist entity was created through terror. The atrocity of the King David Hotel is merely one example. The Israelis were angry with their benefactors the British, for their attempts to hold them accountable. So, they attacked them. They bombed the British headquarters of Palestine. Their intent was to create vast carnage and, then, blame it on Muslims. Dressed like desert Arabs they entered the hotel, carrying milk cans filled with TNT to the basement (note that in the World Trade Center bombs also exploded in the basement). Yet, the plot backfired.

They would have succeeded in blaming the Muslims, but an alert British agent confronted them. A shoot-out ensued, but the Irgun successfully lit the charges, destroying the hotel. Said W. L. Hull in his book *The Fall and Rise of Israel*:

> The loss of life was terrible—some ninety-five persons, including British (that is Christians), Jews, and Arabs. For several days army engineers toiled day and night, lifting huge blocks of concrete and iron girders, seeking to rescue

those who had been buried under the debris. Over all hung a thick cloud of dust. Living bodies were uncovered up to three days after the explosion, but most of these subsequently died. The terrorists bombings were successful...

The Zionists, mere thugs, murdered these people. The victims included fellow Jews. The fact is the Israeli entity is based upon such acts of terror. The Israelis kill people and cause unknown numbers of others to suffer, all to further their own wicked aims. What's more, they have never been held accountable for these acts.

The destruction of this hotel is reminiscent of various crimes in the United States, where buildings were bombed, mercilessly crushing people to death: Oklahoma City, the World Trade Center attacks, and the attack on the Pentagon. In these cases rather than Zionists or other hidden operatives the Muslims were blamed, although in Oklahoma City this was quickly retracted. Yet, only the Zionists have a proven history of committing such acts.

There is no Islaamic precedent of bombing public buildings. In the entire history of Islaamic civilization, a period of nearly 1,000 years, there is not a single case of a such a bombing. The destruction of buildings by set charges or planted bombs is a Western, rather, European, invention. This method was prevalent throughout the entirety of the World Wars. What's more, today, it is a mainstay of Israeli attacks against Palestinians.

Even sympathizers, such as W. L. Will, fully acknowledged that the Jews achieved their power only through "a reign of terror." Notably, these Zionists claimed that 'terror was the only way they would achieve statehood.' So, since it worked for them in the past, it would be expected that they would continue to use these methods. Again, only the Zionists willfully bomb public buildings, deliberately targeting the innocent. What's more, incredibly, only they been caught in the act. They were caught bombing the King David Hotel and more recently attempting to do so in the Mexican Congress. During the 1950s in Egypt they were captured attempting to destroy U.S. installations. During the September 11 attacks they were caught celebrating as people were being roasted alive and jumping thousands of feet to their deaths.

Also, astonishingly, on 9/11 Israeli nationals were apprehended with a van full of explosives. Due to the detailed maps they held the target was the George Washington Bridge. Alert law-enforcement officials apparently prevented another catastrophe. These Israelis possessed detailed maps of American landmarks, along with box cutters and cash stuffed in socks. The cash was used for purchases, that is to avoid any paper trail.

This is easy for them to do. This is because they are fully funded to create mass terror. In contrast, any Muslim armies are comparatively poor. The Israelis are given carte blanche by the United States many billions of dollars every year. These monies fund international terror acts. Then, who would truly believe the PR blurbs from the Israelis regarding the source for terror? The fact is they are its inventors.

Deir Yassin

This was a massacre of an entire village. The Zionists, mostly Europeans, were fierce invaders. Their goal: through terrorism to drive people from the land. The notorious Irgun gang, a group of thugs headed by Menachem Begin, entered the defenseless village and slaughtered the inhabitants. Some 200 people, mostly women and children, were killed, the bodies thrown into a well. The survivors were stripped of their clothes, packed into a truck and taken to Jerusalem, where they were paraded about naked. Clearly, this was to create fear in order to further Zionist expansionism: to drive the Palestinians en masse from their homes. This was a war crime of unprecedented proportions, equal in severity, rather, more extreme, than Nazi acts.

In her book *Armageddon in the Middle East* Dana Adams Schmidt describes this massacre as a "systematic act of terrorism." Its purpose: to create "panic" in an already frightened people who were beginning a mass exodus. It was a vile atrocity, and word of it spread quickly. This created mass panic. The fact is the Deir Yassin massacre was so calculated, so utterly brutal, that hundreds of thousands of Palestinians immediately began to abandon their homes and take distant refuge. This exodus was already instigated by the Israeli "dynamiting of their villages." Yet, wrote Schmidt, it was the Israelis themselves who confirmed the truth of these statements, when a top Irgun member told him that the use of "terror, bombs, and assassination...(is) the only way" to achieve their goals. This brings into dispute the common myth that the local people, Muslims and Christians, as well as indigenous Jews, "invited" the Europeans to take their land. Here, it is said, the local people "felt bad" for the supposedly displaced foreigners, and, therefore, accommodated them. There was no such invitation. Nor was there any welcome. Rather, the locals continuously resisted the encroachment. The land was merely stolen, and this was through terror, coercion, murder and tyranny.

Sabra and Shatila

Ralph Shoenman in his book the *Hidden History of Zionism* gives perhaps the most succinct account of this atrocity. These were refugee camps, utterly squalid. In fact, their existence was a consequence of Israeli oppression. Long before, the people were driven into these camps, and their homes and land confiscated by the Zionists. The camps housed exclusively women, children, and older men. There were no Palestinian fighters in the camps.

In 1982 during the Israeli invasion of Lebanon Israeli troops fully encircled the camps. Then, they orchestrated the terror. Using Israeli-trained Christian militia as their henchmen the camps were invaded and the inhabitants slaughtered.

As documented by *Time Magazine,* a less than sympathetic outlet, the crime was organized by the chief Zionist Ariel Sharon. What's more, it was no spontaneous act. Weeks prior Sharon had planned to exterminate the inhabitants: these were the wives, children, and family members of Palestinian fighters, who had been recently driven out of the country. The Israeli news journal *Haaretz* reported the quote of the then Chief of Staff General Raphael Eitan, "All four Palestinian (refugee) camps are hermetically sealed." As reported in the *New York Times*, as if to memorialize Sharon as a globally recognized premeditated murderer, "Sharon told the Knesset that the General Staff and the Commander in Chief of the Phalangists met twice with Israel's ranking generals (regarding) entering the camps, which they did the next afternoon."

The Israelis met with the militia only a few days before the slaughter. According to a militia member 12 uniformed Israelis came to them to prepare them for the act. They swore them to silence, that is to prevent the revelation that this was an Israeli operative. Yet, the Christian fundamentalist militia was wholly dependent upon them: for guidance, advice, and military equipment. Without doubt, this was entirely an Israeli operation. The militia was merely an extension of the Israeli terror squads, and their equipment was U.S. in origin. Yet, the direct Israeli role in the slaughter is never reported.

The Jewish journalist and eyewitness Schoenman documented proof of the Israeli involvement. Quoting Christian militia members:

> At about 10 p.m. we climbed into an American army truck that the Israelis had given over to us. We parked the vehicle near the airport tower. There, immediately next to the Israeli positions, several such trucks were already parked. Some Israelis in Phalange (Christian militia) uniforms were with the Party. "The Israeli friends who accompany you," our officers told us, "…will make your work easier." They direct us not to make use of our firearms, if at all possible. "Everything must proceed noiselessly."
>
> We saw other comrades. They had to do their work with bayonets and knives. Bloody corpses were lying in the alleys. The half-asleep women and children who cried out for help put our whole plan in danger, alarming the entire camp.
>
> Now I saw once again the Israelis who had been at our secret meeting. One signaled us to move back to areas of the camp entrance. The Israelis opened up with all their guns. The Israelis helped us with floodlights.
>
> There were shocking scenes that showed what the Palestinians were good for. A few, including women, had taken shelter in a small alley, behind some donkeys. Unfortunately we had to shoot down these poor animals to finish off the Palestinians behind them. It got to me when the animals cried out in pain. It was gruesome…at about four in the morning my squad went back to the truck. When there was morning light, we drove back into the camp. We went past bodies, stumbled over bodies, shot and stabbed all eyewitnesses. Killing others was easy once you have done it a few times.
>
> Now came the Israeli Army bulldozer. "Plow everything under the ground. Don't let any witnesses stay alive." But despite our efforts the area was still teeming with people. They ran about and caused awful

confusion. The order to "plow them under" demanded too much. It became clear that the...plan failed. Thousands had escaped us.

Yet, there was an enormous death toll in the camps: some 3,800 women, children, old men, and young boys but no fighters. The latter were driven out months prior to ensure no resistance. Thus, not only were the attackers cold-blooded murderers but they were also cowards. Now consider the brutality of this Israeli-trained terrorist, as he closes his statement:

Far too many Palestinians are still alive. Everywhere, now, people are talking about a massacre and feeling sorry for the Palestinians. Who appreciates the hardships that we took upon ourselves...just think. I fought for twenty-four hours in Shatila without food or drink.

The accuracy of this account is demonstrated by the fact that the reporter and author, Schoenman, was in Lebanon when this happened. Within a few hours he interviewed numerous eyewitnesses and visited the camps. He also confirmed that during the invasion of Lebanon some 20,000 additional civilians, Palestinians and Lebanese, again, mostly women, children, and the elderly, were slaughtered. The war left some 400,000 homeless.

Schoenman notes that after taking control of south Lebanon the Israelis stole all that could be taken: all heavy machinery, warehouse inventory, industrial equipment, machine tools, agricultural equipment, in short, all that they could haul away: all taken to Israel. Even the water was stolen, that is through the diversion of the Litani River, plus thousands of tons of topsoil was stripped from the land and hauled away.

This is the very Israel that the so-called Christian fundamentalists support: an evil entity that violates everything

Christian. What's more, the very victims of this brutality are largely Christian, since the Lebanese are nearly 40% Christian. Thus, incredibly, by supporting the Israeli entity Christian fundamentalists are supporting the slaughter of their fellows in faith.

This is planned and plotted terrorism which was truly achieved against Christians, Muslims, and Jews. The Israelis show no bias towards whom they brutalize. Their fellow Jews, particularly those of Middle Eastern origin, are usually treated with contempt. What's more, they inflict such atrocities for mere material gain: the gains of wealth, land, power, and status. Then, again, who can believe after realizing this that Islaam is the source of global terror? Schoenman was there during the "final day of the slaughter." He knows precisely what happened.

Yet, Islaam holds the religious Jews in high regard, giving them complete freedom of worship. Thus, the God-fearing Jews are given greater freedom and respect under the auspices of Islaam than even within the Israeli entity.

The Lavon Affair

As reported by the *London Times* during plans for an Israeli invasion of Egypt (mid-1950s) the Israelis were perturbed by a hesitant U.S. presidency. They wanted the U.S. to aggressively support them. So, they attempted to bomb a U.S. facility in Egypt, blaming it on the Muslims. However, the plan was wrecked when the spies were caught and confessed, creating a major scandal. This is known as the Lavon Affair after the name of its organizer, then Israeli Defense Minister Pinhas Lavon. An analysis by *American Free Press* is revealing:

Perhaps the best-known instance in which Israel used a "false flag" to cover its own trail was in the infamous Lavon Affair. It was in 1954 that several Israeli-orchestrated acts of terrorism against (Western) targets in Egypt were carried out. Blame for the attacks was placed on the Muslim Brotherhood, which opposed the regime of Egyptian President Gamul Abdul-Nasser. However, the truth about the wave of terror is found in a once-secret cable from Colonel Benjamin Givli, the head of Israel's military intelligence, who outlined the intended purpose behind the wave of terror:

"[Our goal] is to break the West's confidence in the existing [Egyptian] regime. The actions should cause arrests, demonstrations, and expressions of revenge. The Israeli origin should be totally covered while attention should be shifted to any other possible factor. The purpose is to prevent economic and military aid from the West to Egypt."

To further their agenda Zionists will destroy and kill *by any means necessary*. The following is yet another attempt of brazen killing, true terror, to achieve political ends. This proves that the Zionists have over a 50 year history of fabricating terror events as well as a willingness to freely kill even their allies.

The U.S.S. Liberty

In 1967 during the Six Day War the United States began espionage activities. This was to determine the origin of the conflict. The spying vessel, the U.S.S. Liberty, was stationed off the coasts of Egypt and Israel. The commander determined that Israel had, in fact, initiated the war. This was contrary to the global news, which promoted the Israeli claim that it was the victim of aggressors.

This claim was a total fabrication. The commander of the Liberty was in possession of proof otherwise. The Israelis were 'politically' threatened: if this had become common knowledge, it would have been a public relations disaster. In fact, it would have proven that the Israelis were liars and that the entire basis for the "disadvantaged Israeli state" is a fraud. They wanted the world to believe that "poor little Israel" was a victim of 'Arab' aggression by numerous countries and only sought to defend itself. This was a lie. The Israelis were strictly the aggressors.

The Liberty was the only impediment to this agenda. Its intelligence would prove that the Israelis were exclusively the aggressors. Thus, Dayan gave the order and unmarked Israeli jets, all U.S.-issue, were dispatched and mercilessly bombarded the defenseless vessel. Torpedo boats launched numerous torpedoes, which scored direct hits. Per the American 'ally,' Dayan, the order was to sink the vessel, killing all aboard.

The Israeli attack was well planned. Initially, the Liberty's radio towers were struck to prevent any contact with the nearby Sixth Fleet. The U.S.-issue Israeli fighters relentlessly bombed and strafed the ship. As a result, 34 American servicemen and hundreds of others were wounded. The Israelis even machine gunned the life rafts, which had been deployed in the event of an abandon ship order. Like previous Israeli terror acts the intent was to blame the event upon the Muslims. However, the courage and ingenuity of the Liberty crew prevented a total disaster. What's more, suspiciously, the U.S. Naval commander refused to respond to the cries of the Liberty's crew for help.

By then the captain and crew knew that the Israelis were the culprits. They reported this to the military, but the Navy took no action. Thus, there was an international conspiracy to disguise the truth. To the high powers the lives of young Americans were of no consequence compared to maintaining the status quo.

When news of the attack became known, the Israelis lied. They said they had nothing to do with it, and, in fact, instead blamed it on the Muslims. As reported in national news the impression at first was that it was a revenge attack by an 'Arab' country due to the United States' support for Israel. This is the same kind of reasoning used to explain the now disproved claim of an Islaamic 9/11. Here, the Zionist-controlled media told blatant lies. Yet, in this case there was no way for the Zionists to fully disguise it. There were too many eyewitnesses.

Thirty-four U.S. servicemen were slaughtered by the Israelis. Yet, there was never an official inquiry. Rather than open warfare this was a terror attack done under stealth. It was a murderous "take no prisoners" strike, complete with disguised airplanes. What's more, incredibly, it was an attack against an unassuming ally. Yet, as always there is no way for the Israelis to completely disguise their plots.

The Israelis are obvious murderers. They even murder their allies. Thus, their claims regarding the sources of terror must be disregarded. The fact is if the Israelis would do this to their committed friends—the American people—who, in fact, fully finance their capacities—why would they hesitate to kill other Westerners, for instance, the people in the World Trade Center?

Jordon's war against the PLO: the Zionist connection

People often accuse Middle Easterners of being inherently violent. Yet, virtually all the violence in the Middle East is the result of outside interference. In the 1970s tens of thousands of Palestinian refugees were brutally killed by what would appear to be their fellows: the Jordanians. As quoted by Pastore an excellent exposé regarding this massacre is found in the *American Free Press*.

> In 1970 King Hussein of Jordan was provided incriminating intelligence that suggested the Palestine Liberation Organization was plotting to murder him and seize power. Infuriated, Hussein mobilized his forces for what has become known as the "Black September" purge of the PLO. Thousands of Palestinians living in Jordan were rounded up, some of the leaders were tortured, and in the end, masses of refugees were driven from Jordan to Lebanon.

King Hussein directly ordered this massacre. The King was a 'swinger' and loved to party. He had a number of affairs. New data, discovered after the murder of two Mossad agents in Cyprus, proves that one of these affairs was with a top Mossad agent, Sylvia Roxburgh. She purposely seduced him, a relatively common practice of Israeli operatives. Her purpose: to incite the King to attack and destroy the Palestinians. She achieved this by telling him that elements of the Palestinian resistance were plotting his assassination, and she provided false documents to "prove" it. This was the motive behind the King's Palestinian wars. The Israeli plot was truly the force behind the massacre.

Political terror: an Israeli specialty

In 1982 the Mossad spread disinformation about "terror attacks" against the Israelis, claiming Palestinians were attacking the borders. These reports were used to justify the

Israeli invasion of Lebanon. This was a PR campaign: mere lies. Years later, even leading Israeli spokesmen, such as former Foreign Minister Abba Eban, admitted that the reports of "PLO terrorism" were fabricated.

The Israelis also kill their own dissidents, blaming it on others. The attempted assassination in London of Israeli ambassador Shlomo Argov was initially blamed on the PLO. This was also used as a justification for the 1982 invasion. This diplomat was one of the Israeli's more mild mannered types and aimed at a peaceful solution to the conflict. Thus, the stage was set for the massive invasion of Lebanon. The result was the destruction of an entire region, a sovereign nation, plus the deaths of over 25,000 innocent individuals.

London bombings

That Mossad is the culprit is more plausible than any lone Muslims. It had foreknowledge of this act and was the only one capable. Mossad has an extensive espionage organization in England. In contrast, there is no Muslim spy or intelligence agency in this country. Also, numerous British citizens have previously been assassinated by Mossad operatives.

Mossad works in concert with American and British spy agencies to commit espionage. This espionage includes coups and assassinations, in other words, murders. Rather than the Muslims only the Israelis and the secret services of Western countries commit organized terror acts. For decades these agencies have committed global crimes against humanity, slaughtering world leaders, perceived enemies, and the common human. In fact, such entities have invaded entire continents. Since this is their history and there is no Islaamic precedence of such acts, then, it is exclusively the West which is the source for global terror. Suspicion against the Muslims is baseless.

In its arrogance the Mossad often reveals its crimes. It wants to be the most respected one, the organization that Westerners admire, that is that it "really has its act together." Thus, it usually flags its operations to take a kind of credit for being all-knowing. This is part of its false front, a means to create a kind of awe or fear. So, again, when it is to its advantage, the Mossad reveals all. In news reports everyone was reminded "the Mossad office in London received advance notice about the attacks, *but only six minutes before the blast…*" The old adage surely applies here, that is "thou doth protest too much." People are supposed to worry about the plots of Muslims, such as bin Laden, az-Zarkawi, and Zawahiri, while the Mossad continues to unabashedly plot its crimes and while claiming foreknowledge warns no one.

How could Mossad know what no one else could tell? Even eyewitnesses had no such knowledge. What's more, according to the Scotland Yard in the initial London bombings the men who were accused looked completely innocuous. They showed no apprehension: no signs. They appeared absolutely normal: everyday Londoners going about their business. The fact is there was within the Muslim community no advance warning, and there were no "leaks." Other than the Israelis no one knew that there was going to be a bombing. So, the only way that the Mossad could know was if it was the perpetrator.

The claim by the Mossad of short notice was due to the potential repercussions of saying the opposite. If there was an admission of significant advance knowledge, then, they would have been accused of duplicity for failing to warn the people. So, they concocted the "six minute warning" as a ruse.

The six minute warning was a part of the cover up. This is because in their previous announcement they admitted they knew of the attack some 32 minutes before the bombing (about 8:15). Yet, no one warned the authorities. Then, of what value is such an organization, set up exclusively to spy, if it can't even give warning—even when it has supposedly absolute evidence? Rather than an espionage agency this is a fraud. In fact, its very purpose is to to create lies, all to disseminate blame against others.

There is only one way the Israelis could have know in advance. They had to be involved, rather, they were the perpetrators. Think about it. Blame is placed upon four men, who gave not a single hint of this act. No friend or relative had even an inkling of the crime. Scotland Yard reported there was nothing in their behavior that would indicate their purported intent. Furthermore, British authorities dispute any claim of suicide bombers. From Scotland Yard's analysis even these men were unaware of their fate. The fact is according to these investigators they behaved "normal." Obviously, the Israelis, having full control of the security, provided British authorities with these tapes. Yet, these tapes offer no proof of a crime.

Even so, how could the Israelis know? How could the Mossad know with such certainty that they penned an article about the bombings days prior? No one else knew about it, not even the closest loved ones of the accused. Then, according to Scotland Yard there is no supposed mastermind behind this. Are people to believe that these four men who casually knew each other, acted alone to commit one of the most well coordinated and successful terror acts in English history, the first subway bombing ever? Yet, this was done under the full view of thousands of security cameras? Then, where is the evidence that they did it? Films should show them directly entering the bombing sites. There are no such films. Thus, these men were never there.

Without doubt, Mossad, as well as the Israeli leadership, admittedly knew of it. What's more, they were the only ones who had such knowledge. Yet, according to the BBC this would appear to be hardly a random terror act: "Three bombs on London underground trains on Thursday exploded *almost simultaneously*, police have said. Scotland Yard said the attacks took place within 50 seconds of each other (that is it was a professional job)." As reported in the *Chicago Tribune*, July 10th, 2005, said Tim O'Toole, managing director of the London Underground, "It was bang, bang, bang, very close together." This could only be achieved by remote control detonation.

Only a professional espionage agency could have achieved such a crime. Only the Mossad admitted advance knowledge; the time frame given by it varied. The other organization which claimed knowledge, The Secret Organization of Al-Qaeda in Europe, doesn't exist.

Yet, perhaps it does exist: as a shill organization. Its Web server has been traced by experts to Maryland and Austin, Texas. These are regions where U.S. espionage agencies, as well as the Mossad, are active. The point is rather than Islaamic the organization was invented by spies. What's more, these spies were non-Muslims. This phony organization alone refutes the possibility of an Islaamic source.

Yet, who are the people responsible for seeding this blame? Obviously, it is Islaam's enemies.

There is another suspicious element which points to professional espionage. During the first hour or so after the destruction the press was told by an unknown agency that there were no explosions. Rather, they were deliberately informed that the horror in the Underground was due to a power surge. This was repeated until 10:00 a.m., over an hour after the blasts. Yet, these claims, which circulated among the media, did not apparently arise from British authorities. In fact, the report by clandestine sources of a power failure was done maliciously, perhaps to delay any response by the authorities. Incredibly, these are the same groups which said not a single word about the crime, even though they had advance knowledge. Thus, instead of warning the authorities they spread false rumors, which surely delayed the rescue effort. Such disinformation may well have cost lives. Thus, obviously, the people responsible for this disinformation campaign are connected to the bombing. This is further proof that the avowed purpose of the bombers was to create hatred for a people and to mark Islaam as a terror source. This is because it was all planned, that is this method of blame. So, without investigation and with malicious intent the English press immediately blamed the Muslims. This is despite the fact that they had no evidence of an Islamic plot.

As confirmed succinctly by the writers of What Really Happened, an e-newspaper, despite 'knowing' in advance the Mossad issued no warnings. The editors state: "How long does it take Mossad to pick up the phone?" Surely, it wouldn't have taken an hour. Yet, the fact is the Mossad only calls when it suits its purpose. There will never be any calls from it to warn anyone. Thus, the bombings were surely a Western operation, the Mossad playing the primary role. The fact is it was the London National Grid authority which at 10:00 a.m., over an hour after the Mossad was 'warned' said that there had been "no problems with its system." Thus, the statement of a power surge came from other sources. The English workers were honest; the Mossad was deceitful. Someone was buying time, and it wasn't the Muslims. Nor was it the British authorities. Again, the Muslims have never bombed British civilians. Rather, only the Israelis have done so. Even so, this raises another question: Who warned Mossad?

The Muslims are avowed enemies of the Zionists. Thus, the Zionists attack them through any means possible. Then, should this surprise anyone, that is that Islaamic terror is fabricated?

Jack Straw, the Zionist puppet, immediately revealed the true source of this crime. He said that this had "the hallmarks of an al-Qaeda-related attack." Then, shortly afterwards there was the bogus al-Qaeda posting. This is highly suspect, this immediate targeting of the Muslims, because, without doubt, the public's eyes al-Qaeda is associated with Islaam and its 'activities' constantly give the latter a black mark. Without evidence Straw maliciously branded the Muslims. Rather, the evidence is to the contrary, pointing instead to the Zionists, who Straw well knows have a history of committing violence against British citizens.

The posting itself reveals the source. Any sensible British diplomat who would read the following would find it suspect. Say the claimants:

> Rejoice, Islamic nation, Rejoice, Arab world. The time has come for vengeance against the Zionist crusader British government—in response to the massacres Britain committed in Iraq and Afghanistan.

Yet, according to MSNBC translator Jacob Keryakes the posting contained an error in one of the Qur'anic phrases it quoted. For a true Muslim this is inconceivable. Would an orthodox Christian misquote the Bible? What's more, vengeance is prohibited in Islaam. All that is allowed is to legitimately fight the oppressors. Even so, why should anyone trust the issuances of the Mossad at such a critical juncture? Netanyahu says these terror acts are "good" for the Israeli regime. In contrast,   Muslim countries have universally condemned such acts. Furthermore, it is the

Mossad which has its own sophisticated spy base in England, so it alone is positioned for any devious acts.

Bus bombing: suicide or planted bombs?

Revealing eyewitness accounts tell the real story of this bombing. These eyewitness statements were twisted by the press, notably Fox News, to give an opposite effect. This is what one witness said:

> "Some guy came and sat down and...(immediately) exploded." The friend of this passenger said, 'the guy sat down and "the explosion happened."

Another witness, Richard Jones, was often quoted. He has given a vast array of contradictory statements. He said he saw an Asian man, who kept digging into a bag, although he never identified this bag as the pictured rucksack.

At first he said he thought the person was fiddling with, perhaps, a bomb, possibly "setting a timer." Yet, why would anyone do so in full view of all others? Later, he changed this story, saying it was probably only a palm pilot. The repeated digging, he said, made him nervous, so he *got off the bus just before it exploded.* Interestingly, Jones is a former worker in an explosives factory. No one has bothered to analyze why a former explosives worker, as well as the bus driver, disembarked, while the remaining passengers were bombed.

The other two witnesses, 20-year-old women who reported what they saw to nurse Terence Mutasa of the University College hospital, provided the more reliable view. In fact, their reports corroborated each other. Both these young women gave the nurse precisely the same story, while in four different interviews Jones' story changed drastically. Yet, Jones is insufficient as a witness, because, unlike the young women, he did not see the actual bombing. In fact, since the women saw the bomb explode, only their testimonies are reliable.

A senior police source said: "There are two bodies which have to be examined in great detail, because they appear to have been holding the bomb or *sitting on top of it.* One of those might turn out to be the bomber." Supposedly, a decapitated head was found at the bus scene. The media emphasized that *in Israeli experience* this is the sign of a suicide bomber. Here again, the Israelis are 'on the scene,' being quoted. Yet, Scotland Yard said these were not suicide acts. Thus, the disinformation by the Israelis is continuous.

Again, the sources of "proof" are Israeli. For instance, there is the much hyped disinformation statement that 'Israeli police have revealed that the explosives used in the multi-pronged terrorist attack in London last week were materially identical to the explosives used by two British Muslim suicide bombers, who struck in Tel Aviv more than a year ago.' Yet, this is the opposite of the statements of independent military analysts, who confirm that the bombs were industrial, that is military. Thus, this former statement by the Israelis is fraudulent.

Terror in America: Mossad, MI6, and/or CIA?

The question is could 9/11 have been a set-up? Rather than an Islaamic act could it have been an internal attack? Or, could it have been an attack by an international crime syndicate, that is the Zionists? It was top U.S. Army analysts who provided a compelling assessment of the true nature of Mossad. A "ruthless and cunning" organization, they said, in any terror event they are a "wild card." What's more, they have the ability to make it appear that the Arabs that is

Muslims, did it. This revealing assertion about America's supposed ally was reported in the *Washington Times*, incredibly, on September 10th, 2001. This was one day before 9/11. The timing surely is suspect. Yet, despite this telling report the acts of September 11 are exclusively and erroneously blamed on Muslims. According to Michael Collins Piper of *American Free Press*:

> This serious charge by U.S. Army officers against the Israelis appeared in a 68-page paper prepared by 60 officers at the U.S. Army's School for Advanced Military Studies...Then, just hours after the terrorist tragedies a well known pro-Israeli analyst, George Friedman, proclaimed Israel as the primary beneficiary.

In a kind of brutal indifference, which is typical for the Israeli hierarchy, Friedman wrote, "The big winner today...is the state of Israel. There is no question...that the Israeli leadership is feeling relief..."

How could anyone speak such cruel words, while people were being roasted alive in a most gruesome death and also falling from thousands of feet to the most frightening deaths conceivable? Surely, while Muslims throughout the United States shuddered in fear and grief the Zionists were remorseless, rather, gleeful. Zionist commentators were admittedly pleased at this act. Wickedly, they reveled in the deaths of Americans as well as hundreds of foreign nationals.

Yet, after 9/11 no Zionists were victimized, even though various Israelis were caught attempting to commit terror acts in several regions, for instance, in the Midwest and in Mexico City. There were no Jews or Zionists in the United States who were gunned down, beaten to death, wrongfully imprisoned, and/or tortured. In Gauntanamo or Abu Ghraib there are no Zionists. This violence is only perpetrated against God-fearing Muslims. Rather, it is the Zionists who largely created these prisons.

Only Muslims are wrongfully imprisoned in the concentration camps, Gauntanamo, Abu Ghraib, and others. Only they were/are brutalized in such camps. In contrast, no Jews receive such treatment. Yet, it was the Zionist Jews who had an indisputable role in 9/11. Only they were caught on September 11 in New York City with sufficient explosives to destroy the George Washington Bridge plus cash stuffed in socks, along with box cutters. Yet, the image created internationally was that the Muslims bore these: all lies. What's more, the fact is only the Israeli entity has profited from this act. On 9/11 essentially no Israeli nationals were killed, and on the front lines in the war in Iraq no Israelis are being slaughtered. In contrast, American soldiers do the Zionists' bidding. Yet, as a society only the Muslims gain torment, while the Israelis are free to do as they please. Thus, truly, regarding 9/11 and the subsequent wars in the Middle East Israel is the exclusive beneficiary. This entity benefits, while the United States is bankrupted.

The driving out of the Iraqi Jews

This bears repeating, since it is truly telling of world events. In Iraq the Muslims have been accused of genocide against the Jews. This is to portray Islaam as intolerant. This is regarding the exodus during the 1950s through 1960s of Jews from Iraq. The destination was Israel. What's more, until the establishment of this entity regarding these Jews there was no such exodus. Prior to the Zionist invasion in this region for centuries Muslims and Jews lived together in complete tolerance. Again, rather than Semites the Zionists are Europeans of non-Semitic blood. This demonstrates that it was non-Semites who uprooted the Semitic Iraqi Jews.

The fallaciousness of the official story is documented by the Jewish scholar Naeem Giladi, himself an Iraqi. As reported by the Islaamic researcher Ansar, Giladi's book details how during the 1950s Zionist gangs committed terror acts against Iraqi Jews for the purpose of sewing discord. As a result, over 95% of the Jews in Iraq fled to Israel. Giladi was one such Iraqi Jew. This is a clear example of Jews attacking their fellow people for mere material gain, a propensity mentioned in the Qu'ran. Thus, the exodus was exclusively Jewish, rather, Zionist, in origin. In other words, the Muslims of Iraq were never the the instigators. Despite this blame has been heaped upon the Muslims. This is another example of the lies told against the Islaamic people.

Are Middle Easterners terrorists?

Regarding Middle Easterners the Israelis are responsible for the negative image. They relish in creating, in particular, the image of the 'Arab' as a brutal being. This was the purpose behind the image of the notorious Abu Nidal. The name itself is recognized as 'evil.' Yet, it is the Jews who make use of the word 'Abu' in numerous infamous titles. This is reminiscent of the cartoon Popeye and the 40 Thieves, with the Arabic-appearing character, "Abu Hassan" and with the sword-wheeling scene, "Hassan Chop." Yet, in Arabic Abu is a mere pronoun and has a dignified meaning. In fact, it means "Father of." So, Abu Hassan means "Hassan's father."

This is a racially charged cartoon. It falsely depicts Muslims as "thieves and killers." The supposed source of the image, *The Arabian Knights*, was the very source of much of Western literature. It had a major impact upon Western culture. Without doubt, the Arab terrorist is a Zionist/Hollywood creation. The effectiveness of this is demonstrated by the fact that in a recent survey of Americans on the streets when asked what terror meant to them nearly 90% responded, essentially, 'Muslim, Islaam, and/or Arab.' This is despite the fact that the majority of the people in the Middle East are non-violent, rather, dignified. Thus, the Hollywood image is false and, is done maliciously.

In virtually all instances these infamous Abus are deemed impostors: for instance, Abu Nidal and Abu Hafs Brigade. Their real signature is Israeli, and in real life many of the namesake Abus are Zionists posing in disguise.

This is surely true of Abu Nidal. The fact is this man was merely a Zionist *posing as a Palestinian.* The question must be asked, of course, if he was so notorious, why was he never caught? Thus, the claim that Muslims are ruthless, for instance, Abu Nidal, is fraudulent. The fact is Abu Nidal is strictly a Western creation. This was done to mark the Palestinians, as well as Muslims, as bloodthirsty.

Abu Nidal was no Muslim. Nor was he a Palestinian. Rather, he was an Israeli spy. This is easy to prove. Over half his victims were Palestinian. Palestinians are notoriously nationalistic, and they rarely if ever kill each other. Plus, he never supported any Palestinian cause. Nor did he fund or support the impoverished. He gave not one cent to any peoples' cause.

With his vast wealth did he build schools and mosques? Also, he was indiscriminate in his killing. He assassinated numerous Muslims and to a lesser degree Christians in cold blood. His killing of Jews was more rare. Furthermore, his appearance is far more Jewish than Muslim. Both French and Jordanian anti-terrorism experts agree that the only possible explanation for his vicious acts is that he was an Israeli agent.

True, Abu Nidal has attacked Israeli elements, for instance, machine gun assaults in Rome and Vienna at El Al Airline counters. Yet, this is nothing new in the Zionist agenda, since to advance that agenda, even its own infrastructure is fair game. However, curiously, unlike legitimate resistance groups Abu Nidal had never attacked the Israeli entity itself. Rather, all his attacks were exterior of it, particularly in Palestinian territories.

Again, the claim that he was a Palestinian operative is unfathomable, attacking and assassinating, as he did, his own people. It was finally his attack on the Achille Lauro which established the Palestinians as "heartless killers." To this day this attack is attributed to Islaam and Muslims Thus, because of it, still, Muslims are tormented. This is despite the fact that Islaam completely bans such acts. It is also despite the fact that this act had nothing to do with Islaam, Muslims, or any Islaamic revenge.

Such an attack would have been truly bizarre for the Palestinian establishment, since the Palestinians were well aware that the socialist-leaning Greeks were sympathetic to their cause. The Greek Prime Minister, Andreas Papandreou, often defended Palestinians rights. Would the besieged Palestinians, so sensitive to public opinion, truly have done the very deed, which would alienate their only friends? Yet, perhaps even more revealing is the fact that despite attacks upon Israeli interests Abu Nidal's 'organization' has never been attacked by the Israelis.

The Israelis could have easily killed him, as they had assassinated and continue to assassinate countless legitimate Palestinian resisters. What's more, Abu Nidal was never involved with any legitimate resistance organization. Nor did he support in the least the peoples' movements such as the infitada. The Palestinian people didn't even know who he was. He never helped his people in their struggle for freedom. Thus, there is no possibility that he was Palestinian. So, what was he? Middle Eastern males seemingly cannot be cleansed from this scar. Even so, even if he was Palestinian, there would still be no Islaamic connection to his acts.

The Achille Lauro: a Zionist crime

Regarding the Achille Lauro the official story has been disputed by Israeli insiders, for instance, Ari Ben-Menashe, a former Israeli Defense Forces arms dealer. In his book *Profits of War: Inside the Secret U.S.-Israeli Arms Network* Ben-Menashe states that the entire act was ordered and funded by the Mossad. What's more, true to form the Mossad achieved the desired objective. The fact is why would the Palestinians, already under siege, do anything so destructive? For the murder of a single innocent tourist would they truly bring the condemnation of the entire world upon themselves? Rather, this would be an act achieved exclusively by their enemies.

Ben-Menashe says that the Israelis routinely engaged in operations to portray the Palestinians and, in fact, Muslims in 'the worst possible light.' "An example," he wrote, was the attack on the Achille Lauro. That, he said, was an Israeli 'black' propaganda operation to show "what a deadly, cutthroat bunch the Palestinians were." Certainly, although largely unknown it was the Israelis who orchestrated this hijacking/murder. This demonstrates how truly erroneous are most peoples impressions of this world. What's more, this revelation is directly from Israeli sources. According to Ben-Menashe in a bid to affect world opinion Israeli spymasters created a plan to mar the international image of the Palestinian cause. They arranged the attack through "abu'l

Abbas, their Palestinian front man, who to follow such orders was receiving *tens of millions of dollars* from Israeli intelligence officers posing as Sicilian dons under Israeli guidance. Abbas...gathered a (paid) team to attack the cruise ship. The team was told to 'make it bad,' to show the world what lay in store for other unsuspecting citizens if Palestinian demands were not met. In a gruesome scene which all people remember they then selected a pitiful crippled elderly Jewish passenger, Leon Klinghoffer, and brutally killed him. Then, they threw his body and wheelchair overboard. Incredibly, this was videotaped and broadcast globally. Yet, the entire operation was conceived, plotted, and financed by the Israelis. Even so, this is the exact opposite of the world view. This was to, once and for all, turn public opinion against the Palestinian resisters.

Yet, this organization killed randomly. Abu Nidal claimed responsibility for killings that stretched globally. Some of these killings were inevitably committed directly by the Mossad under the guise of Abu Nidal. All the while Muslims, as well as Arabic-appearing people in general, took the blame.

As noted by Ben-Menashe it was a convenient way for the Mossad to achieve its goals simultaneously: to kill any potential adversaries, while portraying its supposed 'enemy' as wicked. In this they were spectacularly successful. People assassinated by Abu Nidal or at least for which he claimed responsibility included Israeli Olympic athletes (1972), a Kuwaiti diplomat in Spain, Issam Sartawi, a PLO official in Lisbon, a Jordanian diplomat in Rumania, Ismail Darwish, an Arafat supporter in Rome, the British High commissioner in India, and in Rome PLO official, Husayn Kamal. To this day all such acts are acclaimed as examples of Islaamic terror: pure lies.

It must also be noted that many of the aforementioned victims were Muslims. Christian Palestinians were also killed. Their killings greatly disabled the Palestinian movement. Thus, the real nature of this agency becomes obvious.

Again, there is no possibility that this organization was Palestinian in origin. There may have been within it Palestinians, even Muslims (in name), but they were working for a different master.

Incredibly, as these examples demonstrate the claim of an Islaamic threat is based upon fraud. Rather, it is Zionism which is the threat to global peace. This is the source of the terror which is destroying the world.

Institutions attacked by Abu Nidal a.k.a. Mossad included the Saudi Embassy in Paris, Damascus' Semiramis Hotel, the Syrian Embassy in Rome, the Syrian Embassy in Pakistan, the Jordan Occupied International Hotel in Amman, a synagogue in Vienna, a synagogue in Rome, a hotel in Khartoum, Sudan, the LaBelle Disco in Berlin, the Neve Shalom Synagogue in Turkey, and a restaurant in the West Bank. For the Palestinians none of these institutions have any military significance, rather, many of these organizations/countries supported their cause.

Of the eleven sites attacked seven were in Muslim countries. The fact is this is, historically, the Israeli pattern. The tactic is to kill dissidents and enemies, particularly progressive Palestinians, while maintaining a continuous barrage of global terror attacks, even against Jewish targets.

True, Jewish sites were desecrated. However, this seeming contradiction is easily explained. Terror against Jews outside Israel is a Zionist strategy. This is largely to promote Jewish exodus. In contrast, Israel is promoted as a safe haven. Had the feared Abu Nidal operated freely in Israel this would have slowed emigration.

It becomes evident that the world Jewry is the main if not exclusive fomenter of global strife. This wicked element, which must not be confused with the legitimate religious and God fearing Jews, plots, as well as enacts, every conceivable terror act. What's more, these aggressors do so relentlessly. It is not that they are so smart: they are often caught. It is just that their agenda is the same as Western powers—where the twain meet—and, so, they are rarely if ever prosecuted.

If in the Western World a Muslim were to commit such acts, this person would suffer dire punishment. Surely, the Muslim would be imprisoned, as well as beaten, tried and convicted as a terrorist. In contrast, the Zionist would be merely deported. This is a diabolical trend. It gives the Zionists carte blanche to do whatever they will, including tormenting, killing, and raping of the innocent. Then, they wickedly blame it upon others. By giving such criminals free reign all people suffer, particularly the defenseless— particularly Muslims but also Christians.

The Zionists have as their avowed agenda to destabilize the Muslims as well as the Islaamic faith. To a degree they have achieved this. Yet, God is great, and He has His own far-reaching plan. Even so, precautions must be taken.

It is a fact that there will be further terror attacks on U.S. soil as well as in other Western regions. It is also a fact that these attacks will be blamed exclusively on Muslims. Even so, Muslims have yet to be proven as the sole provocateurs of any terror attack in the United States. Even the original World Trade Center disaster was largely an inside job, involving both the FBI and the Mossad. This means that this act was plotted by the U.S. and Israeli governments.

Regarding the original World Trade Center bombing the FBI has admitted "it was a sting," even confirming it created the bomb. Yet, was it so important to blame this act on the Muslims that the government would harm its own citizens? One official has stated publically that if it were not for government aggression, the bombing would never have occurred. The role of the government is demonstrated by the fact that its agents, and, therefore, the government itself, knew of the bombing in advance and, what's more, refused to stop it, which they could have easily achieved. A government informant, who had been paid a half millions dollars, actually watched the bombing unfold.

This government-sponsored act, which led to the devastation of an American landmark, can be easily explained. It is because, like the Zionists, the government's goal is to create controversy and, particularly, to mar Islaam. It is to create a hateful enemy to justify a military agenda.

The fact is Islaam *is* a threat. Globally, people are vigorously adopting it. They thrive on its inner truths. It weighs heavily against corruption, which is endemic in the United States and the rest of the world. It is against all forms of oppression, including the active promotion of the murderous military-industrial complex and the creation of wars merely for profit. It is resolutely against any such acts which could for mere material gain lead to the killing of the innocent and the destruction of public buildings or any other landmarks.

Global terror acts: government-sponsored or Islaamic?

Globally, the Zionists have infiltrated Islaamic groups with countless spies. This infiltration is an avowed objective of global Zionism, and all Western countries are participants. A good example is the second group of London bombers.

Incredibly, many supposedly radical Muslims aren't even real Muslims. Rather, they are spies disguised as

Muslims. Their purpose was to create a negative impression of Islaam. True, in every religion there are extremists. However, only Islaam is targeted with imposters, people who create terror acts, so these acts can be attributed to it. Obviously, this is to discourage others regarding it. For example, consider Osman Hussain. In the London attack he is the only person who has fully admitted to setting a bomb. Yet, his real name is Hamdi Adus *Isaac*. The Muslim name is a forgery. Thus, incredibly, *the only admitted bomber is a Jew*. This proves the extent of the Zionist plot. Note that in comparison neither of the two Muslims in the United States who are in prison, John Lindh and Zacharius Moussaoui, have committed an act of terror. Regarding the latter he said he signed a confession, because he was tired of fighting the system but is fully on record saying he had no knowledge of or involvement in 9/11. Recently, he denied having any involvement in a terror act

Yet, in London the Mossad blundered greatly. Undercover Zionists attempt to state that the Mossad never spies upon its Western allies nor commits terror. The capture of Isaac is proof that such statements are baseless. The fact is the Zionist code mandates spying. It also mandates the speaking of lies.

Upon entering London in the 1990s Isaac created fake documents; he assumed an Islaamic name and claimed to be a refugee from a Muslim country. However, as demonstrated by Italian police these are all fabrications.

Rather than Islaamic three of the suspects bear strictly Jewish names: Hamdi Isaac and his brothers Remzi and Fati. Ethiopian Jews commonly use the first names Hamdi, Remzi, and Fati. The latter name may be derived from the ancient African region of Lake Fati, where much of the Ethiopian Jewish community had its roots.

Yet, this is not how the world sees it. The entire world has already pegged these people as Muslims or Islaamic terrorists. Their actions have been trumpeted as "proof that Islaam endorses terror." How incredible: and the only one of the accused London bombers who admits to setting a bomb is a Jew.

For the second bombing regarding the four accused bombers the names given are Mukhtar Said-Ibrahim, Osman Hussain, Yasin Hassan Omar, and Ramzi Muhammad. All are Muslim-sounding names, although so far at least one of these has been found to be operating under disguise, even falsely representing himself as "devout." Regarding the latter he purposely disguised his Jewish ancestry in order to commit acts of terror. What's more, this bomber used this disguise to terrorize the local Muslim community. He was head of a group, which routinely terrorized mosque elders, even beating them. His goal was to create a brand of fanatical Islaam in order to destabilize it.

The extent of these bombers' efforts to foment terror—to demonize Islaam—is compelling, as demonstrated by this report from the *London Times*:

> Police are investigating allegations that the four suspected July 21 bombers collected more than £500,000 in benefits payments in Britain.
>
> The claim was made as the Bank of England moved to freeze financial accounts belonging to the men. Bank officials also disclosed the financial details of the suspects, Ramzi Mohammad, Yasin Hassan Omar, Muktar Said-Ibrahim and Hussain Osman. These showed how the men, all in custody, have used multiple aliases and addresses in recent years.
>
> Mr. Ibrahim, is said to have had six aliases. Some are also shown to have claimed several nationalities, ages

and national insurance numbers while in Britain. Investigators believe that bogus names were used to make some benefit claims.

Two are also alleged to have obtained asylum using bogus passports and false names and nationalities.

All the addresses registered to the suspects were in Greater London, and each man is known to have had at least one national insurance number.

Yet, it is the true teachings of Islaam, as well as Judaism, which categorically prohibit theft as well as corrupt acts. Thus, there is no possibility that these men are 'devout' Muslims, because this word means the peaceful surrendering of the self to God. This includes surrendering to God's laws as well as just civil laws. Thus, Islaam prohibits opportunism. However, when the aforementioned Times article was posted online, there were a host of comments, for instance:

Kill all Muslim Islaamic militants and any who support or abet: now.

Kill all Muslims, like you would mosquitoes.

I'm glad Blair is going to start throwing them out. The US should follow suit.

Yet, incredibly, the basis of such statements is a bombing by a non-Muslim, the Zionist agent and Jewish youth Hamdi Isaac. No one said after learning of this man's identity, "Kill all Jews and Zionists."

This is not to say that such people, those who make these comments, are never provoked. Certainly, the media wrongfully stirs such hate. There also the occasional disturbed individuals who might perpetuate the stigma. One such individual, Omar Bakri, a self-professed Muslim scholar, is particularly well known for his provocations.

Incredibly, he called the 19 hijackers of 9/11 "the magnificent nineteen," while deeming the London bombers "the fabulous four."

This man justifies terror. Yet, his comments seem more like publicity stunts than Islaamic scholarship. Yet, obviously, such comments would generate hate.

This is the rare individual. The vast majority of Muslims make no such comments. Bakri may be a Muslim, but his comments prove that he is at a minimum misguided. The fact is regardless of an individual's beliefs there is nothing magnificent or fabulous about terror. Anyone who supports the slaughter of the innocent is truly deranged. Yet, deranged, too are British and American rulers, who claim that through their Iraq escapade they are, somehow, doing God's work.

There is much focus in the media on certain Muslims who are, perhaps, overzealous, and who make comments which are provocative. In their ignorance some Muslims might claim 9/11 is 'justified' or 'good.' Some remote individuals may have even praise the hijackers as well as the London bombers. This brings great hate against a people as well as the Islaamic system. Yet, such comments are the opposite of Islaam, because it never condones terror. Yet, in contrast, a major public figure Binyamin Netanyahu called terror "good." However, no hate was spewed at him or Jews in general. He said the same thing that the rare 'Muslim' might say, but there were no condemnations. Thus, it becomes obvious that without warrant Islaam is routinely attacked, while atrocities committed by people of other faiths remain unattached, that is such terror acts are rarely if ever deemed "Jewish," "Hindu," or "Christian."

One reason for this are the statements given, again, by a supposed Muslim, London's Omar Bakri Muhammad. Yet, there may be a more sinister explanation for his extremist position. Evidence is dominating that this man is an espionage operative. For certain, his views are completely discounted by any knowledgeable Muslim. Even so, it takes little provocation for people in the West to attack Islaam and even call for its destruction. Bakri's views are horrifying and are diametrically opposed to the views of Britain's Muslims. He has no significant followers in this country. His views are unIslaamic. Interestingly, as soon as Muslims showed serious concerns about his extremist statements, even indicting that he could be a British or, perhaps, Israeli operative, he disappeared.

According to the *London Times* Bakri, who was supposedly under intensive scrutiny for his views, had managed to fly out of England 'without being noticed' and "would never return to Britain." Here is a report by Daniel McGrory from London regarding Bakri's actions:

> Only days after Tony Blair gave warning that the activities of radical preachers would no longer be tolerated, Ahmed Choudary said: "The sheik has left the country and I don't think he will come back. He has said that he is willing to destroy his British documents

Noted The Times:

> He has described the July 7 bombers as "the fabulous four." He has received tens of thousands of pounds in benefits payments and told followers to claim as much as they can while doing all that they can allegedly to "wage war" against Britain.

Yet, here, there is a serious question: how does a man who is essentially, under house arrest, who is a known fomenter of hate—who is the only Muslim in all London who publically praises the bombers, gloating in the carnage—how does such a man "slip away?" What's more, how does he virtually immediately upon his arrival in Lebanon gain an interview on that country's most popular TV station? Is it not true that the Zionists largely control the global media?

Since the early 1900s Jewish and British spies have masqueraded as Muslims. Even now—even in the Iraq war—the Israelis, Americans, and British all do this: all to mar Islaam. Blair calls the Muslims extremists, yet consider his blatant acts of terror, as reported by Matt Hutaff in *Canon Fodder*:

> A car driving through the outskirts of a besieged city opens fire on a police checkpoint, killing one. In pursuit, the police surround and detain the drivers and find the vehicle packed with explosives—perhaps part of an insurgents plan to destroy lives and cripple property. If that isn't enough, when the suspects are thrown in prison, their allies drive right up to the walls of the jail, break through them and brave petroleum bombs and burning clothes to rescue their comrades. Incredible, no? Yet, this story took place in the southern Iraqi city of Basra…the drivers of the explosive-laden car were not members of an insurgency group—they were British Special Forces. Their rescuers? British soldiers driving British tanks.
>
> …(thus) two members of the British Armed forces disguised as (Muslims) killed a member of the Iraqi police…when the people of Basra rightfully refused to turn the murderers over to the British government, per Coalition "mandate," they sent their own men in and released over 100 prisoners in the process.

The British soldiers were dressed as Middle Easterners. Thus, they were to create a terror act, while blaming it on the Muslims. According to the Geneva convention this is a war crime. Their gear included assault rifles, machine guns, an anti-tank weapon, radio gear, explosives, detonators, and bushy black wigs. The source of many of the constantly emphasized Islaamic suicides is now exposed. It is Western operatives whose entire purpose is to mar this faith. What's more, they maliciously attempt to create divisions—to cause people to attack each other. In contrast, Islaam prohibits wanton violence. Yet, it does urge fighting. This is against all sources of tyranny. Here, the fight is to the death.

The British/American/Israeli plot against this religion continues unabated. It is a rendition of the original Crusades. This is to support a most vile agenda. In England it is to neutralize any resistance to the war machine as well as to fight the rise of Islaam.

It worked in the United States. The British hierarchy also needed a mini-9/11 to prevent protest. This is to mollify the British public before the attack on Iran, which is fully planned. The British, as well as the Americans, regard Iran as strategic due to its oil wealth and due to the fact that rather than Western ways it represents Islaam. The Iranians are a God-fearing people. They worship the one God. What's more, like the Iraqis, as well as the Palestinians, they have never attacked the United States. Thus, on what basis must these Muslims be denigrated and attacked?

CHAPTER 5

Caught in the Act

Non-Muslims are posing as Muslims. Then, they commit violent acts *in their names*. Then, the perpetrators escape and the Muslims are blamed. This is done to portray Islaam as a sponsor of terror. The Adus Isaac debacle is merely one example of this. So is the capture by the Iraqis of British or perhaps Israeli secret service agents, fully disguised as Muslims. So, is the premeditated rape and murder of an Iraqi girl by drunken U.S. soldiers. This vile crime, which included setting the girl's body on fire and killing her mother and sister, has been fully confirmed by U.S. officials. Then, the soldiers concocted a crime scene to make it appear that it it was committed by insurgents.

Usually, the culprits are not so easily caught. This time the evidence is damning. The soldier, private Steven Green, has been essentially proven guilty. Too, the guilt of Zionist Adus Isaac has been proven, since he freely admitted to his crime. He was definitely acting as a spy for the Zionists to foment strife against Muslims. Thus, rather than terrorists Muslims are victims of terror.

That is why they attempted to assassinate him. Instead, they killed the innocent Brazilian, Charles de Menezes.

That Western powers have infiltrated the Muslims is undeniable. They are doing so to create terror acts in their name. The Zionists have been caught numerous times doing this. In India they masquerade as Muslim preachers, in Iraq as so-called insurgents, in American mosques as 'Islaamic' leaders, and, of course, in the London tube bombing as the Zionist Adus Isaac, who was captured by Italian police after imitating a Muslim subway bomber. In Iraq they, along with Americans, kill, rape, and maim, while blaming the insurgents.

While the latter person, who posed as a Muslim, was caught, this was a professional operation. Interior Minister Giuseppe Pisanu said Isaac had evaded police searches with the help of contacts within Italy's Ethiopian and Eritrean immigrants. This network was extensive, that is it was difficult to penetrate. In contrast, there are no similar Muslim espionage networks. Rather, only the Israelis have such networks. What's more, why not—they have been impersonating Muslims for centuries and are experts at doing so. Said the authorities, "From the investigations it has been possible to identify a *dense network* of individuals belonging to Eritrean and Ethiopian communities in Italy believed to have helped him *cover his tracts* (italics mine)." The fact is the entire group of the second accused London bombers are either Eritrean or Ethiopian. Thus, rather than as portrayed in the media, that is of an act of vengeance "due to anger over Iraq," this was an espionage operation. These men had no love for the Iraqi people nor any 'religious' commitment. Thus, the statement that they are radical Muslims is a lie.

The extensive support network encountered by Italian police demonstrates a pre-existing infrastructure. This is proof of Israeli involvement. Yet, it is not in the interests of Western police to blame the Jews. That would violate the

Western agenda, which is the creation of a deliberate war against Islaam. After all, such a war is supposedly "good for business."

Yet, rather than due to any role in terror Islaam is attacked because of jealousy. It is a vital, vibrant way of life, which draws into its fold vast numbers of people. Every year untold thousands of individuals adopt this faith. It is the source of human revival. It gives people hope. It creates for them a purpose. It gives them a solution to their woes. What's more, because of the message of the Qur'an and the teachings of its Messenger it gives them guidance.

There are people who hate the Islaamic way to such a degree that they would do anything to destroy it. The fact is they would even create terror attacks as if Islaamic: all to diminish it. They wish to see this religion weakened and even defeated, while Muslims are systematically slaughtered. What's more, they are achieving this on a routine basis in Palestine, Iraq, Chechnya, India, Nigeria, Sudan, Egypt, Algeria, Thailand, the Philippines, Indonesia, China, and more.

Any terror attack that can be blamed on Islaam, legitimate or otherwise, creates vast interest. Violent words against Muslims and their religion are blared. Yet, no one even considers the continuous terror fomented by the West, for instance, the entire history of modern Iraq—the Western installation of the brute Saddam Hussein and, then, the fraudulent and brutal Western wars against this country as well as the installation of the murderous and former Shah of Iran. The untold millions of people who have died in Iraq and Iran under the oppression of the West: how can this even be remotely compared to any supposed Islaamic terror? These are the horrors inflicted upon countless groups of Muslims, as well as numerous Christians: the global wars against the Palestinians, Chechans, Uzbeks, Indonesians, Philippinos, Moroccans, Kazakhs, Sudanese,

Saudis, Bosnians, Algerians, Iraqis, Iranians, and Egyptians, that is through, for instance, the Eastern/Western puppets Karam Islam of Uzbekistan, the former Indonesian ruler and brute Suharto, and the mega-rich American puppet and ruler of Egypt Hosni Mubarak, the latter being a decided non-Muslim. Through such tyrants the Muslims are constantly under siege.

No one considers that the entire Islaamic world is ruled by "synthetic" rulers. Each of these brutes has been installed by Western and/or Eastern powers. This is the dilemma of Islaam: to be blamed, while the Muslims endure vast atrocities, while this faith is attacked from all fronts. Incredibly, with the exception of Iran the remaining 'Muslim' countries are under the authority of the West as well as the East, that is Russia. In other words the policies issued by these governments are ultimately controlled by the United States, Britain, the European powers, Israel, and Russia. There are no independent Islaamic governments in these countries.

Do not forget that there is no way to invade or attack the Muslims, for instance, to attack Iran, without first demonizing them. This is precisely what is being achieved.

They ask, "What in Islaam causes all this terror: no other religion is like this?" They don't ask, "What in Judaism allows the creation of four million refugees, the Palestinians, while killing. imprisoning, raping, robbing, and torturing them?" Nor do they ask, "What in Christianity allows the deliberate genocide against the Native Americans, the wicked enslavement of the black Africans, the relentless provision of murderous weapons to the Israelis, or the bombing into oblivion of Iraqi civilians?"

Yet, is there anything in the words of the magnanimous ancient prophets, Abraham, Moses, and Jesus, which would allow this: the killing of the innocent, a deed which the American 'Christian' hierarchy achieves every day? Until the American war on Iraq in that country there were no violent civilian killings, for instance, of Iraqi children, shoppers, and/or workers in Baghdad. There were no car or suicide bombings. There were also no beheadings. So, since these deaths are only post-occupation, who is truly responsible?

Beheadings: Islaamic or bogus?

Since the Iraq war Islaam has been associated with beheadings. This was based upon the beheading of an American former espionage agent, Nicholas Berg. People might believe this religion condones such a practice. True, Berg was slaughtered, but it was not by the Muslims.

How could the Muslims do it? The atrocity occurred in the Abu Ghraib prison. There was no means for them to gain access to that fortress. What's more, at the end of the video a voice can be heard, saying, "Thy will be done." This can definitely be heard. Also, at the end a man's head pokes into the screen wearing a U.S. military-issue green cap. Thus, these men were merely masquerading as Middle Easterners and were, instead, Westerners. Therefore, upon careful investigation there is no doubt that this was fabricated. No Muslims were involved. This was all a lie to displace blame from the true terrorists.

In Iraq this disguising is continuous, as proven by the recent capture in Basra of two British secret service agents. These Westerners were dressed as Middle Easterners and were in possession of enough military hardware to blow up a city block.

Too, the timing is suspect. Through the Abu Ghraib atrocities the Muslims gained a degree of public sympathy. The powerful people of the West could not tolerate that. So, they concocted a terror event, so that the Muslims could, again, be marked. What's more, there is no allowance anywhere in Islaam for public beheadings or to brag about it. In other words, such acts are not a part of this religion. Rather, this is largely a European creation. Even in Saudi Arabia the beheadings have no Islaamic basis. Rather, they were instituted by the Kingdom. This practice was adopted in the 1950s after the European model. Then, the ruler, Ibn Saud, was a paid U.S. agent. This was to create a repressive state based on fear, all to maintain American hegemony. Thus, since its invasion in the 1930s by American interests there has been no 'Islaamic' rule in Saudi Arabia. Even today it is a puppet state.

Islaam prohibits rule by king. Only God has the right to rule. Thus, the entire concept of the so-called Kingdom of Saudi Arabia is a violation. Undoubtedly any act instituted by this Kingdom is corrupt, including the gruesome display of beheadings: a kind of terror tactic to portray Islaam as if bloodthirsty. The Kingdom is a U.S. operative. Nothing about it is Islaamic.

Beheading is un-Islaamic. The diabolical habit of holding up the severed head, as if a prize, is also condemnable, also un-Islaamic. In fact, this tactic has its origins in ancient Mongolia and Persia as well as, certainly, Western Europe. There is no Islaamic precedent for it. This is a Western crime foisted upon the local people by Western powers. It is to prevent rebellion in order to maintain power over the oil wealth as well as, supposedly, strategic territory.

Regarding the true basis of Saudi Arabia the words of former President Franklin D. Roosevelt are revealing. On his battle-carrier in the Persian Gulf, 1944, he told the British, essentially, 'Hands off Saudi Arabia: Ibn Saud is our man, and so is this country. Instead, you British can have Iraq and Iran.' This was the superpowers' agreement for colonization as well as for the theft of these countries' resources. These powers continue to, essentially, steal these resources: oil, minerals, and gas. Surely, the effects of this colonization are easily demonstrated. It is demonstrated by the poverty of the common man in Iran, Iraq, Jordan, and Saudi Arabia. From Western meddling the people never benefit. What's more, try as they might no one can deny it: the aforementioned words of the former colonizing president tell all.

Americans say, "Oh, I don't think that our government is really colonizing." Then, what did Roosevelt mean when he said it was "ours?"

The oil resource in Saudi Arabia is worth trillions of dollars. It is all easy money. The Americans and British have the power to control these assets. Does anyone really believe that they wouldn't exert that power? Thus, the tyrants of this modern world would do all that is necessary to maintain their power, even the institution of public beheadings, to 'control' the masses. Incredibly, in their efficient use of their propaganda apparatus Western powers have effectively represented a Western act, the gruesome public beheading, as if it is an Islaamic practice.

Crisis in Sudan

This is another example of misplaced blame. There is absolutely no evidence of Islaamic atrocities in this country. True, Sudan is under siege. However, it is not from the Muslims. Nor is it from the so-called Arab militia.

There is no Arab militia in this country. This is a decoy created by PR groups, all to create indignation against the Muslims. It is also to prevent people from investigating this faith. This is proven by a simple fact. The area of concern, Darfur, is virtually entirely Muslim. It is also *oil-rich*. Now, the reason for the war and atrocities in this region becomes apparent.

Proof of a plot against the Muslims is compelling. That the crisis is a Western one is equally compelling. As documented by the authoritative article by F. Huwaidi *Israel's Fingerprints in*

Khartoum it is primarily the Israelis who have destabilized Sudanese society. This is because the Sudanese have a love for Islaam and recently have attempted to create an Islaamic government. The fragmentation in the Sudanese capital and the claim for a separate state is not the working of the people. Oppression of the Christian masses is never an Islaamic policy. Says Huwaidi from the beginning this was an Israeli operative. The purpose: to prevent the independence of the Muslim world of North Africa, from colonial rule. What's more, notes the author, rather than his words or any bias these ware the words of Israeli spies.

Huwaidi quotes a book published by the Dayan Institute called *Israel and the Sudanese Liberation Movement* written by ex-Mossad officer M. Fergi. The terminology used in this book is telling. Incredibly, regarding the infamous happenings in Sudan the Israelis are the clandestine sources. They describe their goals metaphorically, that is the "pulling the limbs then cutting them off." Pulling means building relationships with minorities, making them powerful. The 'cutting off' can then occur, that is the creation of an autonomous state within the Muslim state. This is why the Sudanese government is essentially sharing power with the Southern government. Rather than to protect against the persecution of forlorn Christians this was an Israeli act, which served only Zionist interests. The purpose is to destabilize Muslim countries. This is so Israel can continue its criminal expansion. What's more, the Israelis have followed the same process in Kurdistan, creating a group which serves rather than Islaam secular interests. These people have even become loyal to the Israelis. Thus, the entire Kurdish and Sudanese national wars are rather than local religious disputes, instead, Israeli, as well as American, creations. In Lebanon the Christian/Muslim War was also largely a Zionist provocation, which the Zionists are now attempting to repeat.

The Israeli espionage in Africa began, notes Fergi, in 1956. This is fully confirmed by the Ugandan Henry Kyemba in his book *A State of Blood*. The Zionists had established good relationships with numerous African countries, concentrating on the Horn of Africa (Ethiopia, etc.). Yet, they proved to be opportunists. While there they stole some of the land from the disadvantaged natives, and created businesses and resorts.

To the Israelis this region is highly strategic. Thus, they hand-picked operatives, concentrating on the notorious brute, John Karnak. They "prepared" him and, then, backed him, "so that he challenges the (Sudanese government) and *imposes himself on it...*" In addition, notes Fergie, the purpose was/is to create pressure on the Muslims in Egypt and Sudan to weaken these nations.

The reason this is important is that the Muslims are blamed for destabilizing Sudan and for any atrocities, especially against supposed Christian minorities. Does this make any sense? The Sudanese have never attacked each other previously. Rather, wars in Sudan have been largely fought against colonial invaders. There problem has always been invasion, not civil war. Then, it makes greater sense that an outside power is attacking and corrupting it. This is what Fergie proves. He says that since the 1960s Israel sent aggressive missions into Ethiopia, the Congo, Uganda, and Kenya, with the ultimate goal of destabilizing Sudan. This is because the objective of the Israelis is to "control" this country through an artificial government.

Said the Mossad the success of this operation, first in Ethiopia, was "absolute." Israeli entities have complete control of the security organizations, as well as the police, in this country. They have fully infiltrated the Ministry. In other words, in a secretive manner they run the government. This enabled the Mossad and Israeli military to have "unprecedented control" in order to pursue at will further conquests, focusing primarily on Sudan and, ultimately, Egypt. Ethiopia was merely their base of operations. By the early 1960s a separatist movement was well under way through the infiltration by Israel of some 600 Jewish 'advisers.' This led to the flow of various weapons of Israeli and U.S. origin. The Israelis captured many of these weapons while warring with Muslim countries and, then, sold them to the Africans, all to further destabilize the Muslims.

In 1993 when Eritrea gained its independence this was an example of what Israel could achieve, that is the creation of isolated states. Then, they armed the country extensively to achieve their political desires. The result was the systematic slaughter of tens of thousands of Africans. This is why the Mossad considers this country "Israel's strongest strategic ally in the African continent." In 1996 Eritrea was the main country to take Israeli military aid, and by 1997 some 650 Israeli advisers operated there plus numerous spies. Eritrean intelligence units, each masquerading as Muslims, complete with *falsified names and IDs as Muslims*, were then sent to spy in Yemen and Sudan.

For their own selfish interests they created these brutal conflicts, again, to destabilize the region. It was also to sell armaments, even drugs. In this regard to them the common man is dispensable. These Zionist elements pursue their agenda recklessly, with complete disregard for all others, particularly the poor and disadvantaged. The point is the Muslims have been blamed for the Sudanese conflict with all its horrors, when, in fact, they are not to blame. Rather, they have been attempting to ameliorate it. The Israelis who created this conflict are responsible for the atrocities, and exclusively created the rebellion. They created the various sub-states. Thus, it is they alone who must be held responsible for the vast crimes, even for any Christian deaths. This ethnic strife is no Muslim creation: it is a premeditated Zionist crime, proven by the Zionist's own publications.

Israel, notes Huwaidi, "used its influence to insure the separatist fighting goes on" by *making it appear* that there is a true struggle between the occupying 'Arabic' north and the impoverished 'African' Christian south. Yet, these lies are proven by the fact that all Sudanese are Africans. What's more, there are virtually no Arabs in this country as has been falsely reported in American news.

The separatist movement was headed by an Israeli agent, John Karnak. Eventually, there was a lull in the fighting and relative peace, and Karnak and the northern government signed a treaty. Then, oil was discovered in the south, and the hostilities were resumed. Through Ethiopia the Zionists delivered millions of dollars worth of weapons plus strategic support. For propaganda purposes a radio station was built. This was all done using the American public's money. Even fighter planes were delivered. Then, the U.S. provided additional support to the rebels, rather, mercenaries, through satellite pictures of northern government forces. In addition, Israel sent a number of military experts to assist the effort. This is proven by the fact that in battles in 1988 which led to the occupation of Sudanese cities two Mossad Colonels were killed. This proves that regarding any ethnic strife the Israelis are the instigators. They are the real aggressors. Yet, the United States is also involved in the atrocities. Regrettably, the money and weapons with which Israel supplies the rebels originates from this country.

It is easy for the Israelis to create such mini-wars. In their aggression they purge the American treasury. Then, they use this money to create terror against Muslims as well as the minority Christians. They "submerge" minority groups with money, creating so-called "liberation armies," which are in reality mercenaries. Thus, it is money from the Western public which is used to fuel global ethnic strife.

According to the Mossad before recommending him the Israelis studied the personality of the future dictator, John Karnak, much like they studied the personality of the Shah of Iran. The latter was also an Israeli operative. This was because they would be entrusting such men with weapons and money; they didn't want them to become traitors. Then, regarding Karnak they got him a scholarship in America and a doctorate degree in economic agriculture, which enabled him to access American military training. In other words, once again, the tyranny in the Sudan is largely a U.S. creation through the creation of a brutal tyrant. Thus, Karnak was nurtured as a U.S.-Zionist operative, all to plot against the people of Africa on behalf of the certain powerful 'globalists.' After that in Israel he joined the College of National Security for further training, particularly in espionage.

This is the man—this Israeli-trained spy—who operated the southern Sudanese war. This is the very war for which the Muslims are blamed. Not once was it mentioned that the chief architect of this war is an Israeli agent and that the war is fully funded by Israel and the United States, particularly wealthy Zionists. Rather, it is portrayed as a struggle against the 'tyrannical' Arabs of the north. There are no such Arabs. These are deliberate schemes.

Blame is falsely laid upon Arabs and Muslims. Yet, throughout Sudan it is exclusively the Muslims who are being slaughtered, all with U.S.- and Israeli- issued weaponry.

As Huwaidi demonstrated, ultimately, through murder and deceit, the Israelis achieved their objective. Karnak is now Sudan's vice president, and his movement "has become part of the ruling force in Khartoum." This is the source of the corruption and strife which has plagued Sudan and which has led to the deaths of the innocent. Estimates vary, but it is believed that approximately one to two hundred thousand innocent people have perished. This is an Israeli crime—true genocide—although the connection is never mentioned.

Like the Iran-Iraq debacle the Muslims did not create this war. Sudan was invaded by foreign elements and, in fact, this war was started and maintained by the Israelis, with tacit U.S. support. Yet, the hate is registered, the Muslims are blamed, and Christian people believe it is Islaamic. It is as if a confirmation that Islaam breeds intolerance and that if the Muslims are in power, they will kill all Christians. This is the message that the Zionist-controlled media spreads, yet, it is absolute lies. The fact is for over a thousand years the indigenous Muslims and Christians lived in this region in peace. Until Israel intervened in Sudan there were no Muslim-Christian wars. Any supposed Muslim-Christian fighting in this region is orchestrated by the Israelis. Yet, since Darfur is over 97% Muslim the entire claim of such a war is a ruse. Even so, if any Christians are being slaughtered, it is the Israelis who are responsible.

It might be said, "This is a Muslim's opinion. It is biased." Yet, incredibly, the source for the aforementioned is non-Muslim, specifically Zionist. This is confirmation that the media has purposely fabricated the Sudan crisis. Then, Darfur is oil-rich, a relatively recent discovery. This surely plays a critical role in any destabilization. Thus, the blame against the Muslims is both false and malicious. People who have invested in this region wish to drive the peoples from their land, so the latter can have no claim for their wealth. That is strictly the cause of this 'conflict.'

Assassination of a president

This is an excerpt from the book *By Way of Deception* by Victor Ostrovsky, a Mossad whistle blower. It regards a planned assassination attempt against former U.S. president George Bush, Sr., who fell into disfavor with the Israelis. The assassination was to occur in Madrid, Spain:

> The Madrid Royal Palace would be the safest place on the planet at the time, unless you had the security plans and could find a flaw in them. That was exactly what the Mossad planned to do. It was clear from the start that the assassination would be blamed on the Palestinians, perhaps ending once and for all their irritating resistance and making them the people most hated by all Americans. Three Palestinian extremists were taken by a Kidon unit from their hiding place in Beirut and relocated incommunicado in a special detention location in the Negev desert. The three were Beijdun Salameh, Mohammed Hussein, and Hussein Shahin. At the same time, various threats, some real and some not, were made against the president. The Mossad clique added its share, in order to more precisely define the threat as if it were coming from a group affiliated with none other than Abu Nidal (an Arab-appearing Mossad agent). They knew that name carried with it a certain guarantee of getting action and keeping it. So, if something were to happen, the media would be quick to react and say, "We knew about it, and don't forget where you saw it first."

Several days before the event, Ostrovsky notes, it was leaked to the Spanish police that the three terrorists were on their way to Madrid and that they were probably planning some extravagant action. Since the Mossad was in control of security it would not be a problem for this clique to bring the "killers" as close as they might want to the president and, then, stage a killing. Thus, the Israelis feel immune to any consequences. They are true international criminals. Then, why should the American people support such criminals?

Ostrovsky continues:

> In the ensuing confusion Mossad agents would kill the "perpetrators," (and, therefore, eliminate the only witnesses to their crimes), scoring yet another victory for the Mossad. They'd be very sorry that they hadn't been able to save the president, but his protection was not their job to begin with. With all the security forces involved (that is for the cover-up), and the assassins dead, it would be very difficult to discover the source of the security breach, except that several of the countries involved in the conference, such as Syria, were regarded as countries that assisted terrorists. With that in mind, it would be a foregone conclusion where the breach was.

This proves that the Zionists are the true international terrorists. Without hesitation, they plot the assassination of an American president. Then, in the epitome of wickedness they blame it on another people, while murdering any scapegoats. Yet, if this would have been achieved, no one would have suspected the Israelis. Instead, full blame would have been placed on the Arab-appearing patsies.

They have done this before, that is feigned Islaamic terror. Surely, 9/11, Bali, Madrid, and the London bombings wouldn't be exceptions. This group has plotted to kill a U.S. president. Thus, there would be no hesitation to kill few thousand people in high rise buildings, everyday workers from the United States and various other nations, including several hundred Muslims.

The postings

The media broadcasts claims of responsibility, known as postings, as if they are truth. These include various claims of responsibility for terrorist acts. None of these organizations or postings are legitimate.

In the London bombings there were two postings, one from the "Secret Organization of al-Qaeda in Europe" and another from the "Abu Hafs al Masri Brigade." Neither of these organizations exist. They are phantom 'groups' used to create false images. Incredibly, these organizations have no members. Even U.S. intelligence agencies dispute them. Yet, despite suspect e-mails confirmed as bogus by espionage experts their postings "sowed anxiety and drew instant headlines all over the world."

According to Bryan Bender and Farah Stockman of the Globe Staff specialists "there is no evidence these organizations exist. Consider, for instance, the Abu Hafs Brigade. E-mail messages purporting to be written by the group previously claimed responsibility for everything from the North American blackout to a 'suicide' attack in Iraq that killed 20 Italian policemen. However none of those claims have proven true. Then, after 9/11, this phantom group predicted that there was a "90% chance" that another attack would occur in the United States. Could this relate to the illegal aliens—Israeli nationals— who were caught attempting to blow up a nuclear plant?

Abu Hafs Brigade and/or Abu Hafs Army are fabrications. These are false fronts for Zionist operatives who, again, seek to make Islaam appear diabolic. This is to distract attention from their own murderous attacks. Again, Abu merely means father of, in this instance, father of Hafs. It is the Zionists who caused this to be associated with terror. For resistance groups Muslims rarely if ever use this term. Thus, like the Popeye cartoon when such language is used, it must be held suspect.

Top authorities fully dispute the validity of the various postings. Specialist Ben Venzke, CEO of IntelCenter, a private firm specializing in analyzing terrorist messages, made a simple analysis: "they are not credible" and, further, "none of the brigade's e-mails have ever proved authentic..." Then, if they are not authentic, this is proof that the Muslims are being falsely accused. The source of these accusations are the Zionists.

Yet, the objective was already achieved: to tarnish Islaam in the eyes of the masses, so that atrocities against them can be perpetrated—so that their oil can be stolen and their wealth usurped. It is also so that the Zionists may continue to commit evil acts, without consequences.

In summary, regarding the London bombings a list of the various facts that point to non-Muslim versus Islaamic sources are:

- A phony posting attributed to the so-called Secret Organization of al-Qaeda, which is non-existent and which, therefore, has no members. This is in order to divert blame from the real perpetrators

- A phony posting of the second bombing by the so-called Abu Hafs al-Masri Brigade, an organization which top U.S. intelligent officials claim as bogus. There are no known or admitted members of this group. What's more, all e-mails from it have proven unsubstantiated and, in fact, fabricated.

- The fact that all four accused bombers from the initial bombings had no known motives for the killings and are conveniently unable to defend themselves

- The fact that these initial four had every reason to live and showed no signs of anger, discontent, frustration, or any desire to kill themselves.

- Eyewitness accounts dispute the official statements that the bombs went off on actual people with rucksacks or even from any such bags left on the subway/tube carriages or bus. One eyewitness said, essentially, 'There was no such bag where the bomb went off.'

- The fact that a scholarly Muslim, Dr. al-Fagih, was implicated as an accomplice almost immediately after the bombings. Subsequently, this was determined to be a fabrication.

- The fact that this occurred when the Israeli Prime Minister was in town and that the bomb blast, which could in no way hurt him, occurred at a station near his hotel. The Zionists have a history of such faked attacks, using them to gain sympathy. His nearness to the bombing site is highly suspect. He was, then, immediately available for interviews when he called for a kind of World War against the Muslims. If bombers wanted to take revenge on the Israelis, it would have been more likely that they would attack him rather than innocent civilians, since the latter were largely against the war.

- That Netanyahu made comments which were highly suspect and had to be later retracted.

- That the Web server where the posting "Secret Organization of al-Qaeda in Europe" originates is in United States, specifically Maryland and Texas.

- That the bus bombing occurred near an espionage center known for plotting fake terror acts as well as near the address 77 Great Russell Street. The latter is the original site for the office of Chaim Weisman, the founder of modern Zionism. It was at this address that the course for the creation of the Israeli entity was plotted. There was no reason for Muslims to symbolize this, most of whom have no idea what this address represents. To reiterate the likelihood that Muslims would know the significance of this is nil.

- The fact that all four of the accused purchased return tickets and long-term parking tickets. This would, in fact, support the need for large backpacks; it would indicate they were taking a prolonged trip, perhaps an outing. They had also purchased parking tickets for a week, which supports the need for backpacks. The bombing occurred in the summer. Evidence exists that these men may planned a summer outing. They could have easily have been targeted and killed to be used as patsies. This would explain the convenient finding of fully intact IDs near the sites of the explosions, including the bizarre finding of IDs from one of the accused at two different sites.

- That in the original posting the Arabic Qur'an was misquoted. This would be virtually impossible for a Muslim to do. Muslims, particularly highly educated ones, as many of these men were, would only carefully render the Qur'an for any quote.

- That the bombing was a public relations disaster for the Muslims and was devastating to any Muslim cause. The accused were highly educated. It is unlikely that they would give no consideration to the derogatory consequences of such acts.

- That for the original bombings many of the official and well-published statements about the bombings are wrong. For instance, the respected news journal the

Scotsman noted that the four accused men gathered together the night before at a distant site, Lutton, departing the next morning on the 7:20 train. From there, so reports the *Scotsman*, they set about do "a day of carnage." This is erroneous, because they could have never made it to this train. The video places them merely entering the train station at approximately 7:20 (the train actually departed at 7:24) In their casual pace it would have been impossible for them to have bought tickets and made it to the departure deck on time. This may explain why later police reports place them as departing on the 7:40 train. Yet, this train departed, in fact, at 7:50, which they surely could have made. However, incredibly, the train arrived at 8:43, virtually precisely when the bombs began exploding. Thus, there is no possibility that these men could have made it to the involved sites. Rather, they were patsies, preselected for the blame in order to fix Islaam in peoples' minds as a supporter of terror.

To reiterate accepting the official statement as true if these men truly were in Lutton the absolutely soonest they could have arrived in London was at 8:43, while the bombs began exploding five minutes later. Thus, it is physically impossible for these men to have been the bombers. This confirms the observations of eyewitnesses, who state categorically that on the tubes *there were no Muslim bombers*. In a chilling revelation it also means that the video films of these men may have been fabricated.

- That regarding the bus bomb this was obviously planted. Muslims may have been on board, but they were not the bombers. The bus' security camera had been disabled a few days prior. On the day of the bombing was diverted to a region near an espionage center. What's more, just prior to the bomb exploding an individual got off, as did the driver. Yet, the region at which they departed is not a bus stop. This is evidence of a plot. The people who left the bus just prior to the explosion are likely culprits. The bomb blast may have been timed, perhaps, to coincide with the boarding of the Muslim in question, so he could have been incriminated.

• That in the second, that is attempted, bombings the claim of responsibility fails to fit the types of people who have been accused. These were native Eritreans and Ethiopians, who are not violently attached to the Iraq war and who would never say, "Our strikes into the depths of the capital of the British infidels are only a message to other European governments that we will not relent and sit idle before the infidel soldiers will leave the land of the two rivers (that is Iraq, which is situated between the Tigris and Euphrates)." Ethiopians have no moral or religious attachment to this region, nor would they verbalize such a statement. For them there is no 'holy' reason to fight this war. Nor is the statement of the Land of Two Rivers an Islaamic one. Muslims never use it. Rather this is an Old Testament phrase. Nor do they commonly call Westerners infidels. In fact, these are mere schemes to create fear and hate.

• That in the second attack the bombs were all duds. Thus, they were meant at a minimum to sow terror. This is confirmed by the Zionist Adus Isaac, who said that the objective was to instill terror in the masses. Rather, his purpose was to cause people to associate Islaam with terror. They could not be all duds, unless this was a specific plot. The purpose was to create an impression, that is of civilian Islaamic bombers armed with supposedly home-concocted bombs, while avoiding minimal disruption of infrastructure. What's more, after the original bombing the Muslim community was alerted to the dire consequences of such bombings. Too, all community leaders condemned these acts. Therefore, it would now be difficult to find Muslim patsies, that is from the regular community members. So, agent conspirators were selected to create the image of Islaamic terror.

Again, the Zionist Adus Isaac said these bombs were meant only to "sow terror, never to kill." To date no Muslims, particularly true Muslims, including Usama bin Laden, have said such words. A Muslim has no interest in doing this. Rather, Muslims say, "We are fighting the oppressors, who have stolen our land." Or, "We are fighting the evil governments of Israel and the United States, which oppress our people" or similar statements. They never say, "We are sowing terror in the British or American population as pay-back." The fact is the message itself is geared to create terror. The posting continues, 'we will launch a "bloody war,"' which will wreak havoc on the capitals of European countries that do not remove their troops from Iraq within a month. No Muslim organizations makes such statements. In fact, if any such proclamations were made, it would logically arise from the oppressed: the tormented Iraqis.

It is obvious that the Muslims are being targeted. If, for instance, a good 'Christian' American or, surely, a zealous or

'Orthodox' Jew was caught setting off a bomb on, for instance, a New York City subway, would news reports blare, "Christian terrorist (or Christian bomber) or Jewish terrorist/bomber caught attempting to blow up New York subway?" As a result, would Christianity and Judaism be registered a sponsor of terror? Would such a person be imprisoned and never allowed legal representation? This is implausible. Thus, regarding Islaam the bias is obvious and malicious.

CHAPTER 6

Conspiracy to Control

In the media lies are constantly being spread. The people behind these lies are obviously afraid the truth will be revealed. This is to control people's minds. Incredibly, merely a few people control the way people think. Thus, for mere material gain people are being manipulated.

The second London bombing occurred on the day that in the United States the Patriot Act was slated for renewal. This is surely no coincidence.

In England since the bombings the anti-war movement is greatly weakened and may effectively be neutralized. This was surely an objective of the bombings. Then, would a Muslim, who is against the vile wars in the Middle East, seek this goal? What's more, draconian measures have been authorized to 'deal with' any protesters. This would never be the objective of any devout Muslims. This sets the stage for another war, such as an international, that is Western, attack on Iran. For instance, England cannot afford to fight two battles, one in the streets of London against the anti-war movement, while another in the streets of Teheran. The same is true of the U. S. hierarchy. 9/11 effectively neutralized any resistance.

Regarding the initial bombing in London the official story is heavily in dispute. Eyewitnesses fully contradict the government story. A second bombing would serve government interests by distracting the public from the disputed allegations.

The contradictions are extensive. For instance, initially, government officials said it was a suicide bombing. Scotland Yard rejected this. What's more, within days the government accused four young Pakistani Muslim men. Eyewitnesses said this was not so and that, rather, the bombs were likely planted under the carriages. These eyewitnesses include those sitting directly across from the precise sites of the explosions.

This means the official story is a fabrication. Any videos released supporting it are also fabricated. There is only one group that has the ability to do so as well as manipulate the media response. These media accounts are spread by the Zionist cartel. This cartel controls the security operations for the London Underground and also the media. They have the security operations, as well as the political power, in place, so they can perpetrate any level of lies. Instead of eyewitness accounts people rely on the news or so-called experts. Thus, they are easily misled.

Let there be no doubt about it, the bombs blew up beneath the trains. This is the same methodology used in the Madrid bombings. If there was a bomb which was visible, someone would likely have seen it and, then, the plot would have been disrupted.

No one can dispute it; just like in London the Madrid bombings were professional jobs. The organization which took credit and which was represented globally as the culprit is now confirmed as bogus. Then, if the organization is bogus and if there are no Muslims who have claimed responsibility, what is the basis for blaming Islaam? This is merely further corruption aimed at destroying it. What's more, the Egyptian Zahawiri did not say he plotted or conceived the bombings. Rather, the likely culprits are whoever created the false postings. This is because, surely, this posting was created by Islaam's enemies.

Whether 9/11, Madrid, or London the Muslims had nothing to do with it. Rather, as will be demonstrated later in this book they attempted to warn the authorities about potential attacks. What's more, the fact that these bombings occurred in concert with attempts to legislate the Patriot Act is incriminating, that is against the global powers. There was also the 'coincidence' of the G8 conference occurring in Scotland. Here, too, the bombings would neutralize any resistance. What's more, since the bombings in London occurred nearly simultaneously with the mandate by the British government to withdraw from Iraq huge numbers of troops, this too points to a Western source. Already, there had been bombings against war resisters. Australians were struck in Bali. There was also the attempted bombing against the Mexicans for refusing to support the war.

In all this terror the evidence points to the Israelis. After all according to British historians, including Christopher Sykes in his book *Crossroads to Israel* they have the world's first terrorist state, that is an entity established exclusively through terrorism. What's more, the arrival in the United States within hours of the London bombings of Israeli officials demanding 2.2 billion dollars in free aid, rather, charity is surely suspect. Can anyone deem this a coincidence? What's more, why believe anything the Zionists say? They have never told the truth previously. Why would they do so now? The fact is whatever the orthodox media says must be held suspect, because it is based upon a singular purpose: the maintenance of the evil Israeli empire.

Obviously, the Israelis have committed multiple terrorist crimes, while blaming Muslims. There are also American elements which seek to perpetuate the impression that Islaam is tyrannical. There are even Christian organizations which have as their agenda the destruction of this religion. Yet, there is no purpose in Islaam for attacking the United States or the Christian people. What's more, there is no Islamic agenda of usurping the wealth of any Christian nation. Christians need to look elsewhere for the source of harm. In fact, historically, the Islaamic system has always been their supporter. After all it is only the Muslims, along with their Christian brothers, who revere Jesus and the Virgin Mary as high. In contrast, regarding the latter it is only the Zionists who say vile words regarding them.

It was Brigadier general James J. David who reported the true source of the harm that is striking America. In his letter to the editor sent to the *Atlanta Journal-Constitution* General David said:

The news reports were initially as follows:

> Two Middle East men who led Tennessee police on a high speed chase in a rented Ryder truck are now being held without bond pending an investigation by the FBI. It seems that the two Middle East men refused to stop while being chased for three miles by Tennessee police. Officers say the men threw something something from the truck while being pursued and later the officers found a vial containing an unknown substance along the roadway.'

> After forcing the vehicle to stop officers found a "Learn to fly" brochure in the truck leading officers and others to express concern about the security at the nuclear fuel services plant nearby. These two men also

gave authorities fake Florida driver's licenses and fake identification cars.

Just weeks after 9/11 this should have been a massive story, but it received no headlines. Soon after this, there was in Florida the notorious arresting of Muslim medical students who were reported as 'suspicious' while they were eating in a restaurant. The latter were proven innocent, but the point is their arrests and the accusations which followed were national news. Yet, this, a potential attack on a nuclear plant, plus lying to an officer and false IDs—plus hiding and destroying of evidence which could be of danger to humanity—this receives no press? Had these men been of Arab origin it would have been blared all over the world. Instead, because they were both Israeli Jews nothing was said. The gross bias is obvious.

The "learn to fly" brochure is telling. This was the very evidence used to falsely implicate Muslims. This event is further evidence that the people who laid this blame on the Muslims were Jewish spies.

Operation Northwoods

Regarding global terror the Israelis are not the only culprits. Is anyone really surprised that powerful entities, for instance, world governments, would commit terror? Must it only be a Muslim propensity? This is perhaps best illustrated by a U.S. government document, 1962, known as Operation Northwoods. Titled *Justification for U.S. military action in Cuba* this document was signed by the then Chairman of the Joint Chiefs of Staff, L. L. Lemnitzer. Therefore, it is official and real. The memo, listed as Top Secret, describes the methods used by those in power to exert control over the civilized world. It demonstrates that they are ruthless. This was never meant to be seen by the trusting public, since it was released by an insider. Says the document (an abridged version):

- The Joint Chiefs of Staff have considered the attached Memorandum for the Chief of Operations, Cuba Project,...which would provide justification for U.S. military intervention in Cuba.

- The Joint Chiefs of Staff recommend that the proposed memorandum...suitable for planning purposes... (Note: nothing in the military is left to chance: this is typical military jargon).

- Further, it is assumed that a single agency will be given the primary responsibility for developing military and para-military aspects of the basic plan. It is recommended that this responsibility for both overt and covert military operations be assigned the Joint Chiefs of Staff (remember, the U.S. president is the Commander in Chief, even above this unit).

The problem

As requested by the Chief of Operations, Cuba Project, the Joint Chiefs of Staff are to indicate brief but precise description of pretexts which they consider would provide justification for U.S. military intervention in Cuba.

Facts bearing on the problem

It is recognized that any action which becomes pretext for U.S. military intervention in Cuba will lead to a political decision which, then, would lead to military action. Cognizance has been taken of a suggested course of action proposed by the U.S. Navy relating to generate instances in the Gauntanamo area.

Discussion

The suggested courses of action…are based on the premise that U.S. military intervention will result from a period of heightened U.S.- Cuban tensions which place the United States in a the position of suffering justifiable grievances. World opinion and the United Nations forum should be variably affected by developing the *international image* of the Cuban government as rash and irresponsible and as an *alarming and unpredictable threat* to the peace of the Western hemisphere.

Recommendations

(The goal is to develop) adequate justification for U.S. military intervention. Such a plan would enable a logical build-up of incidents to be combined with other seemingly unrelated events to *camouflage the ultimate objective* and create the *necessary impression* of Cuban rashness and irresponsibility on a large scale, directed at other countries as well as the United States. The desired (result) would be to place the United States in the apparent position of suffering defensible grievances from a rash and irresponsible government of Cuba and to *develop an international image of a Cuban threat* to peace in the Western Hemisphere.

…Inasmuch as the ultimate objective is overt military intervention, it is recommended that primary responsibility for developing military and para-military (mercenary-like) aspects of the plan for both overt and covert military operations be assigned the Joint Chiefs of Staff.

Pretexts to justify U.S. military intervention in Cuba

(The plan is as follows):

* Since it would seem desirable to use legitimate provocation as the basis for U.S. military intervention in Cuba a *covert and deception plan*, to include requisite preliminary actions...could be executed as an initial effort to *provoke Cuban reactions*. Harassment plus deceptive actions to convince the Cubans of imminent invasion would be emphasized. Our military posture through execution of the plan will allow a rapid change from exercise to intervention if Cuban response justifies.

* A series of well coordinated incidents will be planned to take place in and around Gauntanamo to give the *genuine appearance* of being done by hostile Cuban forces.

Incidents to establish a credible attack (include):

a) Start rumors (many). Use clandestine radio

b) Land friendly Cubans in uniform "over-the-fence" to stage attack on (the U.S.) base

c) Capture Cuban (friendly) saboteurs inside the base

d) Start riots near the base main gate (friendly Cubans)

e) Blow up ammunition inside the base; start fires

f) Burn aircraft on air base (sabotage)

g) Lob mortar shells from outside of base into base. Some damage to installations

h) Capture (fake) assault teams approaching from the sea or vicinity of Gauntanamo City

i) Capture (fake) militia group which storms the base

j) Sabotage ship in harbor; large fires—naphthalene (Napalm)

k) Sink ship near harbor entrance. Conduct funerals for *mock-victims*

United States would respond by executing offensive operations to secure water and power supplies, destroying artillery and mortar emplacements which threaten the base. Commence large scale United States military operations.

- A "Remember the Maine" incident could be arranged in several forms:

a) We could blow up a U.S. ship in Gauntanamo Bay and blame Cuba.

b) We could blow up a drone (unmanned) vessel anywhere in the Cuban waters. We could arrange to cause such incident in the vicinity of Havana or Santiago as a spectacular result of Cuban attack from the air or sea, or both. The presence of Cuban planes or ships merely investigating the intent of the vessel could be fairly compelling evidence that the ship was taken under attack. The nearness to Havana or Santiago would add credibility, especially to those people that might have heard the blast or has seen the fire. The U.S. could follow up with an air/sea rescue operation covered by U.S. fighters to "evacuate" remaining members of the non-existent Crew. *Casualty lists in U.S. newspapers* would cause a helpful wave of national indignation.[1]

- We could develop a Communist Cuban terror campaign in the Miami area, in other Florida cities and *even in Washington (D.C.)*. The terror campaign could be pointed at Cuban refugees seeking haven in the United States. We could *sink a boatload of Cubans enrooted to Florida (real or simulated)*. We could foster attempts on lives of Cuban refugees in the United States, *even to the extent of wounding* in instances to be widely publicized. *Exploding a few plastic bombs* in carefully chosen spots, the arrest of Cuban agents, and the release of *prepared documents* substantiating Cuban involvement also would be helpful in projecting the idea of an irresponsible government.

- *Use of MIG type aircraft by U.S. pilots* could provide additional provocation. Harassment of civil air attacks on surface shipping and destruction of U.S. military drone aircraft by MIG type planes would be useful as complementary actions. A F-86 (properly painted) would convince air passengers that they saw a Cuban MIG, especially if the pilot of the transport were to announce such fact. The primary drawback to this suggestion appears to be the security risk inherent in obtaining or modifying an aircraft. However, reasonable copies of the MIG could be produced from U.S. resources in about three months.

---

[1]This is reminiscent of the 9/11-related casualty list. Could these lists from the various airlines be falsified? Only further research will tell.

- Hijacking attempts against civilian air and surface craft should appear to continue as harassing measures condoned by the government of Cuba.

- It is possible to create an incident which will demonstrate convincingly that a Cuban aircraft has attacked and shot down a chartered civil airliner en route from the United States to Jamaica, Guatemala, Panama, or Venezuela. The destination would be chosen to cause the flight plan route to cross Cuba. The passengers could be a group of college students off on a holiday or any group of persons with a common interest to support chartering a non-schedule flight.

Aircraft at Eglin (Air Force Base) would be painted and numbered as an exact duplicate for actively registered aircraft belonging to a CIA proprietary organization in the Miami area. At a designated time the duplicate would be substituted for the actual civil aircraft and would be loaded with selected passengers, all boarded under *carefully prepared aliases*. The actual registered aircraft would be *converted to a drone*. [2]

Take off times of the drone aircraft and the actual aircraft will be scheduled to allow a rendezvous south of Florida. From the rendezvous point the passenger-carrying aircraft will descend to minimum altitude and go directly into an auxiliary field and Eglin Air Force Base where arrangements will have been made to evacuate the passengers and return the aircraft to its original status. The drone aircraft

---

[2]A drone is an unmanned aircraft, which is flown, as well as destroyed, via remote control.

meanwhile will continue to fly the filed flight plan. When over Cuba the drone will begin transmitting on the international distress frequency a "MAY DAY" message stating he is under attack by Cuban MIG aircraft the transmission will be interrupted by destruction of the aircraft which will be *triggered by radio signal.* This will allow ICAO radio stations in the Western Hemisphere to tell the U.S. what has happened to the aircraft instead of the U.S. trying to "sell" the incident.

- It is possible to create an incident which will make it appear that communist Cuban MIGs have destroyed a USAF aircraft over international waters in an unprovoked attack. Approximately 4 or 5 F-101 aircraft will be dispatched in trail from Homestead Air Force Base, Florida, to the vicinity of Cuba. Their mission will be to reverse course and simulate (fake) aircraft for an air defense exercise in southern Florida. These aircraft would conduct variations of these flights at frequent intervals. Crews would be briefed to remain at least 12 miles off the Cuban coast; however, they would be required to carry live ammunition in the event that hostile actions were taken by the Cuban MIGs.

  On one such flight, a pre-briefed pilot would fly tail end Charley at considerable interval between aircraft. While near the Cuban Island this pilot would broadcast that he had been jumped by MIGs and was going down. No other calls would be made. The pilot would then fly directly west at extremely low altitude and land at a secure base, an Eglin auxiliary. The aircraft would be met by the proper people, quickly stored and given a new tail number. The pilot who had performed the mission under an alias would resume his proper identity and return to his normal place of business. The pilot and aircraft would then have disappeared.

At precisely the same time that the aircraft was presumably shot down a submarine or small surface craft would *disburse F-101 parts, parachute, etc.*, at approximately 15 to 20 miles off the Cuban coast and depart. The pilots, returning to Homestead, would have a true story as far as they knew. Search ships and aircraft would be dispatched and *parts of aircraft found.*

On 9/11 suspicious-appearing aircraft parts, were found near the Pentagon. These airplane parts were obviously planted. The jetliners which struck the World Trade Center were not passenger planes. Rather, they were drones. What's more, the passenger lists were also falsified. In other words, there were no people on the planes. The use of this as a tactic was explained in Operation Northwoods. Grey in color they had no windows. Now, does anyone doubt the real source of global terror? How can anything the U.S. government says be trusted? Obviously, it regards itself above all decency, with impunity to terrorize. What's more, the powerful ones in this government regard themselves immune to any consequences. Only such people would wantonly inflict terror on the masses. Only such criminal elements would brazenly lie and through these lies place untold millions at risk. Regardless, the critical point is that there were no Muslim hijackers. Nor did any Muslim plot an attack against the United States.

This official document makes it clear who is the real source of global terror. These terrorists are internal. In other words, they are Westerners. This is proven by the fact that 9/11 and the London bombings were committed by non-Muslims. What's more, the Western role in these murderous acts is definite. The evidence for an internal 9/11 is particularly damning. What's more, the evidence is obvious. Terror is committed and then blamed on others, all to further the agenda of the vested few.

The satanic actions of such powers are obvious. The nearly 5 million Iranian and Iraqi corpses tell all. These powerful ones disregard the consequences, all the innocents they kill. Rather, they only care about their own personal gain. The people never benefit from their vile plots. Nor do the nations who uphold them achieve any gain. Thus, their actions are a detriment to the people and their countries.

People wish to be patriotic. They claim that it is their solemn duty and that they will live and die as patriots. However, do they wish to be patriotic to this type of entity, the very power, which even blindly murders its own citizens? The fact is that is devil worship.

In contrast, in Islaam there is only one possibility, It is he complete giving of the self to God. This is where the greatest peace lies. There is no worship of country or heritage, rather, only of God. Patriotism is unknown: almighty God is the sole source of adoration. Rather than national pride, which is hollow, the fight is in the name of God against injustice. What's more, this war is non-denominational, that is universal. He is the beginning and the end: He is the Source of all authority. He alone is the ultimate power. He is the fount of love, the truly compassionate One—the only One capable of giving mercy—the only One who can forgive.

Why would any other be adored? Anyone with even the slightest wisdom would realize that there is only one way to succeed, and that is the path that leads directly to almighty God. All other powers are impotent, rather, destructive.

International terror: a Western plot

9/11 and the London bombings are reminiscent of disasters of the past: the Battleship Maine, the Reichstag, Pearl Harbor, the King David Hotel, the Bay of Pigs, the Iraqi invasion of Kuwait, and the Gulf of Tonkin. In all such cases violent acts were used to justify war, that is by Western powers. What's more, in all cases blame was laid on outsiders. Now it is known that these events were fabricated. On their basis thousands, rather, millions, were murdered. The same is true of 9/11 and the London bombings. Like previous acts these were fabricated to make them appear Islaamic. Yet, the fact is in 9/11 and the London bombings there were no Islaamic invaders: no Afghan, Saudi, Palestinian, or Iraqi connections. Thus, the waging of war against foreign nations is baseless, rather, a vast crime. Entire countries which had nothing to do with the attacks were invaded. In fact, such countries condemned such horror. Yet, they are brutalized by Western armies? No doubt, the civilized peoples of this world reject this madness. All people must stand up against it.

Only the criminal elements of the United States, along with their Israeli cohorts, have the power and resources to create global terror. What's more, as proven by Operation Northwoods they are they only ones who systematically created the plans to do so.

Pentagon insiders often brag about the terror they create. The fact is it is they who train and equip terrorists, who have the actual training camps for international aggression, and who are the true progenitors of global terror. What's more, without consequence, they kill at will whomever they deem.

There is no need to scrutinize Islaam for terrorism. It means peace, and it seeks to create peace on this earth. True, it commands its people to fight all tyrants. However, regarding the deliberate slaughter of the innocent it has nothing to do with it. This is exclusively a Western practice. The Civil War, the Native American wars, the systematic killing and enslavement of the blacks, World War I, World War II, the Korean War, the Vietnam War, the slaughter in Cambodia, the Gulf Wars, the Iraqi invasion, and the Afghanistan debacle are merely a modicum of examples. Such *Western* wars have resulted in the deaths of tens of millions of people. Islaam has nothing to do with such crimes. Those who quote isolated portions of the Qur'an and claim that Islaam is barbaric should give serious thought to who are the only documented barbarians and who is it who have by far the greatest amount of blood on their hands.

The whole purpose of Islaam is to fight terrorism, rather, to fight every conceivable tyranny known. Says the Qur'an, essentially, "fight (all perpetrators of evil) until there is no longer oppression on this earth."

David killed Goliath. For this he is admired. What if he would have lost? No one would respect him. God urges His people to be powerful and to win. He best loves the strong. The fact is God himself is a warrior against tyranny. What's more, He desires that His people be His tools. The Muslim— the one who truly gives the self to God—is His weapon and His source of truth: to fight every conceivable evil element until it is crushed into oblivion.

Corruption is the destroyer of this earth. Thus, all sources of corruption must be purged. Islaam means peace, but this is the peaceful surrendering to God. All who refuse to do so must be fought. This is the Muslim's duty. It is the true believers' duty, rather, obligation, to fight. What's more, they must do so with all their might, even with their lives.

With the British government since the tube bombings there has been much opportunity to talk. Certain actions have been taken against the Muslim population. The British hierarchy claims that it will fight hate mongering. These powerful ones say this while they create hate. It is they who have wrongfully targeted the Muslims as the committers of the London crimes. Thus, rather than any Islaamic extremists they are the ones who are creating hate.

They have no proof for it. Rather, the proof is to the contrary. Eyewitnesses thoroughly dispute the official claims. What's more, rather than an act of supposedly vengeful Muslims the events favor a government operation. So, again, rather than Islaam it is the Western powers which disseminate hate and which have a proven history of doing so. For instance, they are the ones who wrongly created the Native into the image of a 'savage,' the black with the image of dense and lazy[3], and, now, the Muslim or 'Arab' as the terrorist.

The Israelis make it their purpose to portray Arabs and Muslims as barbarians. This was surely achieved through the September 11th attacks, which were immediately portrayed as Islaamic. This is so that attention can be deflection from the real terrorists, so that the Palestinians and the Muslims in general can be slaughtered at will.

Ultimately, it is to gain Western support for Israeli expansionism, so they can torment and kill, without consequence. It is so this policy of race extermination can be

---

[3]If certain people of black origin do have a slower mentation, or even muscular fatigue, it has nothing to do with innate intelligence or ability. Rather, it may be due to a change in climate. The activity of the neurons of the brain are controlled by the thyroid hormone. Black people have been removed from a hot climate, where there is little need for this gland, to a cold or temperate one. This greatly stresses this gland, and, thus, such people develop an imbalance and/or deficiency. This may slow the activity of the brain, leading to sluggish thinking. Then, if such a person were to relocate to a truly hot climate the brain activity would normalize. Thus, in a black person a slow or depressed mind is likely due to a thyroid imbalance. For a natural means to support the thyroid see the Web site, P-73.com.

perpetuated, without scrutiny. Yet, exterminate who: the very people who these Zionists have driven from their homes and have stolen all that they have, then, exterminate them, all in the full view of 'civilized' humanity? This is the same brutal route taken for the Natives. Who dare do this in the light of modern history? In God's name the decent people of this world refuse to tolerate it. What's more, they will fight with their entire might against it, all together: Native, white, yellow, black, and brown.

Regarding 9/11 the same false front is disseminated. People continue to use this as proof of Islaamic anger. Mere decoys who had nothing to do with it are represented as Islaamic. Even the FBI admits that they have no evidence, that is of Muslim bombers. Rather, they have evidence of something most bizarre. It is the use of unmanned drones instead of commercial or hijacked planes. It is also the arresting of their Israeli agents near the World Trade Center, who participated in heinous acts. What's more, it is the existence of people who were disguised as Muslims—Israeli thugs. On the eve of the disaster these imposters attended a late night party at a strip-tease club. They were drinking and carousing with women. In that raucous environment they portrayed themselves as Muslim pilots. Does anyone truly believe that these were, then, future Muslim martyrs?

The whole basis of the war against terror are these acclaimed attacks by supposedly devout or vengeful Muslims. Yet, rather than the result of any supposed Islaamic hate it is, instead, the powerful ones that rule Western nations who are directly responsible for this crime.

Regarding 9/11, again, how could a group of drunken philandering men, Muslim or otherwise, then, the next day hijack planes? The party was in Florida, and the planes were reportedly hijacked from Boston and Washington, D. C. This makes no sense. Obviously, these men intended to make a scene, to create a memorable eyewitness account. However, rather than Islaamic bombers they were, incredibly, Israelis masquerading as Muslims.

The fraudulent nature of the accusations is supported by the fact that the suicide note is also a fabrication. This note has no basis in Islaam. The fact is it contains ideas never before known. One such idea, completely bizarre, is the importance of prior to any 'operation' shaving various parts of the body. This is a spook ordeal, geared to belittle. Only the Mossad is capable of such denigration. What's more, there is no requirement for a Muslim to shave body parts or wash before entering 'war.' Such a dictum is unknown in Islaamic literature. In the entire history of Islaam this has never been the case previously. If there is a war, the person simply fights. There is no other requirement. Thus, the detailed "to do" list presented as evidence of Islaamic involvement is, rather, proof of innocence.

Throughout history Islaam has shown its elegance. It has demonstrated that it is the most tolerant system in existence. When people were in their most dire condition, it rescued them. Consider the Jews, who, after being expelled during the Inquisition were in their most wretched state. The Islaamic Ottomans rescued and housed them. When the Christians were defenseless in Jerusalem during Salahiddeen's conquest, it was this magnanimous Muslim who protected them. This is why, historically, as described by Byng of all 'religions' it is only Islaam which has shown leniency.

Yet, ultimately, the oppressor can never win. What's more, falsehood is weak. It is baseless, a mere house of straw that will crumble as soon as it is exposed. This is because falsehood is inherently unstable. Islaam is powerful, because it is a divine system. Thus, it is a force to be reckoned with. This is because the fact is it is based on the ultimate truth: divine revelation from almighty God.

The purpose of the divine law is to halt tyranny. This was the very purpose of Moses' mission. It was the way and religion of Jesus. It is the entire religion of the Prophet Muhammad. There is no religion in mere prayer and fasting. The religion of God is the fight for justice. Anyone who is engaged in that fight is a true believer and in God's eyes is utterly high. In contrast, anyone who holds back is inconsequential. What's more, those who resist it, who purposely fight against God's truths, are his vile enemies, true losers.

Yet, why is it that the West must attack Islaam? Constantly, Western agents infiltrate Muslim groups as spies. This is particularly true of the Israelis. Globally, thousands of Zionists are impersonating Muslims. This is largely done to create strife within Islaamic communities. This is also done to create terror in the name of Islaam. According to the CBC quoting a former Scotland Yard officer the four suspected bombers who are used as a thrust to target Islaam are by their behavior non-Muslims. They may have Muslim-appearing names, but this is meaningless. Investigators said they were "dopey" and "not very bright." Unlike true Muslims "who have a degree of professionalism about them, they are so unprofessional." The four, who "drink, smoke dope, and womanize," were said to be susceptible to suggestion by their 'recruiters.' The recruiters were surely Israelis. One of the four, Hamdi Isaac, who lived in England under the guise of an assumed Islaamic name, is, reportedly, a 24-year-old marijuana-smoking play-boy. He had at his behest a vast network of fellow spies and associates, including professional document forgers, a veritable 'international forgery ring.' There is only one source for such ring: the Israeli hierarchy. Thus, Issac was an Israeli terrorist, but he will never be deemed so by the media.

Rather than the Muslims it is the Israelis, the Mossad, the Haganah, and their associates that perpetrated the London bombings. There may also have been cooperation with various powerful ones in Britain. The British must give this serious thought, that is if they are truly sincere about helping their people. What's more, now that the identity of the second set of bombers is confirmed, that is of non-religious men, who were working under cover, the question is who hired them for their dastardly deed, who instructed them to disguise themselves as Muslims? Does it make sense that on the one hand there was a bombing by religious Muslims, and, then, two weeks later a second bombing by marijuana-smoking womanizers? The fraudulent nature of the first bombing is now also being revealed, that is that the official story is bogus. Even so, second crime could help keep the public distracted. Then, it only makes sense that the crimes are related.

According to Carlo De Stefano, head of Italian anti-terrorist police Hamdi Isaac "falsely declared he was a Somali citizen to obtain the status of political refugee and economic assistance…" The question is why would he do so? His girlfriend is in Italy, as is his family. There, he had a comfortable life. There is a compelling reason: he is an Israeli operative, and, what's more, the Mossad, a division of the U.S.-subsidized Israeli government, hired him to perform these tasks. In other words, he was paid to impersonate Muslims and incite terror. Regarding this there can be no doubt. Incredibly, it is Western, in fact, American money, which financed these crimes. The Israelis simply take the funds from the money gifted to them through the U.S. public and use it to perpetrate diabolical schemes.

Still, the media attempts to incriminate Islaam by noting that Isaac and his brother made phone calls to Saudi Arabia, as if this country is a bastion of Islaam. The fact is Saudi

Arabia is a mere puppet state, teeming with espionage agents, including Israeli spies.

Crimes against humanity

The basis of Islaam is the service of God. Yet, what is this service? It is the deep love of humankind. In this regard it is revolutionary. There is no distinction between race, culture, or creed. According to it in God's eyes all people are equal.

The true purpose of this way of life is to work hard. It is to work with every effort against the wickedness of hate and tyranny. The fact is the purpose of Islaam is to eliminate from this globe all vestiges of tyranny. Muslims are merely the tools to do so.

As long as there is oppression the true Muslims will never rest. This is because their entire purpose is to fight this evil: by any means necessary.

Yet, the fact is they must fight. Consider what happened in Fallujah, where the Muslims were slaughtered in cold blood. These people had no desire to attack America or Americans. The fact is they are victims of a brutal invasion. What's more, it is an invasion which violates international law. As documented by investigative reporter Dahr Jamail, who witnessed the events, Western forces destroyed this town, Vietnam-style. When the resistance stiffened, they used Napalm.

As reported by Jamail quoting Burhan Fasaa, a respected Lebanese journalist with the Lebanese Broadcasting Corporation, American forces committed inconceivable atrocities. Said Fasaa, "There were American snipers on top of the hospital shooting everyone." In a dire revelation of the brutality of the American system on November 8, 2004, the military was "allowing women and children to leave the city, but none of the men." Entering through a circuitous route

Fasaa was able to witness the events. "...snipers were shooting everyone in sight," and "rarely a minute passed without the ground shaking from the bombing. "The Americans used very heavy bombs to break the spirit of the fighters in Fallujah," he explained, then holding out his arms he added, "They bombed everything. I mean everything." After two days he saw "Huge numbers of tanks and armored vehicles and troops attempted to enter the north side of Fallujah," he said, "But I filmed at least twelve U.S. vehicles that were destroyed. (Also, there were) at least 200 families who had their homes collapsed on their heads by American bombs."

"Fallujans already need everything, I mean they already had no food or medicine. (There was) a huge number of people killed in the North part of the city, and most of them were civilians." He continued, "The dead were buried in gardens because people couldn't leave their homes. There were so many people wounded, and with no medical supplies, *people died from their wounds.* Everyone in the street was a target for the Americans; even I saw so many civilians shot by them." The military called over loudspeakers for families to surrender and come out of their houses, but Burhan said everyone was too afraid to leave their homes, so soldiers began blasting open the gates to houses and conducting searches."

"Americans did not have interpreters with them, so they entered houses and killed people because they didn't speak English. They entered the house where I was with 26 people, and shot people because they didn't obey their orders, even just because the people couldn't understand a word of English. Ninety-five percent of the people killed in their houses that I saw were killed because they couldn't speak English."

His eyes teared up but he continued talking, "Soldiers thought the people were rejecting their orders, so they shot them. But the people just couldn't understand them." Then, although some of his film was smuggled out, the Americans approached him and took all his camera equipment. At that time I watched one soldier take money from a small child in front of everyone in our house."

Burhan said that when the troops learned he was a journalist, he was treated worse than the other people in the home where they were seeking refuge. He was detained, along with several other men, women, and children. "They beat me and cursed me because I work for Lebanese Broadcasting Company, then, they interrogated me."

He was held for three more days, sleeping on the ground without blankets, as did all the prisoners in the detention camp inside the U.S. military camp. "They arrested over 100 from my area, including women and kids. We had one toilet, which was in front of where we all were kept, and everyone was shamed by having to use this in public. There was no privacy, and the Americans made us do it with handcuffs on."

He then returned to the Fallujah scenes: "I saw cluster bombs everywhere, and so many bodies that were burned, dead with no bullets in them. So, they definitely used fire (that is Napalm), especially in the Julan district. I watched American snipers shoot civilians so many times. I saw an American sniper in a minaret of a mosque shooting everyone that moved. He also witnessed something which many refugees from Fallujah have reported: "I saw civilians trying to swim the Euphrates to escape, and they were all shot by American snipers on the other side of the river."

The home he was staying in before he was detained was located near the mosque, where the NBC cameraman filmed the execution of an older wounded Iraqi man. Said Burhan, "The mosque where the wounded man was shot that the NBC cameraman filmed: that is the Jubilee Quarter. I was in that quarter. Wounded, unarmed people used that mosque for safety. I can tell you there were no weapons in that mosque. People only hid there for safety. That is all."

He personally witnessed another horrible event reported by many of the refugees who reached Baghdad: "On Tuesday, November 11th, I saw tanks roll over the wounded in the streets of the Jumariyah Quarter. There is a public clinic there, so we call that the clinic street. There had been a heavy battle in this street, so there were twenty bodies of dead fighters and some wounded civilians in front of this clinic. I was there at the clinic, and…I watched tanks roll over the wounded and dead there." After a long pause he looked out the window for awhile. Still looking out the window, he said, "during the nine days I was in Fallujah all of the wounded men, women, kids, and old people, none of them were evacuated. They either suffered to death or somehow survived."

According to the Iraqi Red Crescent, which managed to get three ambulances into the city on November 14, at least 150 families remained trapped in the city. One family survived by placing rice in dirty water, letting it sit for two hours, then eating it. There has been no power or running water for a month in Fallujah. People there were burying body parts from people blown apart by bombs, as well as skeletons of the dead, because their flesh had been eaten by dogs. The military estimates that 2,000 people in Fallujah were killed but claims that most of them were fighters. Relief personnel and locals, however, believe that the vast majority of the dead were civilians.

Here, the media casts lies. The entire war is based upon such lies. This has even been documented by U.S. senators, democrats as well as republicans. What is the basis of all this killing? What do the Iraqis have to do with anything? They never hurt even a single American.

For the Western powers there is no justification for being in Iraq. The Iraqis had nothing to do with the September 11th atrocities. This is merely a brutal invasion of a sovereign land. The United States has merely colonized it. Any fighters there are strictly battling for their rights. The fact is the destruction of Fallujah is the most extreme example of terrorism conceivable. This proves a simple fact: Western powers are slaughtering Muslims deliberately. Yet, these are people who have done no harm to the West.

The media calls the Muslims terrorists. Yet, when compared to Fallujah, it is obvious this is fraudulent. Any Islaamic acts are of no consequence compared to the brutality of Western powers. For no reason Western armies destroyed an entire suburb of Baghdad. Fallujans were slaughtered based upon lies. Remember, there was no Islamic 9/11. Thus, the slaughter of Iraqis is a true crime against humanity. The fact is this is a war crime, and all who perpetrate it are war criminals.

It has been demonstrated that the vast majority of the crimes attributed to Islaamic terror were/are fabricated. The fabricators are largely Israelis but also Western powers: American, British, and French. Too, Russia creates criminal acts and attributes them to Islaam. It is well known that the Russian president, Vladmir Putin, bombed Moscow apartment buildings, killing his own people. He did so to create a public furor to support his criminal acts in Chechnya. Bali, the Moscow bombings, Sharam al-Shiekh, the London bus/subway bombings, and 9/11 all are due to Western/Eastern espionage. Then, with all these being committed exclusively by Western powers the claim for Islaamic terror is obviously fabricated.

The acts committed in Fallujah, Gauntanamo, and Abu Ghraib are purely evil. There is no justification for it. Regarding Abu Ghraib U.S. senators and Congress know full well the degree of this decadence. The Pentagon says the publicized atrocities in Abu Ghraib are the tame ones. The yet-to-be revealed ones are of Muslim women being raped by soldiers as well as mercenaries. This is the evidence that the Pentagon is withholding. What's more, these vile acts have been confirmed by credible local sources, including the Islaamic council of the Province of Nineveh.

In Vietnam tens of thousands of women were raped by Americans. The same is likely occurring in Iraq. May such perpetrators be condemned permanently to the fires of hell. Yet, there is additional punishment for such vile ones. The Mosaic Law makes clear the consequences for such criminals. The fact is the face of this earth must be purged of these deviants. This is an obligation for every Muslim.

The Muslims in Iraq have harmed no one. Surely, on U.S. soil they have never attacked a single person. They have done nothing against Americans. The fact is they are fighting for strictly for survival.

Regarding American service-people these, too, are victims. The Zionists and their crimianl associates have placed these men in harms way. Thus, like the Iraqis the service people are victims of the machinations of the powerful ones, who manipulate global events. This includes Henry Kissinger, a mere spy, who specifically proclaimed U.S. soldiers as expendable, that is to serve global agendas.

Yet, the primary victims of these globalists are the various Muslim peoples. The fact is for over 50 years Western powers have held these people hostage, subjecting them to vast horrors. In Iraq they directly imposed the brute Saddam Hussein. In Palestine they impose the Israeli entity. Now, in Iraq they are imposing the brutality more directly, that is through American guns. Saddam, the American lackey, raped them. Now, the U.S. rapes them more obviously.

Even so, as a people the Muslims seek no harm to Americans. The same is true of the Muslims held in Abu Ghraib or the Israeli gulags. None of these people have caused the United States any harm. Rather, they are victims of the most grotesque harm conceivable. What's more, they are victims of a war waged against them based exclusively upon lies.

There is a saying on the streets of Iraq that while Saddam was the student "the U.S. is the master." How dire it is that such people must suffer yet further brutality. First, there was the wicked tyrant Saddam Hussein, fully installed by the U.S. government. Then, there is the direct action of invasion, where the United States has colonized this country.

While brutal American 'mercenaries,' the so-called military contractors, slaughter the innocent—while they even rape Muslim women—Muslims falsely accused of terrorism languish in prisons. Here, they are treated only with contempt. What's more, they are told, "If your religion is so great, where is your God now?" Can this be described as anything other than vileness, in fact, racism? This proves that this is a war against Islaam.

Yet, what is the purpose of taunting a people? If they are truly criminals, there is no use in doing so. The fact is their accusers demean, torture, and beat them: all because of their faith. There can be no other conclusion: the entire war effort has been proven a fraud, since it is based upon lies. Then, can anyone even resist the fact that this is a war against a people, rather, an entire religion?

The source of the terror is easy to define: it is the acts of the governments of Israel, the United States, France, and Britain. It is the terror of the wicked crimes of Abu Ghraib, Gauntanamo, secretive prisons, the Israeli dungeons, the napalm bombing/gassing of Fallujah, the bombing of

Baghdad, the rape of hundreds of Iraqi and Palestinian women, the U.S.-supported Israeli apartheid, the contamination of untold millions of people with American-made uranium, and countless others. All these acts, which maim and kill the innocent—which brutalize the common person—were/are based upon lies.

The President's henchman Donald Rumsfeld lied when he claim that the war was based upon retribution. He proclaimed this knowing full well that Iraq had nothing to do with 9/11. The fact is this is to cover up his own involvement in the crime. Now, he and his cohorts are responsible for mass crimes, including the slaughter of the innocent in both Iraq and Afghanistan.

As a result of the wars in Iraq, Iran, Afghanistan, and Palestine millions of Muslims, as well as thousands of Christians, have been maimed and murdered. What's more, this are all exclusively Western crimes.

CHAPTER 7

Who Bombed London?

In any terror attack most people never question the truth of the official version. Then, they consider all other representations as conspiracies. Yet, regarding the London bombings the official story and eyewitness accounts differ vastly.

Even so, British authorities claim they are fighting a war against an element of Islaam, which they proclaim as 'wicked.' It is, they say, a war of the 'tolerant' British system against 'radical' Islaam. Yet, is a fabricated invasion of a sovereign land an example of tolerance? Is bombing a sovereign people, killing and maiming babies, women, children, and the elderly, an example of liberality? The fact is such a comment is an attempt to demean the Islaamic way, as if the Western way is 'morally' superior. What's more, laws are being changed to "deal with" the Muslims, especially any "extremists", despite the fact that there is not even a shred of evidence for any Islaamic involvement.

Again, in the first bombings there is no evidence that the Muslims were involved. No one saw any Muslims set bombs. What's more, the accused Muslims had no motive, a critical aspect of any murder investigation. As determined by

Scotland Yard from all appearances, that is in the 'infamous' video image, these men's behavior was normal. They exhibited no signs of intent to cause harm. There is no evidence that they carried and/or planted bombs. What's more, none of these individuals had any history of violent acts. There was nothing suspicious about their behavior. Even so, who was it that controlled any video recordings attributed to these men? It was exclusively the Zionist Israelis.

The young Muslim men accused of the original London bombings were murdered. They were not the bombers. Like countless other Muslims throughout the world they were victims of the murderous policies of the Israeli butchers: Sharon, Netanyahu, Kissinger, Perez, and their cohorts. These murderers never distinguish who they kill and how they do so. They merely slaughter people of all backgrounds and denominations. In 9/11 they made the mistake of not killing all the accused. This time they eliminated all patsies.

The Zionists are desperate to maintain their agenda. Thus, they were directly involved in this act, all to create hate against a people. They had the foreknowledge and even bet on this in the London financial market. In contrast, there is no history of Muslims committing such odious acts. Search throughout history. Can anyone find a single example of Western Muslim youths arbitrarily bombing a civilian building or vehicle? Let anyone find an example if he can. There is no such history.

It is necessary to investigate these Muslims individually to determine any evidence, which supports the accusations. Four Muslims, now deceased, stand accused of the bombings. None are capable of defending themselves. Another four men, also portrayed as Muslims, are accused of the second London bombing. Yet, accusations published in the media are insufficient. Culpability must be based upon the available evidence.

Mohammad Sidique Khan

This man had just moved. He was a successful schoolteacher, and his wife is also a teacher. He had a very young daughter and was happily married. His wife is pregnant with their second child.

There was only peace in his marriage, and he was not involved in politics. However, he was deeply religious. According to investigators Khan was highly respected by pupils and parents. What's more, he was entrusted with the care of children and was given full trust by parents. He had never committed even the slightest violent act. He had been previously singled out for special praise in dealing with a transient pupils population from a socially deprived area. He was humble and unassuming. The man was neither desperate nor unhappy. He had no motive to kill himself or anyone else. What's more, in any human bomb, where a bomb is strapped to a human being to strike a target: in all cases there are other parties who are involved. Then, why in his case is there no other element, no bomb maker or coordinator?

Every policeman knows that for a crime to be committed there must be a motive. Police officers are dependent upon this to solve crimes. Regarding this man there is no evidence of a motive to kill himself or anyone else. Yet, Khan's personality has been extensively scrutinized in the media. The Zionist-controlled *Times Online* clearly reveals its bias against him. Reported the Times:

> In 2002 he (Sidique Khan) gave an interview to The Times Educational Supplement about his unusual job, claiming his role helped children to settle. "A lot of them have said this is the best school they have been to," he said.

He also gave a fascinating hint of his own smoldering political anger and dissent. As a Beeston resident, he expressed his discontent with the community's squalor, saying he believed it would be many years before regeneration cash would transform the area.

Is this the best the Times can do? Is this the only 'politically charged' statement that regarding this man the Zionists can find? Can anyone think? His statement has nothing to do with anger: it is a mere observation. What's more, how could such a statement relate to bombing a subway? The fact is Khan worked for the common man. He would never have bombed them. This man was too intelligent to kill himself in such a way, while placing in harms way hundreds of innocent people, including fellow Muslims. Khan was well aware that if he killed any innocent people, Muslim or otherwise, he would be doomed to hell. This is a major reason Muslims do not kill the innocent.

A further report regarding his character was issued by the BBC:

Parents at the school told the BBC the teaching assistant had been highly regarded by both children and parents. "He was a good man, quiet," said one parent, speaking outside the school.

"When I told my daughter she said 'no, he can't do something like that' I had to go and buy the paper and show her." Another parent, Sharon Stevens, told the Press Association how he had been a "big supporter" of pupils and parents.

"He was really understanding and he did work for the children and parents"...Mohammad Sidique Khan (who had been singled out for praise due to his work with disadvantaged children) spoke about his work to the

Times Educational Supplement at the time. "A lot of [the pupils] have said this is the best school they have been to," he said.

He added he believed it would be years before government regeneration cash could transform the deprived Beeston area of Leeds [remember the previous twisted quote form the TimesOnline].

The aforementioned statement is matter-of-fact. What's more, there is not a shred of anger, and, surely, no dissent. A street person might make such an observation. Is, then, that person an example of anger and dissent? This is exceedingly bizarre. This proves bias, rather, hate-mongering, of the media against Muslims. What's more, it demonstrates the obvious lies and the great length that is taken to undermine this faith. The attack is done with contempt. A normal unassuming comment was twisted to malign him. Again, there is no evidence of anger in his statement: the Times has sown lies.

The Zionists send into Western and Muslim countries teams of agents posing as Muslims. What's more, they have done so since the 1940s. They do this to create corruption and to, in fact, destabilize the Muslim countries. They also do so to create negative appearances for Islaam. Furthermore, they foment well planned terror acts and, then, create a black mark against this faith. The fact is they are global experts in inciting terror as well as falsely laying blame. Incredibly, in contrast Muslims never pose as Jews. Nor do they through false terror acts attempt to diminish Judaism. They are not allowed to do so: their holy book prohibits it.

The BBC continues, "In November last year, the teaching assistant travelled to the Pakistani city of Karachi along with *fellow bomber* Shehzad Tanweer. It is not clear what the men did during the three months they spent there, but Pakistani records show the pair left on the same flight in early February." Note here the judgmental statement, calling both men bombers, even though the evidence had yet to be finalized. The report continues:

> Neighbors told how Khan was...a "very pleasant" person. One neighbor said: "He didn't seem to be an extremist. He was not one to talk about religion. He was generally a very nice bloke."
>
> Despite the tributes, Mohammad Sidique Khan detonated enough explosives on a Circle Line train to kill seven people.

A pleasant person who is kind and loving cannot masquerade as a subway bomber. Yet, is the media an expert in criminal investigations? Is it able to act as judge and jury?

Then, to seal the accused Muslim's fate the article closes with:

> Documents belonging to him were found near the Edgeware Road blast.

Yet, the question is if such a person wore a bomb in a backpack powerful enough to blow apart a carriage, as well as blow the bodies to pieces, how did the IDs so precisely survive? Also, how could they be found precisely in the carriage and in or perhaps near such an ideal condition? What's more, what does it mean that they were found *near* the blast site? Furthermore, in particular why were documents from one of the accused Muslims found at two different blast sites? This demonstrates that they were planted.

Edgeware is the most populous Muslim region in London. Khan was the most mature of these men: would he truly set bombs in an area which put fellow Muslims at risk?

In contrast, it would seem, Islaam's enemies would do so. Regardless, documents alone are insufficient proof of guilt. Any bomb of such a degree would have, without doubt, shredded all paper and IDs on the involved person(s). Or, at least such documents would be saturated with blood and largely destroyed. Rather than isolated Muslim bombers it is more likely that these men were slaughtered as patsies and their IDs or other belongings planted. The entire operation was planned well in advance, so it would be "faultless." For instance, this was done previously with Lee Harvey Oswald. Considering their known innocuous nature, as well as the fact that eyewitnesses refute their presence as bombers, this is the only logical possibility explaining any 'evidence.'

Yet, why rush to judgement, that is unless there is a pre-planned, wicked agenda? After the bomb blasts there was a one or two hour delay before the authorities arrived. This is ample time to plant evidence, especially for those who were in charge of security. Claims that these men were carrying bombs and blew themselves up do not match the evidence. Reports in the newspapers are completely different than those of direct eyewitnesses. The newspapers are largely owned by the Zionists, whose bias is proven. In contrast, the eye witnesses have no vested interests. What's more, it is well known that regarding the Israelis they initiated a cover-up from the beginning. Also, only the Israelis knew about the bombing well before the event. There was a specific attempt to delay the process. Then, could the men have been patsies, perhaps killed by espionage agents, their IDs, even DNA, planted? Western espionage agencies have done so in the past. Then, this would imply that rather than suicide bombers the accused Muslims, as well as Charles de Menezes, were victims of murder.

There is another compelling reason to suspect Western powers. The agency which controls the security in the

London underground is Israeli. What's more, the Israelis have been known to deal in body parts, and it is well established that after murdering Palestinians they remove organs and sell them. This fact—this vile act of removing and selling organs—was admitted in the Knesset. What's more, why has there been no chastising of the Israelis for 'failing' to prevent this disaster, since they earn vast sums to supposedly 'protect' the public?

Just four days before the attacks an Israeli company conducted a subway bombing drill. This creates suspicion of malicious intent.

The avowed Zionists, Netanyahu and Giuliani, were also there. They had already previously called for a world war, that is against the Muslims. What's more, the drill was being conducted at the same sites where the bombs exploded. There is no possibility that this is a coincidence. In fact, the odds for this as a coincidence are tens of billions to one. These are serious questions, which must be addressed, that is if the true culprits are to be found. This is more compelling as evidence than any biased news reports.

Regarding Khan the bias against him must be emphasized. The London bombings were perpetrated by the same criminals, who enacted 9/11. They learned their lesson that living patsies are a debacle. So, they were sure to slaughter these Muslims. Khan, now dead, is unable to defend himself.

He made a statement regarding his profession which was innocuous. Yet, this is promoted as evidence of guilt? It is represented as if proof that this man was angry enough to kill people. Has anyone ever killed people because the government was negligent to provide these funds? If anyone thinks that this matter-of-fact statement is evidence for a bomber, this is exceedingly bizarre. The fact is this man's character is so upright that the media is truly reaching to find even the slightest shred of evidence against him.

In England there are funds set aside for such projects. These are the regeneration funds Sidique was alluding to. He was merely urging an upgrade. Yet, this is radical? The fact is there is not even the slightest degree of anger in his words.

The person who wrote this article is a Zionist agent. He/she twisted the facts to create an image of an angry discontented individual. The purpose is to make the Muslims the main 'public' enemy. It is to also distract attention from the real perpetrators of terror. Yet, people who knew him deny this. Then, how does recognizing the need for government funds relate to anger or dissent? Webster's defines dissent as: "to differ in sentiment or opinion; to disagree or to differ in religious opinion or reject the doctrines or authority of…church."

He merely commented that it might take excessive time for government money to be procured. Then, this is used as evidence that he is a terrorist? In fact, he was demonstrating tolerance, since he was merely recognizing that the system is slow. In other words, rather than dissenting he was *consenting.*

Do the authorities expect people to read into this what doesn't exist? Please explain: how does this demonstrate intent to maim and kill? This is proof that there is an attempt to control peoples' thinking. It is also proof of character assassination. This is what the *Times* has achieved through the erroneous and malicious use of mere words.

Regarding this man said a close friend:

> We played football together all the time, we went to the gym every week and we often met at the community

centre. *He was a good man. He and the others put on activities for kids in the area, stuff to keep them out of trouble. Sidique was very committed to his religion, but I never heard him say anything extreme or violent. All this is unbelievable...they're all from really good families.*

Obviously, friends and loved ones are a superior source regarding this man's character than Zionist-owned newspapers.

It must be recalled that rather than being home-made the bombs in question were exclusively military-grade. What's more, they were of a 'high level of sophistication.' This was confirmed by numerous weapons experts. None of the individuals in question had access to such materials. Also, these bombs were detonated virtually simultaneously, which indicates, without doubt, a professional job. It is highly unlikely that a 30-year-old schoolteacher, who is accused of being the 'coordinator,' would be able to achieve such a feat. In addition, the moral fiber of truly God-fearing Muslims would prohibit any such action. Even so, these men are being used as patsies as a cover for the real culprits. Yet, most people find this difficult to believe.

More recently, a video has surfaced, purportedly of this man taking responsibility.[4] Here, it would appear that he is threatening the West with aggression. There is no specific mention of tube or bus bombings. The video became known in September, 2005, over 60 days after the event. Yet, there is suspicion that this, too, is fraudulent. Recall that the belated bin Laden video is a fake. This video of Khan largely

---

[4]This was recently followed by a video, conveniently released on the aniversity of the London bombings, of yet another accused Muslim, Shehzad Tanweer, who was proclaimed as a high school 'drop-out.' This is completely false, as is the video. It was broadcast through the CIA asset al-Jazeera.

neutralized growing doubts about the official claims. Yet, why was it released in so late? What's more, who released it? Furthermore, close associates of Khan have disputed its authenticity.

Hasib Hussain, 18-year-old

Vilified in the media as a trouble-maker this has largely occurred in newspapers owned by Jews. However, the BBC gives this report:

> Neighbors said the 18-year-old had lived all his life in…Leeds. One neighbor described the family as "very nice people." He said: "We all knew (them)….They were just a very nice family."
>
> Hasib Hussain had told his family he was going on a trip to London to visit friends. But when he failed to return on Thursday, his parents reported him as missing to police (Note: this led by the police to an immediate rush to judgement; in other words, the Police were biased in advanced, believing it was Islaamic terror). He had in fact boarded the No. 30 bus in London armed with enough explosives to rip the double-decker apart, killing 13 people.
>
> His driving license and cash cards were found in the mangled wreckage of the bus.

Buses never change their routes. That's why they are called *routes*. Also, keep in mind that the bus was diverted to an unusual location. The location was across from the notorious spy center, Tavistock. This number 30 bus never before took the doomed route. The question is who diverted it and why? Reports that it was due to the subway bombings have no basis. The authorities were still unaware of the bombings, so it was too soon to arrange a deviation. This was mere disinformation from Western spy agencies. Yet, again, the real evidence is found in a simple fact: in all London this was the only bus that was diverted. Then, why did this diversion bring it to the notorious spy station? These are also the very people involved with human microchip technology. Furthermore, suicide bombers always strip themselves of all identification. Why would it be different this time, that is unless the evidence was purposely fabricated?

Another account reads:

> His family later said they were devastated by what had happened. In a statement they described Hussain as "a loving and normal young man who gave us no concern." They continued, "We are having difficulty taking this in."
> One neighbor said: "He lived here all his life. They were very, very nice people."

Hussain's driving license and cash cards were found in the mangled wreckage of the number 30 bus, which blew up in Tavistock Square. This is exceptionally bizarre: anyone who would pack a bomb and blow themselves to smithereens, any ID would surely be shredded, perhaps disintegrated. Even so, if anyone were to do such a deed, would such a person truly carry full ID?

Again, this occurred across from the Tavistock building. This building houses numerous major spy agencies. The Tavistock building was so close to the explosion that it was heavily stained with blood from exploding bodies. A lone Muslim could not have achieved this, nor would such a person have the ability to determine this site. Obviously, the odds that an isolated Muslim bomber would select this spy station as the site for the bus bombing are exceedingly remote, as are the odds that a diverted bus would merely stop there. Rather than the accused Muslim it is the spy station which should be investigated for complicity.

The British Prime Minister needed a diversionary terror act to save his rule. The British hierarchy has previously used such tactics to advance its purposes. Recall that Churchill caused the Lusitania to be sunk to further political aims. Recall also the sinking by the Zionists of their own refugee ships to gain public sympathy. Too, recall that bin Laden and the 19 Muslims were falsely implicated in the World Trade Center and Pentagon bombings. What's more, this was done deliberately. Thus, surely, the London bombings would be of a similar nature, that is instead of the presumed source, Islaamic, it would be Western.

To conclude the account:

> For most of his short life, Hasib Hussain's horizons stretched little further than the lattice-work of narrow streets and Victorian terraces of Holbeck, on the southern outskirts of Leeds city centre. Like his older brother and two older sisters, he went to a nursery 200 meters from home while his father, Mahmood, and mother, Maniza, were at work.
>
> At the primary school next door he was said to be a normal, unremarkable pupil. After school he bought his sweets from...(a)...corner shop, like all the other children, and kicked a plastic football around the street.

A suicide bomber, you say? What type of unusual distress brought this person, this 'baby of the family', to such an act? Yet, the claim of suicide bombing is what billions of people are led to believe. In contrast, Scotland Yard says it has "no evidence" that this is the case. Rather, says the agency, the evidence disputes suicide bombings. Yet, the media is relentless in its attack, fully pinning the bombings on suicide bombers, even though the top officials dispute this.

From *This is London* the following report was issued:

> The family of teenage suicide bomber Hasib Hussain spoke of their "devastation" and described their son as a "loving and normal young man."...they expressed their disbelief that the 18-year-old was involved in the bus attack.

It is recognized that in the West there has always been a great hatred for Muslims. The fact is the Prophet Muhammad has been the subject of vast lies. This is documented by numerous Western historians, including Carlysle and Bernard Shaw. In contrast, the latter give this man much praise. So, if he could be so scandalized, what of these defenseless men? Surely, it is possible that, like Lee Harvey Oswald, they are false images and that there is a far more diabolical force responsible for these acts. The fact is 'someone' targeted common citizens for slaughter. Does it really make sense that it was these young Muslim men? Their various profiles are proof against their involvement.

Shehzad Tanweer, 22, cricketer

This young man had no political inklings. He was very mild mannered and was never involved in violent acts. Nor did he show any hatred for the British or the Western public. The fact is it is impossible that he was involved in a terrorist act.

Tanweer's friends said they *couldn't believe suggestions* he was linked to violence. "It's impossible," said Mohammed Ansar, 19, who said he had played cricket with Tanweer last week "*It's not in his nature* to do something like this, he's the *type of guy who would condemn things like that.*"

Another friend, Azzy Mohammed, 21, called Tanweer "a sweet lad." Described as a good Muslim and "proud to be British," the 22-year-old was an excellent cricketer who had studied sports science at Leeds Metropolitan University.

Tanweer's uncle, 65-year-old Bashir Ahmed, said his family has been "left shattered," adding: "It wasn't him"…he said. Mr Ahmed said his nephew was intelligent, adding: "He was a very kind and calm person. He was respected by everyone."

Tanweer went to Lahore in Pakistan two months earlier this year to study religion, but his uncle denied earlier reports that his nephew travelled to Afghanistan and took part in training camps. Sources said there was "strong" forensic evidence linking him to the blast on the Underground train near Aldgate.

Incredibly, contrary to the view established by the media the Pakistani connection is evidence against radicalization. Tanweer was displeased with the experience, *finding the Pakistani version of religion disconcerting.* Thus, he largely rejected what he had learned. In other words, his trip created no inordinate influence against his personality. Thus, the claim for radicalization is debunked.

It must be noted that regardless of how deeply family members feel about the innocence of their sons, in this racially charged environment they dare not speak out too vigorously for fear of reprisals. Even so, evidence can easily be planted. What's more, espionage agencies have previously done so. Plus, these agencies can readily target such persons, using them as patsies. They did this with Lee Harvey Oswald. Why not here?

Due to the fabrication that the bombs were, in fact, a power surge there was a significant delay in rescue teams reaching the area. Thus, surely, IDs and similar evidence could be easily planted. The Israelis have done the same previously. This planting of evidence is made plausible by the fact that the Israelis purposely seeded disinformation regarding the cause of the blasts. It is also made evident by the finding of IDs from one of the accused, Sidique Khan, at two separate bombing sites. What's more, the Zionists are persistently creating fake IDs of Muslims as well as planting evidence against them. This was done by the Mossad against the mild mannered Mohammed Salameh, who is now serving a life sentence in the United States, related to the original World Trade Center bombing. In fact, this man is wrongly imprisoned for a crime committed largely by the Israelis.

Tanweer's character alone is evidence against any claim for his role. Tanweer is an unlikely fatalistic martyr. This cricketer was absorbed by his sport, even watching a match the night before the bombing. He had nothing to do with this wicked act. Regarding the so-called strong forensic evidence its relevance is thoroughly disputed throughout this book. In other words, where is proof of the bodies being exactly at the blast sites? Surely, if such proof was available it would have been broadcasted globally.

The *News-Telegraph* had this to say:

> Shehzad Tanweer was a God-fearing man with no interest in politics or religious fanaticism, his uncle said yesterday.
>
> Bashir Ahmed said his family was shattered and was struggling to come to terms with what had happened.
>
> Bashir Ahmed, speaking about his nephew, said "...the day before the bombings, he had appeared to be his normal self. He was, Mr Ahmed said, "proud to be British." He added: "I saw him last Wednesday and he

was very calm. We cannot believe what has happened. He gave no idea of what he was involved with or what was going to happen." He also noted, "He became quite a religious person but he wasn't into politics and didn't watch the news or read the papers...He was not desperate, he was not an extremist, rather, he was a decent person loved by his family and well respected in the community."

Neighbors said that Tanweer's father was a "lovely bloke" who cared deeply about his family. One said: "They are such a nice family, always pleasant and well spoken."

The *Wall Street Journal,* July 14th, 2001, wrote:

Shehzad Tanweer often stayed up late to watch cricket matches on television. "He had no interest in anything else," never reading newspapers or taking note of politics, says his uncle, Bashir Ahmed.

There is no possibility that this sports enthusiast would destroy himself. There is only one possibility for his death: he was murdered by espionage agents. The likely murderers were Israeli and/or British thugs.

The media keeps referring to visits to Pakistan. What does this have to do with anything? Since when do people after visiting Pakistan come back to Western cities and bomb them? This has never happened previously. Trips to Pakistan cannot be regarded as evidence. Over the past 50 years millions of Western Muslims of Pakistani origin have visited this country. No one has come back a suicide bomber: why now?

There are those who will say that all these good character points are meaningless, that, in fact, it proves they were suicide bombers: fanatical Muslims in disguise, who had split personalities. They say this despite the fact that Scotland Yard disputes the suicide claim.

Is it that people today have no common sense? Forget for a moment that they were Muslims. There are other people who feel strongly about their causes. Would these people kill fellow British citizens just as pay-back for the sins of their government or for a political issue? These men were common ordinary people, truly British. For instance, Khan and Tanweer were highly intelligent and exceptionally mature: would these men commit the very deed that could lead potentially to the exile and/or extermination of the British Muslims? Would they kill the only Western people who vigorously protested the Iraqi war: the common British citizens? What's more, Tanweer never talked about politics. Also, he never agonized over the Iraq war. His life was focused on sports and studies only. Such a person could never be a suicide bomber.

No diplomats, military men, politicians, or other prominent people died in these bombings. Only the common persons were killed. One of the bombs exploded near Edgeware, the most heavily populated Muslim area of London. What's more, Muslims died in these blasts. A Muslim who murders a fellow believer goes to hell. Thus, the official story defies reason. Even Scotland Yard confirms that it makes no sense that these men purposely killed themselves or anyone else.

Lindsay Germaine, Muslim 'convert'

There is a constant attempt to portray Muslims as radicals. This includes Muslim converts. Lindsay Germaine, a young Muslim father, stands accused of bombing the Russel Square Underground. This bombing led to 21 deaths and hundreds more injured. Close contacts had this to say about Germaine:

"There was nothing to suggest that he was an extremist. In fact, he was shy and calm." His wife denies that it is even remotely possible that he was involved. What's more, she is demanding absolute proof through DNA evidence. This has yet to be provided. What's more, no one saw Germaine plant or set any bombs.

The question will be raised, "If these men are innocent, what about the video footage?" There is no footage showing these men entering the doomed carriages or even standing on the respective platforms. Thus, there is no footage placing them at the bombing sites.

Yet, surely, those in power could fabricate this event. For such people who perpetrate coups against entire countries this would be a minor plot. Without doubt, is they have fabricated even the rule of entire nations, imposing untold terror upon the masses. Consider the fact that, past and present, the entire rulership of certain countries—the rules of the Shah of Iran, Saddam Hussein, Samoza, Batista, Pinoche, Mubarak, the Saudi elite, and Suharto—were/are all frauds, all orchestrated by the West. The Pinoche rule was specifically concocted and managed by the Zionist, Henry Kissinger. These rulers were all installed by outside powers, then, they convinced the population they were righteous. Then, as a result millions of the innocent were/are imprisoned, tortured, raped, and killed. So, the mere fabrication of a single terror operation with a few hundred dead and injured would be a minor issue.

The mild-mannered Germaine, as well as the aforementioned British Muslims, were unlikely mass murderers. This is confirmed by an English counterterrorism expert, who reviewed all available closed circuit TV images of the accused. He clearly observed that none of the accused appeared to be terrorists. Nor were they intent that day on killing anyone. As reported by the London *Independent* this is what an actual expert said:

> I've seen the CCTV footage of these people. They do not appear to be on their way to commit any crime at all. The Russell Square bomber (supposedly Germaine Lindsay) is actually seen going into shops and bumping into people (prior to the attack).

No person packing bombs would be so casual. Plus, the official story places him as arriving at the suspect site with no time to spare. Then, did he have time to go shopping? Then, why would he go shopping if he was going to commit suicide?

Yet, eyewitnesses are the ultimate evidence which prove the fraudulent nature of the official report. Think about it. In any criminal investigation it is eyewitnesses which are sought. These alone can prove the case. These eyewitnesses confirm a finding with vast implications. It is that rather than from Muslim or human bombers the devices exploded within or underneath the vehicles. In other words, the bombs were planted. This means there was no human bombers. Bruce Lait, bombing victim, makes it clear that the bomb originated from *underneath the carriage*. This was proven by the fact that there was a crater under the bombing site. This was confirmed by a local constable, who, in fact, pointed this out to Lait. Neither Lait nor the constable found any evidence of a Muslim bomber. Thus, even if certain Muslims were killed on these carriages they were not the bombers.

There were similar findings at the Edgeware bombing site. When the bomb exploded, the supposed bomber, Sidique Khan, was simply not there. *Guardian* journalist Mark Honigsbaum reported that at this site according to direct communication from eyewitnesses "tiles, the covers on the floor of the train, suddenly flew up, raised up." This is absolute evidence against a human or rucksack bomb. Thus, in the Edgeware blast the bomb was planted. This means that Sidique Khan was innocent. Regardless of media or government statements it proves that there was no Muslim bomber on this carriage. It also proves that all that is said about the accused, is lies. This is because there is no possibility that a bomb on a bomber's body or in a rucksack could lift off the bottom tiles. Such a bomb would have blown outward; the tiles would have never lifted off. This is a physical impossibility. It is basic physics. It could not occur. For the tiles to lift off the explosive device had to be planted underneath. Thus, it is certain that despite the proclamations of the British and American media there were no rucksack bombers responsible for the carnage in at least two of the bombings: Edgeware and Aldgate.

The fraudulent basis of the rucksack claim is confirmed by the government oriented group, Northeast Intelligence Network, which makes it clear that the bomb-blasts were "nearly simultaneous." This, combined with the lack of rucksack bombers on at least two of the carriages, confirms that the bombs were exploded by remote control. What's more, there is no possibility that these Muslims could have achieved this. The fact is rather than Muslims the Israelis control the Underground.

To reiterate at approximately 8:50 a.m. three bombs exploded within 50 seconds of each other. The first was on the Circle Line near Aldgate. It was about 100 yards into the tunnel when it happened. This was the carriage which had entrapped Bruce Lait and his girlfriend. The second bomb exploded, again on the Circle Line, near the Edgeware station, the latter being basically a Muslim community. The third bomb exploded seconds later on the Piccadilly Line deep in the Underground (train #331), as it was travelling southbound near the Russell Square tube station. The explosion occurred in the rear of the train's first carriage. These were all strategically placed explosives. The purpose: to cause a maximum amount of localized damage with minimal destruction of the infrastructure. These were a special grade of explosive that cause quick damage but no fires.

The final explosion occurred in Tavistock Square almost precisely an hour later within a double-decker bus. The explosive device was military grade and, surely, planted. Regarding this terror act there is an interesting statement: "*News reports* have identified Hasib Hussain as the person with the bomb on the bus." The newspapers and TV identify him, but no eyewitnesses have done so? The question is who provided this confirmation to the media? More importantly, who owns the media which disseminates such statements?

According to official records from the Thameslink train authority the soonest that the Muslims could have arrived in London was 8:43. This makes it impossible for them to disperse and set bombs. Also, curiously, not a single witness has confirmed their existence on the train—recall that the official story places these men on the Thameslink train arising from Lutton. Surely, four dark-skinned men riding for fifty minutes on an English train, complete with large military-style rucksacks would draw someone's attention.

Yet, in this book only those elements which can be determined with certainly are confirmed. Thus, two of the accused Muslims can be absolved. This is due to precise eyewitness accounts, the same accounts that the American and European court systems rely upon to convict or absolve the accused. Prosecutors and police thrive on eyewitnesses. Without them, cases are difficult to prosecute, built merely on circumstantial evidence.

Thus, for two of the accused, Shehzad Tanweer and Sidique Khan, any involvement is impossible. There is not a single eyewitness who can corroborate the government's position. Circumstantial evidence cannot be relied upon, because eyewitnesses prove that they were innocent. No eyewitness places either of them on the carriages. Nor did anyone see them transporting any bombs. Nor were they seen planting any bombs. Nor has anyone reported seeing persons on the involved carriages with large rucksacks.

Curiously, initial reports soon after the bombings, fed to the media, stated that the bombs were likely caused by backpacks left on-board, while the culprits escaped. Yet, how could anyone know of this? The report of rucksack-toting Muslims came four days later. Yet, eyewitnesses, including constables on scene, dispute such claims, clearly witnessing that the bombs arose from *underneath the carriages*. Thus, both Tanweer and Khan, are absolved, if for no reason other than the fact that the bombs were obviously pre-planted and, therefore, systematically detonated by remote control.

Here, the goal of the superpowers is obvious. It is to tarnish an entire people for wicked aims. At a minimum they seek global power at any expense. What's more, they will do all that is necessary to achieve it.

Yet, what proof is there that these men even entered the carriages? Where is the evidence that they were the source of the bombs which destroyed the various carriages and the #30 bus? Lait says he was sitting directly opposite the bomb site, in other words, the bomb blew up directly in front of him: *no one was sitting there*. Is there any need for further evidence? There was no rucksack, he noted. Tanweer is accused of being there: but he wasn't there. This would clearly indicate that regardless of any sudden revelations presented by the media these men were mere patsies and that they carried no bombs at all. They may have been blown to shreds, but they were not the bombers. Nor were they intent that day of committing suicide, a fact which has been fully documented by Scotland Yard.

In the video in Lutton these men appear entirely normal. There was nothing suspicious about their demeanor. Suspicion arose after they were accused of carrying bombs in rucksacks, even though there is no proof of any rucksack bombs in the subways. Had this not been nationally reported nothing about them would have aroused suspicion: not their facial expressions, body language, nor what they were carrying. Interestingly, two of them were deemed culprits shortly after family members reported them missing, which, too, is highly suspect.

That they would kill themselves is implausible. What's more, contrary to media insinuations in Britain in the Islaamic communities there are no 'hidden' suicide bombers.

True, people who are oppressed have made it clear they will fight for their rights. However, they are not about to wildly kill the innocent.

These men purchased return tickets for the tube and bus. They had also purchased 8-hour parking tickets, indicating that their trip was routine. Surely, they were on no suicide mission. Furthermore, regarding the released video there is insufficient proof of any bombers. None of these men acted in even the slightest suspicious way. By all representations they were normal. This video gives only minimal information. For instance, there are no pictures showing them entering the involved carriages. This latter video is always available. Yet, the government refuses to release it.

If they have proof that these men truly set bombs, then, let them release it. For instance, they released it for the slain Menezes, showing him lying dead on the floor of the carriage in a pool of blood. Why not here? The video would prove the existence of any Islaamic bombers, silencing any critics. Yet, there is no such video. Instead, some two months later a highly suspect video of a Middle Eastern-appearing Muslim is released, supposedly, Khan. Yet, this is broadcast as evidence, while the truly confirmatory video is never provided. The fact is there is no such video. To reiterate there are no videos showing any of these men setting bombs. Thus, the official statements of an Islaamic attack on London are bogus. It is as if all that is necessary is to show a picture of a Muslim, make an accusation, and, then, this is a terrorist.

Yet, again, just as in 9/11, magically, in the first London bombings identities of the supposed culprits were broadcasted virtually immediately. They were judged as guilty only by the media and 'government' organizations. In contrast, law enforcement officials quickly disputed the official statements.

The crime scene was a tangled mess. Does anyone really believe that the criminals could be determined that efficiently? Rather, the observations of the police on site dispute the media proclamations. People must use their common sense. The fact is no one has even the slightest proof that these men set any bombs or killed anyone. Rather, as established by numerous eyewitnesses there is proof to the contrary. Statements by eyewitnesses differ completely from the government version.

These accused men carried their normal IDs, and there was no attempt to disguise anything. Some of them had clearly the burden of large rucksacks, which if their intent was truly to create these acts, would produce an obvious trail to them. Yet, with amateur bombers there would be at a minimum some evidence of nervousness, agitation, or perhaps a furtive glance. There was no such indication. Also, the fact that they supposedly killed themselves bearing full identification, including check books, credit cards, and drivers licenses, is suspect. No suicide bomber in the past has maintained so many IDs.

Says Joe Gandleman of *The Moderate Voice* "Suicide bombers normally strip themselves of identifying material (to leave no trail regarding the culprit)," while in the case of the accused Muslims, "They carried wallets containing their driving licenses, bankcards, and other personal items."

Now, the official line is readily disputed. Even so, people are trained to believe a certain way and, then, trust it as gospel. The media tells the masses that radical Islaam was the motive. The Prime Minister confirms this. Then, compare these "unconfirmed" statements to eyewitness accounts of a proven atrocity: the killing of an innocent dark-skinned man, Brazilian Charles de Menezes. This was the man who several days after the bombing was killed in the tube by people in plane clothes. The fact is he was murdered in cold blood within the carriage. There are numerous witnesses to this killing. Yet, there are no witnesses proving any involvement of these four Muslims, that is for multiple massive bombings?

Regarding Menezes this was an assassination. The man carried nothing that would have appeared to have been a bomb nor any weapon. He was simply targeted and hit, shot eight times at close range. Despite this reports were purposely seeded to denigrate the victim. He wore, it was reported, a heavy coat that could have concealed a bomb, and he jumped the turn-style. These are fabrications. Eyewitnesses tell the real story:

> I Witnessed The Shooting in London…
> I was there, on the platform, they ran past me.
> What I saw was some men in normal clothes with 1 having a black gun running after an Asian guy, yelling at him to stop, using expletives too.

He ran in, fell and they jumped him, and even though they had his hands clear, they shot him at least 4 times.

At that moment I ran away.

Now what I want to make clear is, if those guys in plain clothes were running after me with a pulled gun, I would run too.

Why did they shoot him when they had his hands clear, (that is they had grabbed his hands?

And why shoot 5 times?

I think I witnessed a murder to be honest...I am still shaking because the way the police described it is definitely not the way it went....they jumped him, gave no warning, grabbed his hands and shot him at least 4 times.

Executed.

I can't believe I witnessed this here in London, this is sick, what have we become?

Mary-Jane

This man was an electrician. In fact, according to the BBC at the Stockwell Tube station, south London, Brazilian Jean Charles de Menezes, 27, was shot seven times in the head and once in the shoulder. He died instantly.

His murder was definitely connected to the London bombings. Why was it so important to these gunmen to slaughter him: to be sure he would die. Plus, who ordered this hit? If such questions are answered, then, the true culprits of the London bombings can be determined.

It is now known that Menezes was a victim of mistaken identity. He was thought to be the Zionist agent Adus Isaac. This is why he was killed, in other words, his assassination was ordered from the highest levels. However, they killed the wrong man. Isaac was targeted, because he was an inside man, and, they knew, if caught, he would talk. In other words, he would expose the Zionists for what they really are: bloodthirsty murderers.

The Zionists knew they were caught, that is impersonating Muslims as bombers. So, they attempted to 'eliminate' the evidence. Proof of this is in the fact that this killing occurred before Adus Isaac was captured in Italy. Before his capture he was known by his "Islaamic" alias. Afterwards, he was described by his Jewish name. Thus, it was realized that if this man were exposed and prosecuted the entire Zionist system would crumble. In other words, the truth about their crimes would be exposed. Isaac, an Israeli spy, was the main agent provocateur of the second London bombings.

Regarding the bus bombing here is another direct account from a person who works in the field: an employee for Stagecoach, Britain's bus service. As reported by Paul Joseph Watson, investigative reporter, this employee noted in his letter that only one bus was diverted from its normal route that morning, and that was Bus #30. So, reports circulated that the diversion was a normal reaction to the tube bombings are false. Buses never deviate from their courses. There is no defensible reason for this bus to meander into this region. What's more, in London bus drivers do not get lost. In other words, the diversion was unheard of. What's more, never before had a #30 bus been diverted to the spy station. Once there, the bus was detonated by remote control.

There was no reason for the bus to be diverted. At the time the bus was diverted and destroyed no one at the bus terminal knew about the tube bombings.

Hussain had to be killed. This was the only way the tale of the Muslim bombers could hold. The remote detonation was surely facilitated from the Tavistock center.

A Muslim, Hasib Hussain, is accused of this bombing. The media freely condemns him as a terrorist and suicide bomber, even a thug. The proof would be easy: every British bus is armed with closed circuit TV cameras (known as CCTV). The culprit could easily be caught on tape, the evidence provided, and the case solved. However, on that day, it is reported, the cameras were out of order. Yet, this was the only bus in London with such a dysfunction? The fact is this alone is evidence that the official story of bloodthirsty, vengeful Muslims is bogus. In other words, there was a far more diabolical hand in this act and, what's more, it wasn't the Muslims.

The employee notes that the cameras are virtually always operational, because they are diligently maintained. They are inspected about twice per month, which is done by specific private contractors well known to the employees.

The Stagecoach employee, who chooses to remain anonymous, said that he was highly disturbed by the inaccuracy of news reports:

> ...when I heard that the CCTV wasn't working on a vehicle that's no more than 2 years old since last June...I'm sorry that's rubbish, I work for the company I know different.

Then, he provided a revelation with vast implications:

> ...last Saturday (July 2nd, five days before the bombing) a contractor came to inspect the CCTV on the buses at the depot. According to my supervisor the person spent more than 20 hours over that weekend, 20 hours to see if the CCTV is working? Also, that person who came was not a regular contractor. For security reasons the same few people always come to the depot to carry out work. This time it was different.
>
> Drivers in the depot already think the so called bombers had inside help—because it was too organized. Some even think it had help from the company.

He also said that there is a strict protocol for keeping the closed circuit TVs operational, because it cuts down on crime and reduces police work loads. For the company it is lucrative to do so: the "police pay the bus company to check it…so all parties benefit from keeping the TV systems working."

Because of his suspicion regarding the reason these cameras weren't operational he speculated: "Was the unprecedented 20 hour inspection a fabrication, a mere front for disabling the camera? Or, was it perhaps even more sinister: the means to plant the actual bomb? This occurred quietly over the weekend. Then, this bus with the tampered camera is the one that is destroyed? The likelihood that this is a coincidence is non-existent."

His suspicions carry him further, when he said, "Were the contractors, *who were not familiar to the bus company employees,* actually placing the bomb?" His conclusion is compelling:

It's beyond doubt that these four Muslims were framed.

A defunct camera and a visit by a suspicious individual on the weekend is proof of a plot. By disabling the camera was there an obvious attempt to conceal? If it were truly a Muslim bomber that was responsible, surely, they would *enable* the camera. Thus, the only conclusion is an intact camera would have shown that this was rather than a Muslim bomber, in fact, a planted bomb. What's more, it was detonated by remote control. Thus, an intact camera might also have shown that rather than the culprit, in fact, Hasib Hussain was a victim of the bombing. Thus, instead of a random act of religious terror this is a government plot to attack Islaam. This is proven by the unprecedented tampering with the bus.

The way the bus was blown apart proves the existence of a planted bomb, especially a bomb placed near the floor. This is confirmed by eyewitnesses. These eyewitnesses have said repeatedly that just after a person sat in a seat, it exploded— underneath that seat. These eyewitnesses confirmed that there was no rucksack bomb.

The rucksack theory has no basis. In three different sites, Edgeware, Aldgate, and Tavistock (espionage) Square, witnesses saw no rucksack-toting bombers. What's more, no one on the bus has identified the accused, Hasib Hussain, as setting off the bomb. This is major evidence against his involvement. Surely, with such an unwieldy rucksack people on the bus would have remembered him. The point is eyewitnesses, while rarely perfect, are more reliable than mere media blarings.

There is another revealing element: the escape of the driver, just after he had supposedly gotten off the bus to ask directions. Then, the bus blows up? Does anyone really believe that a London or New York City bus driver would disembark to ask directions? This alone is unheard of, let alone to conveniently do so, just before the blast. Yet, where did he disembark? It was none other than within a block from the world's most notorious spy center, from which the Mossad, as well as the MI6, operate. Thus, the claim for needing directions is a fabrication. This means the bus driver is part of the plot.

Further evidence of the plot was revealed, perhaps, inadvertently, by the Israelis themselves. This was via former Mossad Chief Efram Halevy. Incredibly, on the day of the disaster he revealed facts about the bombing that were then unknown. Said Halevy:

> The multiple, simultaneous explosions that took place today on the London transportation system were the work of perpetrators who had an operational capacity of considerable scope.

All the way from Israel, and he knows the truth? In contrast, Scotland Yard was unaware of it. Yet, it was originally thought that the bombs went off over a period of nearly an hour, bolstering the theory of random human bombers. Officially, London authorities reported this, yet, at this time the Israelis had a different story. They had already published what would only be discovered three days later. As usual, the Mossad positioned itself as all-knowing.

To reiterate, British officials were unaware of the simultaneous nature of the bombings until three days later. Yet, incredibly, Halevy had written a comprehensive article, describing as fact what Scotland Yard had yet to discover. This article, which is extensive, was *published* the *morning of the bombing*. This proves that the Israelis were the real culprits of this crime. The article was written days, even weeks, prior. Even so, no Muslim organization or government had any such advance knowledge. To reiterate the Muslims did not know, while the Israelis knew. By revealing in detail what Scotland Yard had yet to discover the Israelis proved categorically that they alone knew the exact method of the bombing. They also knew precisely where and when the bombs went off. They even knew the exact day and month of the act. Yet, the Israelis informed no one and, what's more, made no effort to prevent the carnage.

As if to confirm the true source of the bombing Halevy wrote:

> There was careful planning, intelligence gathering, and a sophisticated choice of timing as well as near-perfect execution.

Near perfect execution is correct, that is against the Muslim patsies. These men were obviously assassinated. What's more, the insinuation that a group of Muslims causally entering a tube station could achieve the bombings is ludicrous. It is obvious that they were not criminals, having not even the slightest criminal intent. Yet, the aforementioned was from an article written by a Zionist calling for World War III. Then, who is the obvious perpetrator of this terror? Clearly, this man is promoting global murder. Previous world wars were also based upon such lies.

Mossad knew, but the families of the accused knew nothing? Halevy proves that the Israeli hierarchy was well aware of this strike. At a minimum the Israelis could have prevented it. Rather, they would desire such an act. This is obvious. It is only this organization that calls for massive invasions and international wars, all supposedly based upon Islaamic terror. Such wars will lead to the deaths and maiming of untold millions of people. Then, who are the obvious international terrorists? It is only this group which admits to having death squads to kill whomever it desires, even throughout the Western world. What's more, only the Mossad and similar Israeli elements are licensed to provide security to London's transportation systems. The Muslims have no such access.

In 2004 London authorities awarded the Israelis a thirty year contract to manage security. This is through the Mossad-infested Verint Security Systems. The money they used to buy the rights to London came from the American public. Yet, rather than any constructive purpose they use this access to commit evil.

Verint's supposed job is to ensure security. Immediately, these Zionists plotted their strike. With many rehearsals and much planning they could guarantee "near-perfect execution." Then, obviously, the Israeli corporation, Verint, is directly tied to the bombings. After all, their job according to an official press release is to "maintain London's Underground infrastructure." This includes "ensuring security in trains, stations, tunnels, and bridges." Yet, in London despite decades of terror incidents before Verint there were no subway bombings. However, now that the Israelis operate this system there is terror and murder. Now that the Israelis hold sway there are no videos confirming the bombers. This is bizarre. This also implies that since it was surveillance cameras which led the gunmen to Menezes this, in fact, was an Israeli hit.

In surveillance the Israelis are supposedly the world experts, who according to Verint CEO Dan Bodner provide based upon "significant experience" the delivery of "innovative networked *video security solutions* for the transportation industry." Then, they allowed this to happen? Too, since all of London is under surveillance why are the Zionists unable to provide definitive proof of any Muslims setting bombs? This is because there are no such videos.[5]

There is another fact which proves a Zionist element. This is the appearance in London of both Binyimin Netanyahu and the former mayor of New York City, Rudy Giuliani. Both were well positioned for media appearances immediately after the bombings. How could they merely be there by coincidence? These are Israeli PR men, obviously placed in London in advance. The fact is they were part of a global plot to create international indignation against Islaam. Netanyahu called for a world war. Both offered advice on national TV regarding terrorist acts. Their presence and comments demonstrate a premeditated agenda. Giuliani was "right near the site of the first explosion, perfectly positioned to go on TV to comment..." The same was true of Netanyahu, who,

---

[5]This is a definite fact. English investigators have carefully viewed all available videos. The conclusion: there is no evidence of an Islaamic attack.

conveniently, was supposedly in Britain to raise money. Then, a few days later the Israelis went to Washington, D.C., demanding 2.2 billion dollars.

Yet, right away, despite the obvious Israeli connection, Muslims were targeted. According to the media investigators began searching leads in "Pakistan, Egypt, Jamaica, and the United States." Blair vowed to confront the "evil ideology" of so-called fanatical Islaam. Thus, a terror act was, once again, identified as Islaamic, despite the fact that Islaam had nothing to do with it.

There is no need for him to confront Islaam. He is wasting his time. If he truly wants the answers, all he needs to do is go to the source: the powerful ones among the Zionists as well as powerful British elements.

It is a minor achievement for espionage agencies to fake this event. They have done so numerous times previously. The Reichstag and Gulf of Tonkin were fabricated. So was 9/11. All led to murderous wars. Like 9/11, any Islaamic connection to the London bombings is a lie. The official story is bogus, and there are profuse documents to prove it.

There is no way these young men could have achieved coordinated or simultaneous bomb blasts. Nor was it possible that this remained unknown, even by their closest relatives and friends. People are truly dreaming if they believe that a few isolated Muslims are capable of doing this.

There are a number of variables which make this impossible. Investigators claim all four men entered a train station together miles away from London. This was about 90 minutes before the blasts. Their movements were completely, we are to believe, without suspicion. They are recorded on video apparently entering a tube station at about 8:25 a.m. Yet, the video cannot be correct, since the official story places them on the 7:40 train from Lutton. This train was late. It didn't arrive until 8:43, some twenty minutes later than the 'official' video. Thus, like 9/11 the official story was fabricated.

There had to be patsies. Surely, if the public determined it was an internal act—by the people in power—they would react. Surely, they would call such individuals to account.

Even if giving the government the benefit of the doubt, that is that the Muslims did it, still, a critical question remains: how did the Israelis know in detail about the bombings even weeks before the strike, when no one in the entire world had an inkling? Meanwhile, direct evidence of Muslim bombers is nil. There are no video images showing them entering the carriages in question. Yet, authorities would have us believe that three of the men were in the tube station together, and, then, dispersed with perfect precision to set their bombs off simultaneously. Now, supposedly four Muslims, true amateurs, never trained in explosives, have enacted the perfect crime?

Even more nonsensical is the possibility that one of them could have gone from the train station, through the tube, and then boarded a bus to create there a perfectly timed blast, which just so happened to occur near the original office of the Zionists, the one where the Zionist mandate for stealing Palestine was enacted. People are to believe that this was all a Muslim plot by four men who were so angry due to world events that they would kill themselves, along with defenseless innocent civilians. Yet, how would such acts aid the Muslim cause?

Again, it was an ex-Mossad chief who said he was "impressed" by the supposed Muslim effort: its precision, accuracy, and sophistication and that it was based on virtually simultaneous bomb blasts. Yet, he published this even before these facts were announced publicly. Rather, when he made this statement about simultaneous bombs (on the tube) it was commonly held that each bomb went off several minutes apart. Somehow, Israel's Halevy was the first to know—well before Scotland Yard.

Yet, it is completely implausible that four independent bombers would be able to achieve such synchronous explosions: anyone can imagine the numerous variables against this. In fact, the aforementioned statement proves that the Mossad knew before anyone else precisely what had happened, or, rather, would happen. They knew even before Scotland Yard, even before the constables on the scene. Again, the article appeared the morning of the event. This means the Israelis knew weeks in advance. Even top British authorities had no such knowledge.

People should give this serious consideration. Since Mossad knew, then, they were involved. No one else had foreknowledge. Regarding 9/11 the Israelis, along with the powerful ones of the U.S. government, had advance knowledge. Then, just as much as any accused Muslims the Israelis bear complicity in the crime, if for no other reason than the fact that they knew well in advance and warned no one. In contrast, not a single individual *in the entire global Muslim community* knew about these attacks. Had any Muslim known of it, such a person would have attempted to stop it. Even so, the Muslims are attacked, while the Mossad, as well as Haganah, runs roughshod, bombing, murdering, and maiming at will. What's more, because of the inconsistencies in their stories the Israelis have halted all comments.

The Muslims are being accused based mainly on the video tape. Regarding this the issue that they were together and that they were all wearing rucksacks is emphasized. Yet, the British are also capable of attacking their fellow citizens and blaming it on the Muslims. However, this is unlikely, since as documented by the U.S. Army regarding any international terror act it is the Zionists who are the true wild card, "ruthless and cunning."

Even so, it is well known that the Queen is disturbed by the rapid growth of Islaam as well as the vast interest of English people in this religion. She wants something done about it. In England there is a massive espionage capability, plus virtually everything is monitored. As pointed out by journalist Colin Deane the likelihood of an event of this magnitude catching the British totally by surprise is minimal.

The accused were far from incognito. Someone would have known that there would be an event—surely there would have been at least some communication that would have aroused suspicion: a cell phone conversation, a community gathering, an e-mail. Too, there would have been at least some degree of unusual behavior. What's more, are again, people to believe that the British were completely unaware of this, a supposed terror act by nonchalant-appearing young Muslims plotted and planned with precision?

In England there are cameras everywhere. Thus, no Muslim men would even attempt this act, that is unless they were utter fools. What's more, not a single one of these men left a farewell note. Surely, they would have made some degree of communication with their loved ones.

Apparently, this is virtually the case: only a fool, an idiot, someone who was on a chemical high, would attempt such senseless acts. These describe the second four. Anyone can look, for instance, on the internet at their pictures. They have a completely different appearance than the original group of the accused. They appear crazed. These are proven drug addicts, who admittedly smoke marijuana. The crazed propensity can be seen in their eyes. Compare the eyes and facial expressions of the living bombers to the accused/deceased. There is an enormous difference.

The second group of bombers are alive. The first group are dead, unable to defend themselves. The wives of these men insist they could not be bombers. Again, these wives were unaware of any such act. Remember, unlike Zionism in Islaam there is no code of secrecy. Rather, secrecy and suspicion are discouraged. Yet, the Mossad had advance knowledge, while Muslim wives had no inkling. What's more, as mentioned previously regarding the second group instead of a Muslim at least one of these is, rather, Jewish. This is a certainty. Thus, any statement in the media that these are Islaamic acts is now proven as a lie, since one of the perpetrators was a Zionist in disguise. The media is a Zionist tool. What's more, the role of the Zionists in perpetrating terror is confirmed.

Like 9/11 prior to the blasts the pound was shorted. This means that due to advance knowledge of the bombings millions of pounds were earned. No Muslims were involved. Nor did any Muslim or Islaamic group benefit financially.

Regarding the second set of bombings these were necessary to help counter growing skepticism, rather, to reinforce the original image of actual (Muslim) people carrying bombs. This is because in the first bombing not all went according to plan. In other words, even with all the planted evidence and the seemingly fool-proof evidence against the Muslims in the official story questions began surfacing.

The bombs were created for these men by undercover agents, the same people who created the 'unused' bombs from the first bombings. Regarding the latter these were planted to create a kind of proof against the Muslims. The reason a second set of bombings was perpetrated was because of the high level of suspicion regarding the first one. Thus, the purpose was to create hysteria. The coming forward of witnesses with a clear remembrance of the events, such as Bruce Lait, was unexpected. Nor was it anticipated that the culprits would be double-crossed by the French, who leaked the information regarding the military nature of the explosives. This was truly an unexpected revelation, that these were military-class bombs made of rare materials. The public is unable to access these materials. Thus, the bombings were government jobs.

It is important to reiterate that no Muslim had advance warning. However, the Israelis did. So did the people who bet on the stocks. Again, only Westerners—perhaps secretive British authorities and the Israelis—had foreknowledge of this act. Incredibly, Deane notes that according to the original press reports Netanyahu was warned "an hour before the first explosion" and as a result "remained in his hotel" room. Yet, there is only one way he could know. It is that he was the perpetrator.

Yet, he knew that people would die and told no one? This is criminal. The normal reaction would be to inform the officials or, at a minimum, to call an emergency number. Certainly, the average citizen would do so. Netanyahu has the connections. He has the access, and he did nothing? This is collusion to a crime. What if a Muslim minister would have admittedly known an hour before and did nothing: what would have happened to him? The fact is he would have been arrested, beaten, and imprisoned, perhaps tortured.

Regarding such crimes how is it that the Israelis have advance warning about all issues? They never tell anyone until well after the horror is inflicted. Thus, obviously, they are the ones responsible for these acts. What's more, regarding their allies of whom they claim to have insider information, that is when and how they will be stricken, what kind of ally is this which disguises that very information that, if revealed, could save lives and much devastation? The fact is rather than an ally such a group is the enemy. Only an enemy would withhold valuable information from its associate, information that could only prevent harm. In contrast, it was exclusively the Muslims who attempted to warn the British about the danger of violent fanatics (see pages 272-274).

Yet, the advance knowledge or any feigned warnings are a mere ruse. This is to make it appear that the Israelis have their "act" together and they are a "class operation," while the Americans or British got 'duped' again. It is all a game, albeit a wicked one.

Do not forget: people were taught to believe that Diana was a 'problem.' It is now known that she was a decent, kind soul. Yet, she too was killed by her own government. So was weapons inspector Kelly. So, why would there be any hesitation to kill a few Muslims and use them as patsies? What's more, if it serves international greed, why hesitate to bomb, maim, and murder a few hundred 'commoners?'

CHAPTER 8

Who Bombed New York City?

It is now known that the Muslims had nothing to do with 9/11. Rather, they were among its primary victims. What's more, regarding terror acts the Muslims are being continuously framed. Here, the Zionists are the primary perpetrators. They created the entire concept of Islaamic terror, while the word Islaam is derived from *salima*, which means "security." This is a war of words, a deceptive one. It is all to distract people from the true perpetrators of mass crimes. It is to portray the Muslims as diabolical creatures, so that as a people they can be destroyed. This is despite the fact that regarding the horrors of 9/11 the Muslims had nothing to do with it. The fact is regarding this disaster no one can produce even the slightest degree of evidence of Islaamic involvement. Again, there was no Islaamic role in 9/11.

It is the Zionists who have created the thinking found commonly in the United States of "taking out" the Muslims. They are the ones who have established such a high degree of hate that people now say the most extreme statements, for instance, "kill all Muslims" or even "nuke them, destroy their holy sites." The fact is this is the Mecca which was the home of Abraham, the original true believer. Here, he created the world's first house of God. It would be, essentially, as if 'nuking' the origin of monotheism, including the origin of Judaism and Christianity. Yet, Mecca is already being nuked. This is through the fall-out of uranium-based munitions.

This is a heritage for all peoples. The Muslims are there only because as pure monotheists they follow Abraham more closely than others. Thus, God gave them this sanctuary as their right. According to the Qur'an God does not take kindly to claims that He has a physical son. Thus, the Muslims are the purest of all monotheists. This is why the site of Abraham is preserved for them. Yet, this sacred land is being polluted by the criminal Zionists and there American cohorts.

Certain Christians are prepared to call for the destruction of a holy site, that is the site of almighty God. Yet, this call for destruction is based merely on lies. Would they destroy the heritage of all humankind, merely due to hate and jealousy, merely because of false information, which is planted in their minds by hate-mongers?

The powerful ones of America plot the invasion and destruction of Muslim holy sites. They also plot the invasion and decimation of Iran, which they regard as a lost colony. This is despite the fact that he latter has shown *no* military hostility towards the United States.

The so-called clash of civilizations is baseless. In all history Islaam has enhanced Christian civilization. Any seeming clash is a fabrication. So is the image of Islaamic terror, which is created to justify aggression. The fact is this is the mantra of the armaments industry.

The fabricated nature of Islaamic terror is confirmed by the latest investigations. According to Brigham Young University's Steven Jones, Ph.D, as reported in a chapter in the book *The Hidden History of 9/11* the Muslims had nothing to do with the carnage at the World Trade Center. Rather, he says, these towers were destroyed through an industrial act: controlled demolition. Compared to the powerful explosives within the towers that were deliberately exploded, he says, the jetliner crashes played a relatively minor role.

In the United States in terror acts claims for direct involvement of Muslims are specious. Usually, the Muslims are maligned for acts they had nothing to do with. Or, attempts are made to create stings to pin blame on Islaam. This is particularly true of the 9/11 attack.

It must be remembered that true Muslims are highly inhibited from killing the innocent. They are well aware that the killing of the innocent leads to hellfire. This is a major inhibition which prevents their involvement in terror.

Again, people quote the original World Trade Center disaster as an example of Islaamic terror. Yet, when the blind Muslim Sheik Omar Abdul Rahman was questioned about his role, he said, essentially, 'As Muslims we are guests of this country. How can we attack it and cause it harm—we cannot do so.' These were his words, yet he was vilified, his guilt in advance was established, and there was little if any opportunity to examine the truth. Because he is a Muslim he was deemed a terrorist, and his guilt was sealed. What's more, the evidence against him largely came through a paid government informant. An aggressive trial condemned him as an enemy of the state based on no direct evidence. The fact is the man was framed.

The Sheik did not make the bomb. Rather, incredibly it was made by U.S. government agents. Then, regarding this disaster who are the real criminals? Much of the evidence against him came from Mossad agents, some of which is now known to have been planted.

The FBI was intimately involved in the bomb plot and even helped create the bomb. Thus, this agency had advance knowledge of the bombing and, like the Mossad, failed to halt it. This is because, incredibly, this organization regarded it in the national interest to target Islaam, even if it meant the loss of human lives. Regardless, Islaamic law prohibits the bombing of civilian buildings.

Isn't the FBI supposed to protect the American public? Instead, it plots against it. There are good people in this agency, as there are in the CIA. Yet, such people must rise up against this tyranny of blaming an entire people for the crimes of the establishment. The fact is there is no evidence that devout Muslims seek to harm America's innocents. What's more, their religion prohibits them from doing so.

True, the rare Muslim may falter, that is if, for instance, provoked by devious elements: spies who wish to foment strife and who purposely incite terror. This is precisely what happened in the original trade center disaster. If the Muslims were involved, they were directly provoked, in other words, by the U.S. government as well as Mossad agents. Thus, even in the first World Trade Center catastrophe it cannot be said that this was a premeditated Islaamic act.

The Mossad was directly involved in this disaster. Two of its agents, Josie Hadas and Emad Salem, are notorious criminals. The latter was proven guilty of criminal extortion. So, how can a liar and extortionist be trusted to give reliable testimony? Yet, this is the man who incriminated the Muslims.

The Israelis, as well as the U.S. government, employed these spies to frame the Muslims. This was necessary to demonize Islaam. Let there be no doubt about it, these men were attempting to give this faith a bad name. Yet, few people realize that in addition to Jews Mossad employs people born of Arabic or Middle Eastern heritage. These people are paid enormous sums to do dirty deeds. For instance, for this act alone Salem was given over a half million dollars. The money came directly from the U.S. government. In contrast, religious Muslims earned no money for this crime, rather, they endured only loss. Thus, people are being paid in hard cash to perform terror acts and, then, the Muslims are incriminated. Salem is Arab- or Egyptian-appearing. However, he is not a Muslim, although he posed as one. In fact, his avowed purpose was to target the Muslims by creating a terror act in their name.

An obviously Jewish or Anglo-Saxon-appearing espionage agent would have failed to achieve the desired result. This is the continued invasion and control of Islaamic lands plus, the wanton torment of the Muslim peoples. A Muslim-appearing person was needed to further the plot. This was a government sting, and the fact is even though they knew lives would be lost the government willingly participated in the bombing.

The spies met with the Muslims and urged them to attack the United States. What's more, one of the convicted Muslims, Mohammed Salameh, was entirely framed and had nothing to do with it. He is a tiny man of humble appearance, a perfect patsy. After he was sentenced all he could voice before he was carried away was, "Injustice, Injustice." There is no doubt about it, like Lee Harvey Oswald and Sirhan Sirhan Mohammed Salameh was preselected as a scapegoat.

In fact, it was Mossad agent Josie Hadas who fabricated 'evidence' against Salameh. Hadas had deliberately targeted Salameh as a patsy. Incredibly, according to the FBI, who searched Hadas' residence, there were bomb making materials. Plus, there was a letter with Salameh's name on it. Yet, in Salameh's house no such materials were found. A hate crime was committed against the pitiful Salameh. He had nothing to do with the bombing.

Yet, no Mossad agents were tried and imprisoned: only Muslims were prosecuted. This proves that there is a fulminate conspiracy against Islaam and, in particular, there is a deliberate effort to alter peoples' impressions of it. The fact is Islaam is the truth from almighty God. It is based upon the Qur'an, a powerful and compelling source. Its sources are free of falsehood. This is why it is attacked.

Westerners who investigate it also find it to be true. This is why there is a massive degree of 'conversion' to this religion. No one forces people to become Muslims. Rather, this is no religion: it is a way of life based upon the highest source—revelation from almighty God. This alone is why it is so viscously attacked.

The Israeli connection

The Muslims had nothing to do with 9/11. They were just as shocked and stupefied as all others at this debacle. What's more, there were hundreds of Muslims killed in the World Trade Center. This is why no Muslims would bomb it. Yet, the Israelis are directly tied to the act. News reports demonstrate the following, which few Americans realize (slightly paraphrased for easier reading):

> Angry witnesses reported seeing three separate groups of men at three different locations celebrating as they watched the September 11, 2001 attack on the World Trade Center. One group of men was seen celebrating in Union City. The witnesses reported their license plate to the police, who later arrested them. Witnesses also saw three men in Liberty State Park in Jersey City filming the attack on the World Trade Center. After the attack the men were seen cheering and jumping up and down. Those men were also caught by

the police and arrested several hours after the attack. Sources close to the investigation stated that it appeared that the men were involved in the attack and knew ahead of time what was going to happen.

Witnesses saw another group of five who were filming the smoking New York skyline (note now there are at least three separate groups of Middle Eastern-appearing men). The men seemed quite happy with the spectacle of the burning towers. A neighbor witnessed the men shouting cries of joy and mockery. They all had prior knowledge of the attack and were set up to film it before the first plane hit the World Trade Center. The FBI issued a warning: "Three individuals…were seen celebrating after initial impact and subsequent explosion. FBI Newark Field Office requests that, if the van is located, hold for prints and detain individuals." Another FBI warning was: "Vehicle possibly related to New York terrorist attack. White, 2000 Chevrolet van with New Jersey registration with Urban Moving Systems sign on back seen at Liberty State Park, Jersey City, NJ, at the time of first impact of jetliner into World Trade Center."

How could anyone cry for joy? The fact is this is vile. In contrast, there were no Muslims who had fore-knowledge of this event. Nor were there any such persons who were filming it. Nor was a single Muslim seen "jumping for joy."

Eight hours later those men were arrested and were found to possess maps and other evidence that linked them to the attack. One of the arrestees had $4,700 in cash hidden in his sock; box cutters were also confiscated. Incredibly, this was the very thing that authorities had attributed to Muslims. The latter were accused of wielding these box cutters in the planes, even slitting the throats of airline attendants, perhaps pilots. This was the gruesome image portrayed by the media, again, of the deranged 'Arab' terrorist. Yet, it is all lies. Regarding the known culprits as reported by *ABC News*:

> Perhaps the biggest surprise for the officers came when the five men identified themselves as Israeli citizens. According to the police report one of the passengers told the officers they had been on the West Side Highway in Manhattan "during the incident," referring to the World Trade Center attack. According to the news report the driver told the officers:
> "We are Israeli. We are not your problem. Your problems are our problems. The Palestinians are the problem."

Yet, there has never been a single terror act inflicted upon Americans by Palestinians. Nor has there been a single Palestinian in this country convicted of treason against the nation, nor have any Palestinians been caught conducting covert activities or destroying American or public landmarks. In contrast, all such crimes have been committed in the USA by the Israelis. *ABC News* also reported:

> The FBI also questioned Urban Moving's owner. His attorney insists that his client answered all of the FBI's questions. But when FBI agents tried to interview him again a few days later, he was gone.

Hurriedly, he emptied his New Jersey home and fled with his family to Israel. Much valuable evidence was destroyed. Three months later the *ABC News* program 20/20 photographed the inside of Urban Moving:

> It looked as if the business had been shut down in a big hurry. Cell phones were lying around; office phones

were still connected; and the property of dozens of clients remained in the warehouse.

There is no attempt by the U.S. government to investigate this connection. Nor is there any attempt to prosecute the gleeful Israelis. In contrast, tens of thousands of Muslims all over the world are being held seemingly indefinitely, without charges. Many have been prosecuted and put in jail, some, allegedly, even for connections to 9/11. What's more, as a result of this Israeli act—this 9/11 terror act—Muslim countries have been ravaged, with hundreds of thousands of the innocent killed, tortured, and maimed. Incredibly, while the Jews who had full complicity in this crime are merely deported, innocent Muslims are slaughtered. Other tens of thousands are held under barbaric conditions, without legal recourse. Many are being tortured, others raped, and still others have died due to their wounds or stress.

While known Israeli criminals, who had intent to murder the innocent and to destroy landmarks, were 'let go' it was the Muslims who were given the ludicrous title of "enemy combatants." Enemy against what: tyranny? Muslims throughout the world were appalled by the horrors of 9/11. What's more, nearly one sixth, perhaps even a higher percentage, of the victims were Muslims. In contrast, Mossad agents, who thrilled in seeing the carnage, are set free, without consequence. Had a Muslim done so, surely, such a person would have been imprisoned, perhaps tortured and, certainly, executed.

According to one news report on 9/11 the Israelis were apprehended with a van full of explosives. A plot by these men to blow up the George Washington Bridge was uncovered. Yet, the young Muslim, John Walker Lindh, languishes in prison, enduring a so-called 20-year sentence, even though he had nothing to do with 9/11. The same is true of Zacharias Moussaoui, who while enduring a life sentence is also innocent of any crimes. Why, such men were only fighting the evil and colonial machinations of Wall Street—they never attacked a single American.

Yet, why let the Zionists escape? These are the very people who commit terror acts, even against Americans, and, then, blame Islaam. It was obvious that these Israelis were spies. Obviously, they were engaged in warfare, a crime far worse than, for instance, anything committed by Lindh. What's more, in contrast to the Muslims who were, perhaps, fighting battles outside the United States if any they were waging war in New York City and Washington, D.C. on American citizens.

This demonstrates that bin Laden was correct when he said that the problem in America is that there is a secret government, "a government within a government." He suggested that Americans look within to determine the real sources of sabotage. Then, he said, his fight is not with the American people but, rather, with the government. The fact is the Zionists largely control the U.S. government. They dictate the terms, all for their own wicked gains. In this regard bin Laden showed more insight than many world leaders.

Further evidence supporting the Zionist role is demonstrated by the precautions taken for Israeli nationals. The number of Israelis who typically work in these centers is high: on a daily basis perhaps several thousand. Yet, only one died.

How could it be that there were no Israelis? Virtually all escaped, while all others—non-Israelis—were caught in the catastrophe. In contrast, 20 Columbians, 15 Philippinos, 11 Mexicans, and some 200 British died. What's more, well over 400 Muslims were killed, some 60 from Bangladesh alone. Again, incredibly, in a mainly Israeli building there were no Israeli deaths? Yet, there were deaths of over a thousand *other* foreign nationals. So, the Muslims were slaughtered en mass, while the Israelis escaped. Then, who is the obvious perpetrator of this act?

The Israelis were saved because they simply did not go to work. Their secret service told them to stay home. This is no small issue: the Israelis knew that if they went to the towers, they could be killed. Yet, they withheld that information from all others. This demonstrates full complicity in the crime. Yet, the Israelis have never been held accountable. In contrast, if a Muslim were to have had such knowledge, while withholding it, he would have been prosecuted, perhaps executed. This is precisely the argument against Zacharias Moussaoui, even though complicity has never been proven.

The statement that these buildings were attacked by Muslims is a fraud. In addition to killing any innocents the killing of fellow Muslims is strictly prohibited. Said the Prophet Muhammad, essentially, 'To (purposely) kill a fellow believer earns you hellfire.' This alone debunks the government position that this was an Islaamic act. The fact is the existence of Muslims in these towers would be a monumental inhibition for such an attack.

For the Israelis the death toll was expected to be massive. The World Trade Center was the hub for Israeli activities. The Israeli firms, Goldman-Sachs and Solomon Brothers, had extensive offices there, and many of these offices are staffed by Israelis. Normally, hundreds of Israelis would have been there. However, on September 11th the Israelis abandoned the building, including the various Israeli security officers.

Israeli authorities at first announced what they regarded as a genocide: some 4000 *Israeli citizens* were expected to have died. This was the minimum. This confirms that this was, in fact, an Israeli center. This also proves that the Israelis fully knew that the Trade Center would be destroyed.

This figure was based upon the number of Israelis who worked in or next to this complex. Yet, as confirmed by Alon Pinkas in the towers only one Israeli, a tourist, was killed. Unlike the regulars he failed to gain the benefit of advance notice. The fact is the primary victims were Christians and Muslims. In contrast, a significant number of American Jews were also killed.

How is this possible, Pinkas reasoned—it would have been expected that thousands of Jews would have died? What he was unaware of was the fact that all Israelis were warned not to go to work that day.

Blood money

Much of the content of this section is derived from the book *Stranger Than Fiction* (A. Pastore). When there is a murder, investigators always attempt to determine who profits. This same method must hold true of the World Trade Center disaster. For a successful investigation to unfold the major beneficiaries must be determined. This will surely expose the culprits. Yet, how could anyone profit from this devastation—surely, this would exclusively be a loss. What's more, how could anyone have the audacity to do so?

There is a type of investing through which investors profit by a decline in stocks. During the early hours of 9/11 there was suspicious activity in the stock market. Large amounts of options were placed on airline stocks, specifically United and American. These are known as puts.

Greed may yet uncover the true facts behind this atrocity. Apparently, the airlines, United and American, were themselves involved in these puts, not surprisingly, since both these airlines have filed bankruptcy.

The potential for success in these options is very low. This is why they are "highly leveraged." A slight failure means that all that is invested is lost: a major gamble.

Perhaps the West is so corrupt that huge money can only be made on other peoples' blood. No Muslim would do it. This is Western terror. Where is the money trail to the Muslims? There is none. Rather, the Muslims are being purged of money, their homes raided, their religious centers vandalized, their belongings stolen/destroyed, their life savings confiscated, their charities seized, their buildings raised and burned. What's more, it is only Muslims who, today, are being found buried in mass graves.

The motto of the Zionists is telling, since they say they do "whatever they want" without consequences. This includes the heartless earning of money from the blood and agony of others.

When a stock collapses, the puts increase in value. Only the shrewdest of all people would do this. The Zionists are experts at this. So is the CIA.

Only a relatively small amount of money is needed to make these bets, because they are based upon poor odds. There may have been hundreds of such puts placed on various stocks. As a result, vast profits were made, in fact, tens of millions. People were dying, and all these financiers could think about was their own enrichment.

As reported by Pastore in addition to the massive put options against United and American Airlines there were also large options bet on the stocks of numerous brokerage houses such as Morgan Stanley, Dean Witter, and Merrill Lynch. This may have been a way for the perpetrators in their greed to regain their investments, since, surely, some of the owners of these institutions were privy to the coming events. Even so, the World Trade Center had increasingly become unprofitable. Thus, it was of benefit to the owners that it was destroyed.

Pastore also reports that the space occupied in the World Trade Center by these firms was vast, some 22 floors in each of the towers. The fact is many of these companies were having difficulty paying their rent. Insurance settlements would be handy. Thus, the people involved in betting were well aware that these offices would be destroyed. They bet as if they had no doubt about it, that is that they knew the buildings would fall. Again, it must be reiterated that, here, there was no Islaamic involvement. Thus, rather than a random act of supposed Muslim rage this was a well planned event, highly sophisticated and carefully designed. What's more, obviously, it was rehearsed.

During the destruction of the World Trade Center the Israelis were absent. This is the first time since the inception of this facility that this has happened. The Israeli offices were vacant, while those occupied by Americans and non-Israeli foreign nationals were 'full.' No Muslims or Christians received advance warning of this doom. Nor were non-Israeli Jews warned. Besides the Israelis no one else knew. What's more, only Israeli 'film crews' were on site, recording it in advance. Then, who could proclaim that they were not intimately involved?

When the destruction of the World Trade Center occurred, the prices of each of the aforementioned stocks plummeted. This earned the perpetrators tens of millions of dollars in immediate cash. Pastore reports that as a result of the drop in prices of Merrill Lynch's stocks alone some 5.5 million dollars was profited. This is an enormous amount of money to earn over a mere stock bet. Yet, that was the result of foreknowledge of the attacks. Rather than Muslims the profits were taken exclusively by Westerners. This is further proof that there was no Islaamic connection.

Whoever did this knew about the attack. Incredibly, they also knew the details: the types of airliners that would be implicated, the buildings that would be struck, the financial institutions which would be destroyed, and the ultimate consequences of those strikes. Again, to place exact bets on only the two airlines that were involved demonstrated absolute foreknowledge. Then, bin Laden is blamed? The fact is he had nothing to do with it. In contrast, these financiers, all non-Muslims, had their 'battle plan' in place and fully profited from it. They did so while thousands of people were crushed to death and/or burnt alive. These agents of the West are the true criminals behind this atrocity.

For most people such a degree of evil is unfathomable. What's more, clearly, these profiteers knew that the World Trade Center would be destroyed. As revealed by Pastore according to the *San Francisco Chronicle* the criminals behind this scheme still have funds to collect: some $2.5 million, which is being held at Wall Street. This was made by gambling on or before September 11 on the drop in United Airlines stock. However, after this illegal activity was exposed, no one attempted to collect it.

The fact that the culprits abandoned $2.5 million in profits clearly demonstrates their guilt. What's more these bets could only have been placed by the actual perpetrators: the people who plotted the attack. Obviously, they weren't Muslims. These are the perpetrators responsible for the murder of some 3000 or more people. Rather than the poor and pitiful people of the Islaamic world it is these people who should be attacked.

It is relatively easy to track the actual people behind these activities. Investigators were led, notes Pastore, to the investment banking firm, Alex Brown, Inc., the nation's oldest investment bank. This bank was directly responsible for the 'blood' money made via bets on United stock.

Pastore says that government's complicity is obvious. In fact, the CIA played an intimate role. This is demonstrated by the fact that the former Chairman of the Board of Alex Brown, Inc. is A. B. "Buzzy" Krongard, the now Executive Director of the CIA.

Krongard's recent comments in the *Washington Post* are telling. He said the entire U.S. espionage service is merely an operative for big money, that is the entire espionage infrastructure, including the CIA and NSA, is "nothing but Wall Street bankers and lawyers." In other words, the power of money determines foreign policy. There is never any true effort to help the people, whether patriots or foreigners. Incredibly, America's foreign policy is based upon greed and lust. This is satanic.

The insiders who earned this money bet on enormous risks. If they were wrong, they would lose all. Thus, they knew for certain that, for instance, on September 11th the stocks of these financial institutions would collapse, in other words, they knew they would win.

How could they be so sure, though, that the planes would bring down both towers? Anyone can realize that there are numerous variables. If it was a random attack—a hijacking by angry men—emotions could rage, and errors would be made. The planes could even miss the targets. So, the people betting knew exactly what would happen. They knew that the buildings would be blown internally and that they would surely fall. This proves that rather than a group of young Muslims, mostly students, a far greater force was responsible. What's more, everyone knows that the refugee bin Laden, trapped in the mountains of Afghanistan, couldn't have achieved this.

There would always be the chance that this "perfect crime" would fail. Unless it was precisely rehearsed and massively coordinated it would be far from fool proof, that is that the two planes would do sufficient damage to cause both towers to collapse. No one would bet on the plane crashes alone. They would only bet if they were certain that the buildings would be demolished, that is by set explosives, because *any building bombed with strategically placed charges will collapse.* So, now they could bet with certainty, gaining tens of millions of dollars of quick cash in the process.

These huge and risky bets could only have been taken by the 9/11 planners themselves. *Certain people within the American and Israeli hierarchy were sure the collapses would occur.* Only such individuals had access to these stock trades. Thus, the people placing the bets were privy to the preplanned destruction, that is by the use of demolition charges. Otherwise, the gamblers would have lost their bets and, then, must pay out millions of dollars. The World Trade Center architects designed the towers to survive such collisions. America is the most sophisticated country in the world. There is no possibility that the designers would neglect to ensure the public's protection. The Twin Towers would have remained standing, the fires put out, and the stocks would have eventually recovered. For the stocks to collapse the massive World Trade Center complex must first collapse. Apparently, the espionage agencies were bankrupt. They sorely needed funds to finance espionage activities.

People want to know if it wasn't the Muslims, who was it? Only two groups had foreknowledge: the Israelis and their various high level rabbis as well as certain powerful people in the U.S. government. On or before 9/11 people in such positions took precautions. Wealthy executives from numerous firms were pulled away from work to attend a party by a Omaha, Nebraska billionaire. Israeli nationals were told not to go to work that day. Top FBI and CIA agents were informed of a potential terrorist act and to stay away.

Thus, only Israeli and American officials had forknowledge. Thus, any investigation of the true murderers must begin with these officials. No other nation warned its officials or workers. Nor did any other nation warn its workers, that is at the World Trade Center. Thus, it is at these highest levels where any investigation must begin.

Due to financial interests the media is heavily biased. Thus, it is revealing to quote independent sources. The *American Free Press* is one such source, whose Christopher Bollyn reports:

> Despite reports from numerous eyewitnesses and experts, including news reporters on the scene, who heard or saw explosions immediately before the collapse of the World Trade Center, there has been virtual silence in the mainstream media.
>
> Television viewers watching the horrific events of Sept. 11 saw evidence of explosions before the towers collapsed. Televised images show what appears to be a huge explosion occurring near ground level, in the vicinity of the 47-story Salomon Brothers Building, known as WTC 7, prior to the collapse of the first tower.
>
> Van Romero, an explosives expert and former director of the Energetic Materials Research and Testing Center at New Mexico Tech, said on Sept. 11, "My opinion is, based on the videotapes, that after the airplanes hit the World Trade Center there were some explosive devices inside the buildings that caused the towers to collapse."
>
> The collapse of the structures resembled the controlled implosions used to demolish old structures and was "too methodical to be a chance result of airplanes colliding with the structures," Romero told The Albuquerque Journal hours after the attack. Romero is one of the top experts in the field and has studied for decades the explosive effects of airplanes and bombs on buildings.

Shortly after his statements Romero was muzzled. He never again gave these comments.

Explosions are violent discharges of energy, which radiate outward. Implosions are also violent, but their energy goes inward, a kind of inward collapse. There is evidence that both types of destructive actions afflicted the World Trade Center. What is certain is that there were explosions in this Center both prior to and after the airplane strikes. These were from bombs strategically placed to break the supportive beams, so the towers would collapse.

Eyewitnesses prove that unrelated to the airplane strikes there were a number of violent explosions within these buildings, particularly in the basements. As documented by top authorities, including the maintenance men working within these basements, these violent underground explosions preceded the airplane strikes. One such person, William Rodriguez, was head of tower two maintenance and holder of the master key. He fully witnessed these explosions. He was in the basement when these bombs exploded. Plus, he testified, that these explosions occurred well before the airplane strike. Repeatedly, like numerous firemen, he stated that prior to the plane strikes multiple bombs exploded. This means that the destruction of this landmark was preplanned by people who had access to the buildings. It also means that it was achieved at the highest governmental level. People who had foreknowledge include Paul Wolfowitz, Richard Pearl, Dov Zakheim, Paul Bremer, Douglas Feith, Donald Rumsfeld, Dick Cheney, various Israeli power-brokers, and even the President himself. Presidential involvement is confirmed by the fact that on September 10th FEMA had admittedly set up a crisis center in Manhattan.

Perhaps all Americans realize where they were when this happened. On September 11th I was sleeping late when

I was awaken by a colleague and told to immediately view a TV, that a plane had hit the World Trade Center. I was certain it was a hoax and at worst an accident. I saw a plane strike the south tower. Along with my colleague, Angelica Lord, we watched the unfolding events. Upon seeing the collapse of the buildings many people, including myself, experienced the shock of their lives. My shock was due to the fact that I was confident that the building had been stabilized, the fires were under control, and that further disaster was preventable.

When the south tower suddenly collapsed, something incredible happened. Immediately, my colleague said, "Oh my God they've set charges." This is not something I would normally think. However, after working with Ms. Lord for over 20 years, a highly intuitive woman, I fully trusted what she said. Call it a man's experience with womens' instincts or merely being open-minded, I had no reason to doubt her. The fact is she is the first person to recognize that the official story is a lie.

The *American Free Press* continues:

> Implosions are used to demolish buildings. This is particularly in areas of high building density, such as Manhattan, to prevent damage to surrounding buildings. Precision-timed explosives are placed on strategic load-bearing columns and beams to cause the controlled collapse.
>
> Demolition experts say that towers are the most difficult buildings to bring down in a controlled manner. A tower tends to fall like a tree, unless the direction of its fall is controlled by directional charges. The towers fell with virtual precision, and damage to surrounding buildings, many of which are worth hundreds of millions of dollars, was minimized. It gave all the appearances of a controlled demolition. What's more, they fell...neatly

within the boundaries of their foundations. Collateral damage was minimal, and most of the deaths occurred within the towers.

After being hit by the aircraft, the twin towers appeared to be stable. Then, without warning, at 9:58 a.m., the south tower imploded vertically downward, 53 minutes after being hit. Curiously, there was an exact half-hour interval between the two events. At 10:28, 88 minutes after being struck, the north tower collapsed. "It would be difficult for something from the plane to trigger an event like that," Romero said. If explosions did cause the towers to collapse, "It could have been a relatively small amount of explosives placed in strategic points," he said...

There is other information that lends credence to Romero's suggestions: One eyewitness, whose office is near the World Trade Center, told AFP that he was standing among a crowd of people on Church Street, about two-and-a-half blocks from the south tower, when he saw "a number of brief light sources being emitted from inside the building between floors 10 and 15." He saw about six of these brief flashes, accompanied by "a crackling sound" before the tower collapsed. Incredibly, each tower had six central support columns. This is a crucial finding, indicating the setting of charges. This shows that there was a conspiracy to cause human loss plus loss of life. In other words, it was premeditated.

Eyewitnesses have confirmed Romero's assessment. Set charges blew the foundation beams apart, causing the building to collapse. Consider the firefighter, Louie Cacchioli, 51, who was one of the first to enter the second tower. Said Cacchioli as reported in *People Weekly*, September 24: "I was taking firefighters up in the elevator to the 24th floor to get in position to evacuate workers. On the last trip up *a bomb went off. We think there were bombs set in the building.*" Unless it was real, no fireman would say such a thing. They tend to be conservative. What's more, they are among some of the most reliable people of modern civilization.

The *American Free Press* also reported:

> Kim White, 32, an employee on the 80th floor, also reported hearing an explosion. "All of a sudden the building shook, then it started to sway. We didn't know what was going on," she told People. "We got all our people on the floor into the stairwell…at that time we all thought it was a fire…We got down as far as the 74th floor…then there was another explosion."

The firemen knew there was nothing in these buildings that could explode. Thus, the explosions could result only from pre-set charges, which were being exploded remotely.

Since the firemen made their initial statements about the planted bombs they have been ostracized. No major media is willing to interview them. Thus, they have been effectively silenced.

What the government says about the collapse

The orthodox theory is that the heat of the fires from airline fuel caused the collapse. As the fires raged in the towers, so the authorities claim, the steel cores in each building were heated to 2,000 degrees Fahrenheit, causing the support beams to buckle. Yet, Lee Robertson, a lead engineer who designed these towers, expressed shock that merely due to the jet accident they collapsed so readily. Said Robertson:

> I designed it for a 707 to hit it (same fuel capacity). Another architect of the WTC, Aaron Swirski, lives in

Israel and spoke to Jerusalem Post Radio after the attack:
"It was designed...to survive this kind of attack..."

The Free Press also reported the reaction of Hyman Brown, a University of Colorado civil engineering professor and the World Trade Center's chief construction manager. Brown watched *in confusion* as the towers came down. "It was *over-designed to withstand almost anything,* including hurricanes, high winds, bombings and an airplane hitting it," he said (italics mine).

Brown told the journal that although the buildings were designed to withstand massive impacts from everything from hurricanes to errant aircraft, including a direct hit by an airplane the same size as the 757, even with all this he did say the burning probably weakened the steel. Yet, he never attributed the collapse to the jetliner strike alone.

This expert disputed one of the official theories, that is that the implosion was due to jet fuel fires, which sucked the air out of the lower floors. Regardless, firefighters were on the scene and were busy putting out the fires. Due to the brave efforts of these firefighters, particularly in the north tower, there had been a gradual improvement, with most fires extinguished. So, if the fires were largely extinguished, how could the steel melt?

Even so, steel melts at 2400 degrees, while jet fuel burns at 1500 degrees. This means that the energy needed to destroy the steel beams came from other sources. The only possible source is planted explosives.

The second plane nearly missed the south tower, cutting through a corner. Much of the fuel from this plane burned outside the building. This jet fuel, set on fire, dropped even on a number of civilians, some of whom died. Yet, this building collapsed first, well before the north tower, which endured the full damage from the fuel.

If the official theory were true, the north tower would have collapsed first, since it bore the brunt of a direct hit. Plus, virtually all the fuel burned within the building. Incredibly, the government theory is completely disputed by the original designers of the building as well as by the use of reason. Regardless, by the time the collapse occurred the fires were greatly reduced.

So, there were other factors that caused the sudden collapse of these buildings. Proof of this is based on eye- and ear-witness accounts of actual explosions, many of these accounts being registered by the tower's maintenance men. These maintenance men confirm that well before the plane strikes bombs exploded in the buildings.

University research also documents the disinformation. Columbia University's Lamont-Doherty Earth Observatory measured unusual seismic activity that morning arising from beneath each of the towers. Seismographs scientifically determine the source of any earthly disturbance. On September 11th these seismographs measured two spikes arising from *directly underneath* the World Trade Center. Here, there arose two enormous bursts of energy, which shook the ground beneath these towers. There is only one possible source of such localized subterranean energy: man-made explosives.

A large ground-based explosion measuring 2.1 on the Richter scale was recorded *just before the collapse* of the first (south) tower. A second large ground explosion, which registered 2.3 on the Richter scale, was detected just *seconds before the collapse* of the second (north) tower. There was nothing within these basements which could have exploded, that is unless bombs were planted.

There is nothing else that can explain these seismic variations. They occurred well after the plane strikes. Each increase was followed immediately by the collapse of each of the two towers. This means that the bombs were purposely exploded in the basement, in other words, it was an inside job.

Pools of molten steel were found at the base of these collapsed towers six weeks after the collapse. This is evidence of massive underground explosions. Only a bomb could have caused that degree of heat, that is stored energy. This could have perhaps been a micronuclear device, which surely would create such heat. A thermite and/or barometric bomb is likely. That would explain the heat which kept the steel molten for six weeks. Jet fuel, mere kerosene, could never do so. The exposure to residues of such explosives could also explain the grotesque diseases which have afflicted clean-up workers.

The huge explosions may have literally knocked the towers off their foundations, causing them to collapse. The jetliners were mere decoys for a far more destructive act. The purpose of the jetliners was to convince people of an Islaamic attack.

Obviously, the destruction of the World Trade Center and the Pentagon were inside jobs. The majority of Americans find it unfathomable that the President of the United States, George W. Bush, is a traitor as well as murderer. Yet, there have been numerous other world leaders who have committed similar treasonous acts over the centuries, including several U.S. presidents. The fact is the rulers of the United States are directly responsible for the murder of millions of innocent people, notably the countless innocent civilians in Iraq, Afghanistan, Central America, Vietnam, and Palestine. Yet, in the collapse of the World Trade Center and the destruction of the peoples of Waco they are also responsible for the slaughter of American citizens.

The Israelis are also culpable for much of this murder. What's more, regarding the crimes of the Bush dynasty this is admitted even by this family itself. According to White House reporter Sarah McClendon in her June 1992 newsletter the elder Bush, who was then president, made the following cryptic statement regarding his own treasonous conduct while in power: "If the people were to ever find out what we have done, we would be chased down the streets and lynched."

CHAPTER 9
Endless Terror

Islaam is noble. It represents an elegant way of life. Its purpose is to fight every conceivable evil on this earth. It is to fight the realm of tyranny. It is to halt all oppression against the innocent. Thus, it is to systematically end all terror.

In 9/11 there was no Islaamic role. Furthermore, for instance, to blame Islaam as a source of international terror is ludicrous, since it is a buttress against such terror. Islaamic civilization has no history, for instance, of destroying public buildings. Thus, the Muslims were/are used as a decoy. In the history of such civilization and at the height of its power no public buildings were ever blown up, destroying their residents. Rather, it prevented such destruction. Because of Islaamic 'policies' the innocents—women, children, the weak, and the infirm—were never expelled from their homes, nor were they murdered and/or tortured. Rather, Islaamic civilization accepted the tormented, housing and caring for them. Thus, there is essentially no history in Islaam of the senseless killing of the common man.

It is the Israelis who have such a history. It is they who are the demolition experts. So, when, suddenly, acts of terror occur, that is when buildings are blown up, while innocent people die, rather than the Muslims the first consideration should be the Zionists. They destroyed the King David Hotel, killing nearly one hundred people. Evidence is accumulating that they are behind two bombings in the Sinai, including the recent Sharam al-Sheik catastrophe. They have been implicated in the bombing of the vast marine barracks in Lebanon (1983) and are clearly a culprit in the 9/11 horror. The fact is regarding 9/11 an Israeli company owned the buildings and, conveniently, other than a random visitor and a janitor not a single Israeli died in the catastrophe.

In Palestine the Israelis have demolished entire cities—while they were fully occupied. They have wantonly slaughtered untold thousands of defenseless women, children, youths, and the elderly. For sport they target children, wounding and/or killing them. These acts were/are committed primarily by non-Semitic European Jews. Incredibly, these people of Anglo Saxon race, who have no Semitic blood, torture, kill, and maim the Semites. Then, after driving them away they steal their land. They even demolish entire cities, rather, countries. There is no Islaamic precedence of such acts. Routinely and diabolically the Israelis demolish peoples' homes on top of them, burying such residents alive. The fact is this is pure terror. In contrast, in Afghanistan rather than destroying infrastructure bin Laden built it.

Like the Russians the Americans destroyed much of Afghanistan. They even contaminated its land, water, and wilderness with radioactive chemicals. This is all to further the financial agenda of the international powers. It had nothing to do with any fight against terrorism. The same is true of the destruction wrought in Vietnam, Cambodia, and Laos.

On a daily basis the Israelis demolish buildings. The fact is they are the experts in such destruction. They have over 50 years experience in demolishing public buildings, even those which are fully occupied. They are also the experts in remote control detonation for use in assassination. What's more, they train hostile forces all over the world in demolition techniques.

The murder of Rachel Corrie

It is only the Israelis who are so vehement about destroying buildings that they have no hesitation regarding life, limb, or property. It is they alone who murdered the human rights protester Rachel Corrie. This American citizen, fully marked in fluorescent orange gear, was sitting on the roof of a Palestinian home targeted for destruction. The Israeli tyrants, who operated the bulldozer, purposely ran her over. This is a hate crime that the entire world condemns. Thus, rather than a defensive army, the Israeli Defense or rather, *Demolition* League is a group of thieves and criminals, which is unrestricted in its atrocities. This is that evil entity which uses monies collected from the American people to perpetrate acts of terror. It uses that money to commit the slaughter of the defenseless. Thus, if the innocent Rachel Corrie is dispensable, what about the people within the World Trade Center—mere pawns of no consequence? How utterly vile it is, rather, wicked, that is that the Israelis brazenly commit murder, while the Muslims are blamed. The fact is the latter are often targeted globally for acts they did not commit, rather, acts that were perpetrated instead by Zionists.

Usama bin Laden is university educated. He is well schooled in global events. In Afghanistan he was a refugee, exiled from his native land. Claims for a bin Laden attack on the United States are unsubstantiated. What's more, in all legitimate interviews where he was interviewed by known reporters he categorically denied any involvement. He also made it clear that Islaam is against the killing of the innocent. What's more, unlike the clearly marked and obviously civilian Corrie, who was murdered by Israeli thugs, bin Laden has *never been proven to have killed even a single civilian.* Any such claims against him are speculative. Nor would he ever have murdered the likes of Corrie. The fact is rather than bin Laden it is the so-called Israeli Army, as well as its espionage agencies, which is the great inflicter of terror in the world.

Bombs of terror

Regardless, bin Laden's activities were the proposed basis of the attack on Afghanistan. Now it is known that the basis of this war is fraudulent, because this man had nothing to do with 9/11. So, this bombing was/is purely criminal. What's more, all the death and despair endured by the people is on the hands of the Western and, particularly, Israeli rulership. This includes long-term consequences such as the causing of tens of thousands of yet-to-be-diagnosed cases of radiation-induced cancer.

This persistent bombing has had vast repercussions, not only killing the innocent but also polluting vast tracts of land and water. How ludicrous: here is a man who is living in a relatively primitive environment, and the United States saturates the region with bombs, including nuclear devices. The fact is bin Laden is no terrorist. Rather, it is the Western governments which are the sources of international terror. Obvious examples of Western terror acts include World War I, World War II, the Vietnam War, the bombing of Cambodia, the nuclear bombings of Hiroshima and Nagasaki, the dissemination of Agent Orange, the crimes of Khmer

Rouge/Pol Pot, Waco, 9/11, the installation of Western-sponsored dictators, and countless other murderous acts. Top former CIA authorities have confirmed that American meddling have caused only despair—for all humanity, including Westerners. Then, comparatively, the emphasis on bin Laden and, in fact, Islaamic terror, is nonsensical.

As a result exclusively of Western acts tens of thousands of Iraqi and Afghani children are dying of radiation-induced cancer. Is this anything other than the most grotesque terror conceivable? Yet, the entire war is based upon fraud. Also, why torment bin Laden? He was never involved. What's more, why put American people at risk, since rather than a war to protect the nation, that is from invaders, this is a war to pursue financial interests. This is what American people are dying for. Thus, is there any legitimate reason for bombing these countries into oblivion? The fact is at a minimum 9/11 was an Israeli decoy operation to distract attention from this entity's heinous acts.

Again, regarding the invasion of Muslim countries the justification was to "get" bin Laden. Yet, 9/11 was never a bin Laden act. Thus, the entire invasion of Afghanistan, as well as the attack upon this man, is based upon lies. So is the invasion of Iraq. These are acts of the criminal tyrants, the rulership of the United States, Israel, France, and Britain. As a result of these acts rather than "decency" or "democracy" all that has been created is tyranny. The blood of the innocent is spilled, all for the sake of capital gains. That is apparently the definition of democracy.

The sophistication of Islaam

Regarding Jews and Christians Islaam has always been liberal. For instance, no Muslim has ever walked into a synagogue and gunned down worshippers. Yet, to the

Muslims this has repeatedly occurred at the hands of true fanatics, hostile Jews and Christians. For instance, in Iraq mosques are attacked and invaded, the worshippers slaughtered and maimed. Yet, no such worshippers have posed a threat to the United States. Consider also the al-Aqsa massacre, when the Zionists gunned down in cold blood numerous worshippers, wounding dozens. Yet, in Iraq weapons produced by Christian nations are used to slaughter and maim untold thousands of Iraqis, as well as Palestinians, even innocent children.

Even so, the labeling of Muslims as brutal—as kidnappers, suicide bombers, and insurgents, that is as the source of source of global terror—is baseless. What Islaamic group or country has arbitrarily invaded nations, merely for material and 'national' gain? What Islaamic power has assassinated heads of states in order to create its own puppet regimes? Which Islaamic group has invaded a sovereign land merely to control its oil or mineral wealth? Which Islaamic power has created illegal settlements, even a hostile 'state,' within other peoples' sovereign land, stealing their land and property in order to do so? This system is far too sophisticated to commit such barbarism. Which Islaamic state has erected a wall directly through sovereign territory, isolating innocent human beings from their livelihood, while usurping their every property, rights, and residences? Islaam has never supported such acts, rather, it prevents them. Yet, is anyone to now believe the emphasis on Islaamic terror? What's more, is there any Islaamic group anywhere on this earth, which even remotely matches the brutality of the Israelis?

Consider this degree of horror, exclusive to the Zionist barbarians. It is only the Zionists, true terrorists, who, without hesitation brutally kill children. It is only they who target them, killing them without remorse. According to Chris

Hedges of the Times Middle East bureau, experienced and respected international reporter, the paper's editor-in-chief:

> I've seen kids shot in Sarajevo. I mean, snipers would shoot kids in Sarajevo. I've seen death squads kill families in Algeria or El Salvador. But I'd never seen soldiers bait or taunt kids like this and then shoot them for sport.

It is no surprise that these Israeli terrorists kill without remorse. The fact is they are trained to do so.

In the Israeli entity children are indoctrinated with the Zionist ideology from a very young age. Calls for Muslims to alter their educational systems to suit the desires of the West are highly suspect, considering that these same authorities say nothing about the brain-washing techniques used by the Zionists. As a result of the Zionist propaganda, rather, hate, Israeli children are raised to believe that they are superior to all others. The Israeli soldiers' brutal treatment of Palestinians is a direct consequence of this.

Consider also the following facts elucidated by Odnan Oktar, Turkish intellectual. He describes the work of Roger Garaudy in the latter's classic *The Case of Israel: A Study of Political Zionism:*

> The Book of Joshua, so often invoked today by the army rabbinate in Israel in order to preach holy war, and also made much of in school teaching, dwells upon the sanctified extermination of conquered populations, putting everyone to "the edge of the sword"—"both man and woman, young and old" (Joshua, vi, 21)—as we read in the story of Jericho and of so many other cities.

Writes Oktar, "Garaudy emphasizes that the Book of Joshua and the Old Testament in general are the source of

Zionist terror." In other words, it is in-bred for the Zionists to use it:

> This conception of the "promise," together with the means for its realization as the leaders of political Zionism derive these from the Book wherein Joshua recounts his feats of extermination of the previous inhabitants, which he carried out at God's command and with his support, plus the themes of "the chosen people" and of "Greater Israel," from the Nile to the Euphrates, constitute the ideological foundation of (Zionism)."

Oktar continues, "The memoirs of an Israeli soldier published in the Israeli newspaper *Davar* are an important example of this. The soldier in question participated in an operation to seize the Palestinian village of Ed-Dawayma in 1948 and described the scenes of brutality he witnessed:

> "They killed between eighty to one hundred Arab (both Muslims and Christians) men, women, and children. To kill the children, they (that is the Israelis) fractured their heads with sticks. There was not one home without corpses. The men and women of the village were pushed into houses without food or water. Then, the saboteurs came to dynamite them. The intent: to create vast terror by killing the innocent.
>
> "One commander ordered a soldier to bring two women into a building he was about to blow up... Another soldier prided himself upon having raped an Arab woman before shooting her to death. Another Arab woman and her baby were made to clean up the place for a couple of days, then they shot her and the baby. Educated and well-mannered commanders who were considered 'good guys'...became base murderers, and this is not in the storm of battle, but as a method of

expulsion and extermination. The fewer the Arabs (in fact, Muslims and Christians) who remain, the better."

Revisiting the Deir Yassin massacre, this was instrumental to the creation of the Israeli entity. This proves that rather than the Muslims it is the Zionists who are the true international terrorists. This must remove any doubts in the minds regarding the true progenitors of evil. What follows is fully documented by hundreds of eyewitnesses, including Western authorities. As pointed out by Oktar this would never be common knowledge due to the black-out from the Zionist-controlled press:

> On the night of April 9, 1948, the people of Deir Yassin awoke to the order "evacuate the village" coming from loudspeakers. Before they understood what was happening, they had been slaughtered. Subsequent Red Cross and United Nations investigations conducted at the scene showed that houses were first set on fire and that all people trying to escape the flames were shot dead. During the attack pregnant women were bayoneted in their abdomens while still alive. The victims' organs were mutilated, and even children were beaten and raped. Throughout the Deir Yassin massacre, 52 children were maimed under the eyes of their own mothers, and then they were slain and their heads cut off. More than 60 women were killed and their bodies mutilated.

One woman who escaped alive related the following atrocity that she had witnessed:

> "I saw a soldier grabbing my sister, Saliha al-Halabi, who was nine months pregnant. He pointed a machine gun at her neck, then emptied its contents into her body.

Then, he turned into a butcher, and grabbed a knife and ripped open her stomach to take out the slaughtered child with his iniquitous Nazi knife."

Not satisfied with just the massacre, the terrorists then rounded up all the women and girls who remained alive, removed all their clothes, put them in open cars, driving them naked through the streets of the Jewish section of Jerusalem. Jacques Reynier, the Red Cross representative of Palestine at the time, who saw the mutilated bodies during his visit to Deir Yassin the day after the attack, could only say: "The situation was horrible."

Yet, could there be any group more brutal, in fact, wicked, than this? Now, is there any doubt regarding the real source of terror? Who can now proclaim Islaamic terror? Lemi Bremer in his book *The Iron Wall: Zionist Revisionism from Jabotinsky to Shamir* provides a chilling reminder of the extent to which the Zionists act in order to achieve their ends:

During the course of the attack, 280 Muslims, among them women and children, were first paraded through the streets and then shot execution-style. Most of the girls had been raped before their execution, and the boys' genitals had been cut off.

This is an indisputable holocaust. It is confirmed by independent investigators. The fact is these barbaric acts are more diabolical than the worst recorded war crimes. Yet, where are the comparable crimes against humanity committed by Muslims? The fact is there are none. The Israelis prove they are at a minimum as wicked, rather, more so, than the Nazis. Yet, the people of this world are to believe that the attacks by Western/Eastern armies occurring now in Muslim countries, the fighting against the Palestinians,

Iraqis, Chechens, Afghanis, and others, are justified, and now that also an attack on Iran is warranted? Rather, this proposed attack against Iran is the same Zionist colonialist policy, precisely the one used previously, when these perpetrators installed the Shah. The latter, a fulminant mass murderer, was a full-blooded Jew. He was imposed upon the Muslim masses by Western authorities. These are the facts, that is for anyone desiring the truth.

Regarding the United States there is no danger from an Islaamic Iraq or Iran. Rather, these nations would be ideal trading partners. Open dealings with such countries would greatly boost the American economy. Thus, fears of any harm to America from an Islaamic state are baseless. This is fully proven by the historical record. Byng documents that, historically, Islaam spread peacefully. Forced conversions were unknown. The fact is Islaam gave the West its beginning. This was through the creation of the modern sciences, a fact fully documented by modern historians. The danger to the West is only in the unbridled power of the Zionist cartel, which, wickedly, performs vile deed to perpetuate its purposes.

The true terrorists are the criminal Zionist groups which kill without remorse and, rather, do so for raw pleasure, as demonstrated by the following. This is again taken from the work of Odnan Oktar, and it relates to a Zionist attack on worshippers in a mosque:

> On Friday, February 25, 1994 a terrible massacre occurred in Palestine. In an attack carried out by a Zionist Jew on Muslims gathered for Friday prayers at the Ibrahimi Mosque, more than 50 Muslims died and almost 300 were wounded. Some of the wounded later died from their injuries.

> A Jew living in the Kiryat Arba Jewish settlement in Hebron (a former exclusively Palestinian town) perpetrated the massacre. This terrorist also turned out to be a reserve officer in the Israeli army and a member of a Zionist terrorist organization. Israeli sources reported that he wore military clothing during the attack. The attacker sneaked into the mosque and hid behind a column as the Muslims were performing their dawn prayers. As they bowed their heads in unison, he opened fire on them with a machine gun. According to eyewitness accounts he did not act alone: he was simply busy pulling the trigger. As his clips emptied out, his accomplices replaced them.
>
> Following this incident Israeli soldiers surrounded the mosque and prevented reporters from reaching it. Many (additional) people died when these soldiers opened fire on Palestinian Muslims who had gathered around the mosque to protest the attack.

Obviously, it is the Muslims who are the victims of international massacres. In contrast, the Qur'an prohibits the slaughter of the innocent, as did the Prophet Muhammad. Rather than the Muslims it is the Zionist Jews and their fundamentalist Christian lackeys who brazenly kill—in cold blood.

Qana massacre

In 1996 in the full view of the world community the Zionists bombed a refugee camp. In a typically cowardly act defenseless civilians were bombed into oblivion. These people had no means to defend themselves nor anywhere to hide. The were attacked by American-made jets and with American-made bombs. More than 100 people, mostly women and children, were killed. Many were burned alive.

The terrible scenes of carnage, including those of decapitated children, have never been forgotten. A UN inspection team determined that the massacre was deliberate.

Jenin

Here, in a recent (April 2002) genocidal act the entire town was flattened. Hundreds of residents were buried alive in their homes. Anyone who believes this is in response to terrorism or so-called Palestinian militancy is merely succumbing to lies. The Palestinians are no more militant than were the American colonists, in fact, less so. The people in the Jenin *refugee camp* were there precisely due to terrorism, that is they were/are its victims. As a result of their brutal policies the Israelis created this camp. Then, they revisited these refugees with additional torment, brutally attacking them, destroying their buildings, homes, gardens, trees, and lives. They cut down virtually all fruit trees. In contrast, in Israel there is a surplus of trees, thanks largely to the U.S. public.

Only the Zionists are the true militants, the proven insurgents and terrorists. Only they have committed gross violations of human rights. They are the ones who wantonly tortured and murdered the innocent. They even violate the truths of their holy books, a fact predicted within these books themselves. They are criminals in the eyes of God as well as the eyes of men. Thus, they are the worst of all people. Estimates vary, but it is believed that up to 2,000 residents of Jenin were either killed outright or buried alive in their homes.

Americans are largely against this injustice. This is demonstrated by the actions of millions of Americans, such as anti-war activist Cindy Sheehan and the parents of Rachel

Corrie, including Veterans for Peace, the various war veterans opposed to further atrocities, and other kind, decent Americans, who oppose all oppression. According to all monotheistic faiths each person has a duty to his Maker to do good and to be kind, loving, and gracious to the fellow person. The fact is this is Islaam.

The American people are a good and decent people. They readily feel remorse at any crime. As a people they rarely if ever intend harm. This is demonstrated by a telling interview by the journalist Dahr Jamail (dahrjamailiraq.com), who visiting veterans of the latest Iraqi war (slightly paraphrased):

> As the blood of U.S. soldiers continues to drain into the hot sands of Iraq over the last several days with at least 27 U.S. soldiers killed and the approval rating for his handling of the debacle in Iraq dropping to an all-time low (38%), Mr. Bush commented from the comforts of his ranch in Crawford, Texas today, "We will stay the course, we will complete the job in Iraq."
>
> Yet, just a two hour drive away in Dallas, at the Veterans for Peace National Convention in Dallas, I'm sitting with a roomful of veterans from the current quagmire.
>
> When asked what he would say to Mr. Bush if he had the chance, Abdul Henderson, a corporal in the Marines who served in Iraq from March until May, 2003, took a deep breath and said, "It would be two hits, me hitting him and him hitting the floor. I see this guy in the most prestigious office in the world, and this guy says 'bring it on.' A guy who has never been shot at, never seen anyone suffering, saying 'bring it on?' He gets to act like a cowboy in a western movie: it's sickening to me."
>
> The other vets with him nod in agreement as he speaks somberly his anger seething. One of them, Alex Ryabov, a corporal in an artillery unit which was in Iraq

the first three months of the invasion, asked for some time to formulate his response to the same question: "I don't think Bush will ever realize how many millions of lives he and his lackeys have ruined on their quest for money, greed, and power," he says, "To take the patriotism of the American people for granted the fact that people (his administration) are willing to lie and make excuses for you while you continue to kill and maim the youth of America and ruin countless families— still manage to do so with a smile on your face."

Taking a deep breath to steady himself he continues as if addressing Bush first-hand; "You need to resign, take the billions of dollars you've made off the blood and sweat of U.S. service members all the suffering you've caused us, and put those billions into the VA to take care of the men and women you sent to be slaughtered. Yet, all those billions aren't enough to even begin to compensate (for) all the people who have been affected by this."

These new additions to Veterans for Peace are actively living the statement of purpose of the organization, having pledged to work with others towards increasing public awareness of the costs of war, to…restrain their government from intervening, overtly and covertly, in the internal affairs of other nations and to see justice for veterans and victims of war, among other goals.

I type furiously for three hours, trying to keep up with the stories each of the men shared about the atrocities of what they saw—and committed—while in Iraq.

Camilo Mejia, an army staff sergeant who was sentenced to a year in military prison in May 2004 for refusing to return to Iraq after being home on leave, talks openly about what he did there:

"What it all comes down to is redemption for what was done there. I was turning ambulances away from going to hospitals, I killed civilians, I tortured guys and I'm ashamed of that. Once you are there, it has nothing to do with politics it has to do with you as an individual being there and killing people for no reason. There is no purpose, and now I'm sick at myself for doing these things. I kept telling myself I was there for my buddies. It was a weak reasoning because I still shut my mouth and did my job."

Mejia then spoke candidly about why he refused to return:

"It wasn't until I came home that I felt it-how wrong it all was and that I was a coward for pushing my principles aside. I'm trying to buy my way back into heaven and it's not so much what I did, but what I didn't do to stop it when I was there. So now it's a way of trying to undo the evil that we did over there. This is why I'm speaking out, and not going back. This is a painful process and we're going through it.

Mejia was then quick to point towards the success of his organization and his colleagues. "When I went back to Iraq in October of 2003, the Pentagon said there were 22 AWOLs. Five months later it was 500, and when I got out of jail that number was 5,000. These are the Pentagons' numbers for the military. Two things are significant here: the number went from 500-5,000 in 11 months, and these are the numbers from the Pentagon."

While the military is falling short of its recruitment goals across the board and the disaster in Iraq spiraling deeper into chaos with each passing day, these are little consolation for these men who have paid the price they've had to pay to be at this convention. They continue to pay, but at the same time stand firm in their resolve to bring an end to the occupation of Iraq and to help their fellow soldiers.

Ryabov then begins to tell of his unit firing the wrong artillery rounds, which hit 5 to 10 km from their intended target.

"We have no idea where those rounds fell, or what they hit," he says quietly while two of the men hold their heads in their hands, "Now we've come to these realizations and we're trying to educate people to save them from going through the same thing."

Note: Reading between the lines what he is saying is that they know that this killed civilians, and it hurts his heart so greatly that he can't even talk about it.

After talking of the use of uranium munitions, of which Ryabov stated 300 tons of which were used in the '91 Gulf War, and 2,200 tons and counting having been used thus far in the current war. He adds:

"We were put in a foreign country and fire artillery and kill people and it shouldn't have even happened in the first place. It's hard to put into words the full tragedy of it: the death and suffering on both sides. I feel a grave injustice has been done and I'm trying to correct it. You do all these things and come back and think, 'what have we done?' We just rolled right by an Iraqi man with a gunshot in his thigh and two guys near him waving white flags. He probably bled to death."

Harvey Tharp served in Kirkuk. His position of being in charge of some reconstruction projects in northern Iraq allowed him to form many close friendships with Iraqis, something that prompts him to ask me to tell more people of the generous culture of the Iraqi people. His friendships apparently brought the war much closer to home for him.

"What I concluded last summer when I was waiting to transfer to NSA was that not only were our reasons for being there lies, but we just weren't there to help the Iraqis. So in November of '04 I told my commander I couldn't take part in this. I would have been sent into

Fallujah, and he was going to order me in to do my job. I also chose not to go back because the dropping of bombs in urban areas like Fallujah are a violation of the laws of warfare because of the near certainty of collateral damage. For me, seeing the full humanity of Iraqis made me realize I couldn't participate in these operations.

Tharp goes on to say that he believes there are still Vietnam vets who think that that was a necessary war and adds, "I think it's because that keeps the demons at bay for them to believe it is justified this is their coping mechanism. We, as Americans, have to face the total obvious truth that this was all because of a lie. We are speaking out because we have to speak out. We want to help other vets tell other vets their story to keep people from drinking themselves to death."

When he is asked what he would say to Mr. Bush if he had a few moments with him, he too took some time to think about it, then said, "It is obvious that middle America is starting to turn against this war and to turn against you for good reason. The only thing I could see that would arrest this inevitable fall that you deserve is another 9/11 or another war with, say, Iran. There are some very credible indications in the media that we are already in pre-war with Iran. What I'm trying to do is find a stand Americans can take against you, but I think people are willing to say 'don't you dare do this to us again.' My message to the American people is this: do you want to go another round with these people? If not, now is the time to say so."

The men are using this time to tell more of why they are resisting the illegal occupation, and it's difficult to ask new questions as they are adding to what one another share.

"I didn't want to kill another soul for no reason. That's it," adds Henderson, "We were firing into small towns— you see people just running, cars going, guys falling off bikes; it was just sad. You just sit there and look through your binos and see things blowing up, and you think, man they have no water, living in the third world, and we're just bombing them to hell. Blowing up buildings, shrapnel tearing people to shreds."

Tharp jumps in and adds, "Most of what we're talking about is war crimes, war crimes, because they are directed by our government for power projection. My easy answer for not going is PTSD but the deeper moral reason is that I didn't want to be involved in a crime against humanity."

"(Yet), to fire artillery and kill people—and it shouldn't have even happened in the first place. It's hard to put into words the full tragedy of it, the death and suffering on both sides. I feel a grave injustice has been done. And I'm trying to correct it. You do all these things and come back and think, what have we done?"

Michael Hoffman served as a Marine Corps corporal who fought in Tikrit and Baghdad, and has since become a co-founder of Iraq Veterans Against the War. "Nobody wants to kill another person and think it was because of a lie. Nobody wants to think their service was in vain," says Hoffman.

His response to what he would say to Mr. Bush is simple; "I would look him straight in the eye and ask him 'why?' And I would hold him there and make him answer me. He never has to deal with us one on one. I dare him to talk to any of us like that, one on one, and give us an answer." Hoffman then adds, "What about the 3 year old Iraqi girl who is now an orphan with diseases and nightmares for the rest of her life for what we did? And the people who orchestrated this don't have to pay anything. How many times are my children going to have to go through this? Our only choice is to fight this to try to stop it from happening again."

Earlier this same day Mr. Bush said, "We cannot leave this task half finished, we must take it all the way to the end." However, Charlie Anderson, another Iraq veteran, had strong words for Bush. After discussing how the background radiation in Baghdad is now five times the normal rate, the equivalent of having 3 chest x-rays an hour, he said, "These are not accidents—the DU, that is Depleted Uranium—it's important for people to understand this—the use of DU and its effects are by design. These are very carefully engineered and orchestrated incidents."

While the entire group nods in agreement and two other soldiers stand up to shake his hand, Anderson says firmly, "You subverted us, you destroyed our lives, you owe us. I want your resignation in my hand in the next five minutes. Get packin' Georgie."

Dahr Jamail, a credible independent correspondent, specializes in eyewitness accounts. His works are far more credible than the issuances of the White House, Senate, Congress, or media. For more information based on eyewitness accounts visit his Web site, dahrjamailiraq.com.

Compare the love and regret expressed by Americans versus the hate dispersed by the Israelis. The Israeli terrorists murder all who stand in their way. In contrast, the Americans have hearts. Like the Palestinians and Iraqis—like the Chechens, Iranians, Algerians, Egyptians, and Uzbeks—they are victims of Zionist machinations. This is why all must joint together to halt this tyranny, which threatens the sanctity of the human race.

Zionism is materialistic. There is no religious or divine basis for it. Herzl, the original Zionist, said that the purpose of the Jewish entity was strictly materialistic. In other words, the purpose was/is merely economic: the accumulation of wealth and power. The Zionists, he said, wanted a region that would compete in glory with other superpowers. They would, therefore, act as partners with these massive powers to further their aims. One of these aims is the repression of the Muslims. Yet, due to Israeli policies Christians are also repressed—as well as murdered. This is precisely what has happened today: the U.S. uses the Israeli entity to keep Islaam from reviving. What's more, the Israelis use the American military to do its bidding.

Yet, there is no good reason for it. Islaam is non-toxic. For instance, there is no desire by the Muslims to conquer America or Britain. These are sovereign Christian states. The correct Islaamic attitude is, "Let them be." Rather, the Muslims only desire their own inalienable rights: their own peace and justice—their own freedom, which has been persistently and even violently denied to them by the joint partners, Israel, Britain, France, and the United States. So, the great powers conspire to repress Islaam to prevent Muslims from ever gaining independence. Rather than 'terrorism' this is the sole reason that the great powers plan, for instance, to invade Iran. This is because the fact is in this country alone a person can freely practice this faith. In contrast, in all other 'Muslim' countries a true believer in God will be readily compromised—spied upon, attacked, beaten, imprisoned, tortured, and/or killed This is particularly true of anyone who seeks political change.

Endless lies

Regarding the bombings in London consider the degree of bias portrayed by the media. The scope of the lies is made obvious by the following report by David Leppard and John Follain in Rome (The *Times*):

> Intelligence warns of new wave against soft targets.
> A third Islaamist terror cell is planning multiple suicide bomb attacks against Tube trains and other "soft" targets in central London, security sources have revealed.
> Intelligence about a cell with access to explosives and plans to unleash a "third wave" of attacks was the trigger for last Thursday's unprecedented security exercise. The operation saw 6,000 police, many armed, patrolling across London.

How could there be a third Islaamist cell when there wasn't a first or second one? This is said merely to target Islaam as well as to create fear. For certain the second group had nothing to do with Islaam. What's more, why mention that the future 'cell' will have, essentially, military-grade explosives, that is unless this was an attempt to cover for the original bombing, where industrial/military-grade explosives were used, which was unexpectedly leaked to the press.

This revelation called any Islaamic role into dispute: there was no means for the accused Muslims to procure such explosives. This is proof that the Zionist-controlled media merely spreads lies. It does so to uphold the Israeli entity. What's more, it does this maliciously, that is to create fear and hate. Also, no Muslim has ever used the word 'cell.' As documented by Samuel Katz in *Soldier Spies* this is exclusively Israeli terminology.

The Zionists own most of the major media outlets. They steal money from the great powers and use it to buy media corporations. They also purchase security firms. Then, with the press, media, and security in place they fake terror events and even fabricate rescues. This is to make them appear all-powerful.

Regarding 9/11, as well as the original World Trade Center bombing, no Islaamic organizations were involved. Nor were any such organizations behind the London bombings. Rather, in London Islaamic groups attempted to warn British authorities about potential violence. This claim of Islaamic bombers is a raw lie for all to see. This time a Zionist was caught in the act, that is Hamdi (Adus) Isaac. In fact, it was Isaac who stated categorically that "Religion had nothing to do with it." Now the lies of the Times have been categorically confirmed.

Islaam condemns terrorism. However, it does support one powerful kind of fight: that of the people of God against all forms of oppression. This is where the brutes of the world are attacked and defeated by the God-fearing. This is what David did, when he defeated Goliath. What's more, this is what the Davids of the future must do in order to bring this earth into peace and, more importantly, do their duty to their creator.

For the great powers it is never sufficient to target Islaam occasionally. This attack must be continuous, though based upon fraud. They attempt to prevent people from gaining a true understanding of it. Oh how the powers-to-be seek to blame terror on Islaam. In contrast, again, the proven bombers were secular. Their goal was political, and they had no connection with Islaam: period. Rather, they were Islaam's opposites: party-loving, drinking, marijuana-smoking revelers. Furthermore, as any experienced investigator or physician will attest while committing the act several of them were obviously intoxicated.

Was the drug habit, that is the need for cash, the motivation for this crime? This may never be known. Yet, all Western countries are unified in their hate for Islaam, as demonstrated by the words of the Italians:

Italian police say they are using Hussain's (rather, Adus Isaac) phone records to unpick the international network that has been helping him. Alfredo Mantovano, an Interior Ministry official, said that the network "confirms the presence in our country of autonomous Islaamic cells . . . which could represent a concrete threat." Italy is worried that it is the next target for Islaamic terrorists.

Of what Islaamic terrorists or cells do they speak? There are no Muslims in this man's network. Rather, they were all Zionist agents. If the Italians were truly sincere, they would broadcast instead warnings about, for instance, secular, pot-smoking, womanizing, 'Ethiopian,' Mossad, or Israeli terrorists. What's more, this proves the fraudulent nature of the media proclamations, since, incredibly, rather than an autonomous supposedly Islaamic cell this was exclusively a Mossad operative. Has Mossad suddenly become Islaamic?

Everyone knows that the Israelis wantonly commit terror acts: they do so against all civilized people. The Italians focus instead on Islaam, even though it was they who determined that Hamdi Isaac and his associates were masquerading as Muslims and are mere liars. His brother also an Israeli, runs an internet cafe and coffee house, complete with pornographic access, an unlikely front for a God-fearing person. What's more, this cafe is near Rome's Termini train station, a likely focus for espionage operatives. Does anyone doubt, then, that this was a professional job, though, perhaps, bungled and that this dense network is rather than 'angry Muslims over the Iraq war,' instead, the Mossad?

Yet, even so, does anyone ever see in print looming predictions of the next "Zionist terror attack or the existence of hidden Zionist 'cells'?" The fact is what people hear is screened and adulterated through Zionist control. People are purposely misguided to achieve a wicked materialistic agenda.

The scope of this Israeli tyranny is finally proven. The MI6 and/or the Israelis had attempted to assassinate Hamdi Adus Isaac, because the captors of Isaac would prove a direct Zionist role in the bombings. Incredibly, it was the Muslims who warned British authorities of his aggression. He used a fake Muslim name plus false IDs to make himself appear Islaamic. Apparently, he went about with a woman who was covered. Superficially, he appeared 'Islaamic.' This was Mossad's intent. Yet, he is exclusively Jewish with Jewish first, middle, and last names. This is final proof of the Zionist role.

On Geocities.com Jewish geonologists trace a family name of Tevya Adus, also spelled in European languages as Eidus. In contrast, there is no Muslim or Islaamic Eidus or Adus. Another genealogical name is Nigun Hisva'Adus.

Consider the Eidus (Adus) family tree of an entire Jewish lineage: the Eidus (Adus) Jewish lineage of Latvia. Say the family members, "There are many family lines of Eidus descendants around the world…derivative surnames include Adus, Aidus, Aiduss, Edus, Edut, Ejdes, Ekdes, and others…" This site traces the descendants of Arye Eidus and specifically descendants of his grandson Tevel Eidus. One lineage reported is, "I am the great-great grandson of Tevel (aka Tevya) Eidus. Tevya's son Chaim Eidus (later Adus) married Mary (Mire) Ritz from Belarus. Chaim (Hyman) Adus was my great-grandfather. Chaim and Mary had two children, Israel (Isidore) Adus and Slate (Jennie) Adus."

Ancestry.com provides this account of the origin and use of Isaac, the bomber's last name. Under the heading, "What does the name mean?" the editors write:

Jewish, English, Welsh, French, etc.: from the Biblical Hebrew personal name yisha⁻q 'he laughs'. This was the name of the son of Abraham (Genesis 21:3) by his wife Sarah. The traditional explanation of the name is that Abraham and Sarah laughed with joy at the birth of a son to them in their old age, but a more plausible explanation is that the name originally meant 'may God laugh,' i.e. 'smile on him.' Like Abraham, this name has always been immensely popular among Jews...

The Jews regard Issac (or Isaac), son of Abraham, as their patriarch. Thus, they commonly use this as a last name. In contrast, this name is rarely if ever used as a Muslim last name. What's more, there is no use of the word Adus in Muslim names.

People disguised as Muslims create terror acts. This is to portray Islaam as diabolical. It is to tarnish the reputation of the great Prophet of Islaam. It is to turn people away from this way.

The hate generated from the New York and London bombings is misdirected. People were deliberately misled, all to create a false image of Islaam. This has even led to hate crimes. Now, because of such imposters people of color, especially those of brown skins, are under siege. In contrast, there are laws in the Western world against hate crimes. Yet, rather than any Islaamic groups it is the Zionist-controlled media, along with compromised government officials, which is the spreader of hate. This is done to create panic fear, a fear, even rage, which results in oppression of the innocent. These are the lies committed by the powerful ones of the United States, Britain, and Israel, who have as their goal the destruction of anything Islaamic.

A professional job?

The wars against the Muslims arise from Western powers. The Muslims have never provoked them. The entire War on

Terror is, rather, a War for Business. This is proven by the fact that as provocation there were no Islaamic terror acts against Western countries. Muslims live in these countries peacefully and have done so for hundreds of years. This calls into question the entire basis of these wars.

What if the true culprits behind these terror attacks were other than the Muslims? Would, then, such culprits be attacked with at least equal force, and, then, the attacks against the innocent, in fact, wrongly blamed Muslims, halted?

Regarding the London bombings there is further evidence which disputes an Islaamic connection. Consider the observations of Christopher Chaboud, head of the French Anti-Terrorism Co-ordination Unit. As reported in *Le Monde* newspaper the explosives used in the bombings, confirmed Chaboud, were of military origin. Chaboud was new in the French service and he didn't realize Western protocol, that is not to reveal the facts to the public. He added that the victims' wounds suggested that the explosives, which were "not heavy but powerful," had been placed on the ground, perhaps underneath seats. Here, it is important to note that the video recording of people toting rucksacks is hardly proof of bombers. Chaboud said the bombs weren't heavy. Therefore, there was no need for such baggage.

Military origin means that the person(s) who made these bombs had to have military access. Surely, this wasn't young Muslims. These various Muslims, community workers and school teachers, college students and similar individuals, had no means to procure them. Nor did they have any history of handling explosives. Chaboud noted that he was *certain* regarding the type of explosives used and that the only way to get them was "*out of a military base*." This rules out the accused Muslims as bombers. They may have died in this disaster, but they were not the bombers. UPI News confirms the nature of these explosives. Reported the news wire:

> Traces of the explosive known as C4 were found at all four blast sites…C4 is manufactured mostly in the United States and is more deadly and efficient than commercial varieties. It is easy to hide, stable, and is often missed by traditional bomb-sniffing detection systems, the newspaper said.

If these bombs are easy to hide, why would anyone need a conspicuous rucksack? What's more, isn't a rucksack combined with long-term parking a sign of a number of possibilities, for instance, a prolonged summer outing? These young men told their parents they were going on an outing with their friends. Even so, rather than any need for a large and conspicuous backpack, a smaller sized tote would be ideal for transporting inconspicuously, that is a military-grade bomb, in order to avoid arousing suspicion. Even so, these bombs were planted underneath seats or, more likely, beneath the carriages. The latter is precisely the finding of eyewitnesses.

The traces of C4 are evidence against subsequent reports that these were home-made explosives. In other words, the existence of C4 rules out amateurs. Furthermore, it was reported:

> Forensic scientists told the newspaper the construction of the four devices detonated in London was very technically advanced and unlike any instructions that can be found on the internet.

The fact is to be so well synchronized these would have to be of such sophistication. They would have to be 'professional' devices to blast raw metal in every direction, ripping to shreds a well-built carriage and a bus, vehicles capable of sustaining major crashes. Only military-grade explosives could have caused such destruction. The same is true of the World Trade Center, the Madrid train bombings, and Bali.

Since this revelation there has been a vast cover-up. The media said that these were not military explosives, demonstrating the fear that this revelation will prove the source: a government operative to target Muslims. The revelation by French experts may well be the provocation for the second series of (attempted) bombings. These bombings were used as a kind of 'proof' that these were man-made bombs that any amateur could create.

Regarding the targeting of public transport the use of small or light weight bombs makes sense. There are potentially many witnesses. To be conspicuous would be a mistake. Therefore such bombs were hidden to avoid alerting suspicion, so the mission could be carried out 'flawlessly.' This would explain injuries such as those suffered by the American, Emily Benton of Tennessee. She suffered broken bones in her feet, and skin was blown off *the bottom of her feet.* In other words, the force of the explosion came from underneath. This is direct evidence against a rucksack bomb. It is also proof against a suicide bomber. As reported in the London media "Her feet were badly injured...," indicating that the explosion arose from beneath the carriage. Again, this negates the rucksack theory. Thus, the criminals who committed this act actually planted the bombs under the carriages.

In New York City on September 11th, 2001, while the Muslims were held responsible only Israelis were arrested due to suspicious activity. Only they were caught with incriminating evidence. Also, in London the Muslims are held culpable, even though, again, only the Israelis had advance knowledge of this disaster. Not a single Muslim in England knew about it. What's more, of all the accused, the only person who has confessed to the crime is Jewish. He alone has admitted bombing a subway carriage. According to the *New Zealand Herald*:

> It emerged yesterday that Osman's real name is Hamdi Isaac and that he had also changed his country of birth from Ethiopia to Somalia when he moved from Italy to England...

Ethiopia is largely Judeo-Christian. In contrast, Somalia is exclusively Muslim. Isaac was a paid Israeli spy. His job was to create strife in Islaamic communities. To do so he was given by the Israelis money and false IDs, all through the Israeli entity. The only reason for this was to attack and denigrate Muslims. What's more, in England this was precisely his history.

When Italian judges interrogated Isaac and his brothers— a true Zionist cell—they determined that the latter broke the law by forging documents. The two Ethiopians were initially charged with using false passports, while the Muslim imposter Isaac was also charged with "membership of an *international terrorist group.*"

That international terror organization is the Mossad. This was the organization responsible for the dense terror network that effectively hid Isaac temporarily from police, while destroying incriminating documents.

Those adorable eyes can be misleading. This is demonstrated by this report from the *UK News*, August 7th, 2005. It regards a prominent trustee at a London mosque, who offers an insider account of the true nature of Adus Isaac:

A moderate Muslim leader today told how police chiefs failed to deal with a gang of fanatics, which included one of the 21/7 London bomb suspects, who tried to take over his local mosque.

The father-of-five claims the mob, which included Shepherd's Bush terror suspect Osman Hussain (in fact, Adus Isaac) who was arrested last week in Rome, forced him and his family into hiding two years before last month's failed attacks.

Toaha Qureshi, 46, a trustee at Stockwell Mosque, south London, says he wrote to senior detectives detailing how Hussain (that is the Zionist Adus Isaac) had threatened him and was inciting racial and religious hatred in the community.

"Weeks after the letter, they helped us install CCTV (that is closed circuit) cameras close to the entrance of the mosque, but after that their hands were tied and they could do nothing to stop the gang," says Mr. Qureshi.

"It is frightening. Even though they knew who they were they could do nothing because their hands were tied under the existing legislation—now it seems other members of the gang have simply disappeared."

On one occasion in 2003 the mosque's caretaker had to be taken to hospital after his tooth was knocked out by a fanatic. He punched him when he refused to allow the gang to take over the mosque, because they felt the leaders were too moderate.

During another confrontation at the mosque, Hussain allegedly pointed at Mr. Qureshi's teenage son who was standing nearby and ran a finger across his throat.

"At the time I was trying to engage the wider community because I felt we had to work to foster better relations—Hussain (Adus Isaac) and his gang did not want any outsiders coming into the mosque because they felt they did not belong there (an interesting attitude for a man who freely made love with Western ladies).

"They were quite clearly threatening me and my family. I was extremely worried and contacted the police about this incident, and we had to go into hiding until the matter had died down."

Detailed information about the activities of Hussain and nine other fanatics, including the former's wife, were recorded and passed to the police in a hand-delivered letter to Supt Malvcolm Tillyer, deputy borough commander at the time.

The letter read: "We believe this group is trying to undermine the moderate approach of the centre's management, imams and community and that they have an agenda to turn this centre into another Finsbury Park Mosque. That is to say, an Islaamic centre where extremist views can be expounded.

"While we recognize we have a prime duty to deal with internal problems in-house, we believe problems have now reached a level where police help is urgently needed."

"We kept a note of what they had done and who they were and sent that to the police asking for their help," added Mr. Qureshi.

Undermine, indeed, yet this wasn't by those who were most publicized, that is so-called extremist Muslims. Rather, the perpetrator was an undercover Zionist spy. He was specifically paid to incite this violence. Yet, if the British truly have such a 'civilized' and 'tolerant' system, then, why didn't they take action against this man, who was a known threat to the innocent?

Even so, the fact is to report a parishioner to the authorities would be highly rare for any clergyman, especially a disadvantaged group such as the Muslims. This demonstrates the degree of desperation at the mosque. As proof that mosques and other Muslim organizations, in fact, the entire realm of Islaam, is/are often infiltrated with Zionist elements, the following report from Indian investigators is compelling:

> On January 12 Indian intelligence officials in Calcutta detained 11 foreign nationals for interrogation before they were to board a Dhaka-bound Bangladesh Biman flight. They were detained on the suspicion of being hijackers. "But we realized that they were tabliqis (Islaamic preachers), so we let them go, said an Intelligence official."
>
> The eleven had Israeli passports but were believed to be Afghan nationals who had spent a while in Iran. Indian intelligence officials, too, were surprised by the nationality profile of the eleven. "They say that they have been on tabligh (preaching Islaam) in India for two months. But they are Israeli nationals from the West Bank," said a Central Intelligence official.
>
> He claimed that Tel Aviv "exerted considerable pressure" on Delhi to secure their release. "It appeared that they could be working for a sensitive organization in Israel and were on a mission to Bangladesh (note Bangladesh is nearly 100% Muslim)," the official said."

Yet, they were detained because Indian authorities thought they were hijackers. Why is it so important for these Zionists to falsify their identities as Muslims? The fact is these are true infiltrators, rather, spies, who had already infiltrated at least two Muslim areas, the West Bank and Bangladesh. Thus, it would be no surprise that, dressed and named as Muslims, their purpose was vile. This demonstrates that the Zionists use Israel as the headquarters for international terrorism. They also use the so-called occupied territories for this purpose.

This is terror fully funded by the U. S. government. They may well have been planning a new terror event, to be, not surprisingly, blamed upon Pakistani, perhaps, Iranian, Muslims. Thus, the call by Muslims for the disintegration of this entity is justified, since it is the headquarters of international terror.

This is a criminal Zionist enterprise that all civilized people must resist. Clearly, this impersonating of Muslims to create terror is a crime against humanity, true fraud.

Islaam is against all forms of corruption, including deceit. In this grand faith the torture and slaughter of the innocent is prohibited. Intimidation and harassment is also banned. The tormenting of the fellow man, that is forcing prisoners or other individuals into the most embarrassing, compromising postures and parading them about naked— merely to degrade them—this is exclusively a Western, in fact, Israeli, phenomenon. There is no place for such acts in the Islaamic system.

As proven by Israeli historians it is the Zionists who invented such horrors. Yet, while Islaam stands accused it is revealing to demonstrate the Western system's method for dealing with the common man. This article is excerpted from the English newspaper *The Guardian*, August 4th, 2005:

> Mr. Belay, 52, an Ethiopian refugee who has lived in London for 12 years, believes he is lucky to be alive. Hours before his arrest at a friend's flat, armed police had mistakenly shot dead Jean Charles de Menezes, less than a mile away at Stockwell tube station. It was the day after

the July 21 attacks and tensions were high. "I was just sitting at the table," Mr. Belay told the Guardian. "I heard this shouting, a lot of shouting and the words 'Get in, get out, get in.' "There were lots of them. They shouted at me to stand up, then lie on the floor face down. The laser was on me, then I am in the corridor and they tell me to take off my trousers. I said, 'Yes sir, yes sir.' Then they told me to take off my jacket and my shoes and then my underpants. I was standing there stripped naked. I was completely naked, and then one guy, I will never forget him, he was not in uniform, he started punching me. I was held against the wall; I was naked, I kept asking, 'Why is he hitting me?' and he said 'shut-up' and punched me again. He punched and kicked me like he was a boxer training on his bag. Then, someone intervened and the punching stopped. "They asked my name, they asked my religion. I told them I was a Christian but I have stopped believing. They put my hands and feet in plastic bags and put me in a white suit. They put me in the back of a car. I was angry and that's when the tears started."

Detained under Terrorism Act 2000; released after 6 days. *The Guardian* reports, 'Mr. Belay understands police are doing a difficult job, but he wants a personal apology from the officer who beat him'

The Western rulership is the progenitor of this racism. The fact is it promotes an agenda of hate, even to the degree of inciting violence, even warfare. Consider the following article written, incredibly, the morning of the London bombings. In this there are numerous hidden agendas. The call if for global violence against a people. As reported by Kevin Sullivan of the Washington Post Foreign Service, August 4, 2005, the following was written by an ex-Mossad director, Efraim Halevy. Halevy heads the Center for Strategic and Policy Studies at the Hebrew University in Jerusalem:

> Multiple, simultaneous explosions that took place today on the London transportation system were the work of perpetrators who had an operational capacity of considerable scope. They have come a long way since the two attacks of the year 1998 against the American embassies in Nairobi and Dar-Es-Salaam and the aircraft actions of September 11, 2001.

The man speaks lies. Even the FBI admits that the Muslims did not strike the World Trade Center. Thus, this Mossad agent is purposely sowing strife, rather, terror. This is to create hate against Islaam. Halevy continues:

> (There was a) sophisticated choice of timing as well as near-perfect execution. We are faced with a deadly and determined adversary who will stop at nothing and will persevere as long as he exists as a fighting terrorist force.

The writer continues by extolling the history of the Zionist empire:

> One historical irony: I doubt whether the planners knew that one of the target areas, that in Russell Square, was within a stone's throw of a building that served as the first headquarters of the World Zionist Organization that preceded the State of Israel.
>
> It was at 77 Great Russell Street that Dr. Chaim Weizmann, a renowned chemist, presided over the effort that culminated in the issuing of the Balfour Declaration, the first international recognition of the right of the Jewish people to a national home in what was then still a part of the Ottoman Empire.

We are in the throes of a world war, raging over the entire globe and characterized by the absence of lines of conflict and an easily identifiable enemy.

He continues to portray the Muslims as the bloodthirsty element which people must always be on guard against:

The populations at large are not involved in the conflict and play the role of bystanders. But once in a while, these innocents are caught up in the maelstrom and suffer the most cruel and wicked of punishments meted out by those who are not bound by any rules of conduct or any norms of structured society. For a while, too short a while, we are engrossed with the sheer horror of what we see and hear, but, with the passage of time, our memories fade, forgetting that the war is still raging out there and more strikes are sure to follow.

It cannot be said that seven years after this war broke out in East Africa, we can see its conclusion. We are in for the long haul and we must brace ourselves for more that will follow. The 'Great Wars' of the 20th century lasted less than this war has already lasted, and the end is nowhere in sight.

There will be supreme tests of leadership in this unique situation and people will have to trust the wisdom and good judgment of those chosen to govern them. The executives must be empowered to act resolutely and to take every measure necessary to protect the citizens of their country and to carry the combat into whatever territory the perpetrators and their temporal and spiritual leaders are inhabiting.

The rules of combat must be rapidly adjusted to cater to the necessities of this new and unprecedented situation, and international law must be rewritten in such a way as to permit civilization to defend itself. Anything short of this invites disaster and must not be allowed to happen.

The aim of the enemy is not to defeat Western civilization but to destroy its sources of power and existence, and to render it a relic of the past. It does not seek a territorial victory or a regime change; it wants to turn Western civilization into history and will stop at nothing less than that.

Then, the devious nature of his plot is made clear with:

...the only way to ensure our safety and security will be to obtain the destruction, the complete destruction, of the enemy—(and) while then proclaiming each and every country... "declare itself at war with international Islaamist terror and recruit the public to involve itself actively in the battle...

Yet, on what basis does he call for this slaughter? Is it the bombings of 9/11 and the London carriages/bus? Is it the micronuclear device blown at Bali? Proof of an Islaamic plot in these acts is non-existent. Rather, it is only the Israeli involvement—as well as foreknowledge—which is fully documented. Thus, the entire basis of Halevy's statements is debunked. If anyone must be fought, it is the real culprits: Zionist thugs. He continues his hate campaign with the following, essentially promoting the Nazification of the world:

In the past, governments have been expected to provide security to their citizens. The responsibility is still there, in principle. But in practice, no government today can provide an effective 'suit of protection' for the ordinary citizen. There can be no protection for every bus, every train, every street, every square. In these times the ordinary citizen must be vigilant and must make his personal contribution to the war effort.

The measures that I have outlined above will not be easily adopted overnight. When the U.S. entered World War II, Congress approved the momentous decision by a majority of one vote. Profound cultural changes will have to come about and the democratic way of life will be hard-pressed to produce solutions that will enable the executive branch to perform its duties and, at the same time, to preserve the basic tenets of our democratic way of life.

The fact is Halevy calls for martial law and, essentially, the destruction of the U.S. constitution. He concludes:

...this war is already one of the longest in modern times; as things appear now, it is destined to be part of our daily lives for many years to come, until the enemy is eliminated, as it surely will be.

This man is calling for a Third World War. This is on the basis of terror acts that his own organization has committed. Thus, if any enemy must be eliminated, it must be he and his war-mongering cohorts, because it is the likes of Halevy who are responsible for the incitement to terror. The fact is rather than any Muslim or Islaamic group it was Halevy who knew well in advance about the London bombings as well as 9/11. *Only the Israelis had advance knowledge.* Regarding 9/11 they knew in advance several months before the crime. They had demanded that an internal terror act was necessary to gain U.S. support for their Middle Eastern wars. Thus, the fact is such wars, as well as the acts of terror used to justify them, are strictly Zionist creations.

While the Israelis knew in advance about 9/11 and the London bombings they told no one. For instance, in 9/11 only the Israelis escaped; all Israeli nationals had advance knowledge. Zim Moving, an exclusively Israeli company located in the towers, had several weeks previously vacated its offices. This means that the Israeli government was fully aware of the impending catastrophe. It also means that the Israelis are culpable. According to the government in its trial against Zacharias Moussaoui this is precisely its argument for the death penalty. It is that forenowledge of a criminal act and the failure to disclose it is punishable as a crime, even with death. Then, if this same criteria were upheld top Israeli officials must be prosecuted for imprisonment, even execution. The entire government case was the accusation of foreknowledge which, of course, in Moussaoui's case was untrue. Yet, this is not the case with the Israelis. They knew the towers would be destroyed. Then, at a minimum they are guilty of complicity, since they only warned fellow Israelis, letting all others brutally die. The fact is they even reveled in the crime.

Furthermore, in the London bombings no Israelis were killed. Only Christians, Muslims, and various foreign nationals died. In contrast, for instance, it was a Muslim agency, which specifically warned the British police about one of the culprits, Adus Isaac. Muslim authorities reported him as dangerous and violent. To reiterate, incredibly, only the Muslims gave warning in an attempt to prevent violence, while the Israelis held back. Rather, the latter disguised it from all others, that is except fellow Israelis. This is a crime, fully punishable in Western Society.

It was Halvey's associates, various Israeli firms, which are responsible for security in the London tube. Such individuals control the operations of all closed circuit TV images. It is well known that they have previously faked terror acts, even faking news articles, videos, and TV images.

The fact is the only way Halevy could know about this crime was if he was the progenitor. What's more, the Israelis have criminal intent if for no other reason than the fact that they withheld lifesaving information.

The fact is the Zionists would provoke a world war. The Jews hold virtually all the gold reserves, so strife is to their benefit, since this raises the price of this commodity. Plus, they are major beneficiaries in the dealing of armaments; a bankrupt Zionist cabal would purposely provoke a global war to regain financial power. Compare the words of Halevy to the innocence of eyewitness accounts, people who have no such vested interests. Directly from the streets of England, the following were circulated as e-mails:

> Hi everyone:
>
> Did anyone traveling before the attacks began yesterday notice anything peculiar on their tube journey?
> I catch the Piccadilly line at 7:15 a.m. each morning from Southgate to reach my work in Kensington by 8:00. Normally, all seats are taken by Finsbury Park and carriages are packed by Kings Cross.
> However, yesterday my tube journey was eerily quiet. For the first time ever there were spare seats in my carriage all the way through Zone 1. It was noticeable enough for me to wonder what on earth was going on. This was at 7.45—over an hour before attacks began.
> I've also heard people saying that the Northern Line was being shut down at the same time
> Is there something that we're not being told?

Another member responds:

> yes!
> I was due to pick a work colleague up from Balham at 7:15 am, but when I got there, I was greeted with

Tube emergency vans, police and hoards of people being turned away from a closed station.

All very strange: they must have known something was going to happen; they surely had a tip off. As I drove along the road (which also follows the tubes) they were all shut, and hundreds of people were queuing for buses.

When I reached Oval, which was open, there were two armed policemen in a road next to the station, which for a quiet area like that is extremely rare.

The Northern Line was shut from Morden to Stockwell. They blatantly knew something was going down, they just got it wrong and are hoping no one mentions anything.

This was all at 7:15, nearly two hours before the bombs were detonated. Someone had 'informed' the British about the bomb threat. There are several issues which eliminate any possibility of a coincidence. Days prior to these bombings there were bomb scares in different major cities. Then, there was evidence of advanced knowledge by the Israelis, including the article written *several days prior to the attack* by a former Mossad chief. For the global powers it is also incriminating that they were conducting "terrorist bombing exercises" some four days prior to the bombings and in *exactly the same sites as the bombings.* This proves that the Muslims could not have been the perpetrators.

Can anyone explain how, coincidentally, the Muslims would have bombed these regions, including their own suburb, in the precise area of a terror training exercise? Finally, there was the use of exclusively high grade military explosives, which exploded synchronously, "boom, boom, boom." Yet, who controls access to the military? Surely, it isn't the Muslims. Also, they don't have the technology to achieve it. Nor did they have the necessary material goods.

All these accounts demonstrate that this was a government-sponsored attack. Furthermore, there is no possibility that the simulations in the tube could have been virtually simultaneous with a random Muslim act.

Even so, there is evidence of a more compelling nature which also refutes the official story. As mentioned previously it is the time line for the accused Muslims. This timeline proves that an Islaamic attack was impossible. Officially, it is said that these Muslims departed from Lutton, a town north of London, at about 7:40 a.m. Then, they were supposedly filmed at 8:26 in London at a tube (subway) station. Yet, incredibly, the 7:40 train from Lutton was canceled. There was a 7:48 train, but this was 10 minutes late.

In a monumental revelation this train arrived a full twenty-three minutes late. Thus, it arrived at 8:43. This was the only train that the accused could have caught. The implications are chilling. It means that the video was fabricated. Yet, since the Pentagon-issued bin Laden video, as well as the 9/11 video of al-Omari, have also been proven fraudulent this would be no surprise. Then, why would anyone believe the issuances of this entity: its entire basis is to promote warfare.

Thus, even though the police and major newspapers, the latter including the London *Times*, reported that these men arrived on the 7:40 train this was impossible. The 7:40 train was cancelled. Then, it could be speculated that they took an earlier train and the police didn't know this. However, the only other train was the 7:24, and for them this was impossible to catch. These men were supposedly taped as merely entering the outside of the station at 7:22. Everyone knows to get in cue, procure tickets, and make it to the train would take at least several minutes. Plus, as filmed, they were walking casually.

So, how could they have been filmed entering the King's Cross tube station at 8:26? It was impossible for them to have been there at that time. Thus, like the 19 fabricated hijackers of 9/11 these men were mere patsies for a globalist operation, which serves a diabolical agenda. It was a kind of decoy operation conceived at the highest governmental levels. The primary perpetrators are the Israeli secret services. At a minimum the Israelis were fully aware of it, since they control the entire security apparatus.

There was no possibility that these men could have made it to London in time to commit the bombings. This is directly supported by eyewitness testimony. These eyewitnesses prove that these men, particularly, Shehzad Tanweer and Sidique Khan, were not on the carriages as reported. This coincides with the fabricated time line. These men were simply not on the carriages to either blow it up or kill themselves. Relative at least to Khan and Tanweer it is all lies.

Yet, even with all this suspicious activity and cover-up who also gets immediately blamed? It is an intellectual Muslim. He is blamed, so that this would appear to be an Islaamic conspiracy. This is another example of how the innocent are viscously attacked. This is in regards to the highly refined and intelligent Saudi exile, Saad al-Fagih, Ph.D. He was immediately and wrongly blamed as a perpetrator. This was again done to seed hate against the Muslims, which is further proof of a plot. The media created stories about him, none of it true:

> The claim was posted on a website run by a London based Iraqi-born doctor, Saad al-Fagih, from a house in Wimbledon, south-west London. Dr al-Fagih, head of an organization called Movement for Islaamic Reform in Arabia, had his assets frozen in December by the Bank of

England after the U.S. treasury claimed his website had been used to send clandestine messages to al-Qa'ida affiliated groups.

U.S. prosecutors also claimed that Al-Fagih had provided a satellite telephone for Osama bin Laden to help co-ordinate attacks on the U.S. embassies in Kenya and Tanzania. On 21 December last year the U.S. classified Dr al-Fagih as a specially designated global terrorist.

Dr al-Fagih yesterday said his Website was "in no way connected" with al-Qa'ida. He added that his daughter was traveling on the Tube to Aldgate at the time of the bombings.

All this is based upon lies. Who are these U. S. prosecutors who make these "claims?" No one bothered to investigate who posted it. It is merely that the Zionists are attempting to crush him due, incredibly, to his outspoken views against the Saudi regime. Yet, it became obvious that he had nothing to do with it. The fact is his daughter was riding on the tube at the time. "She was going to work…" he said. "Would I really let my child travel on a train if I was behind the explosion?" Al-Fagih simply spoke the truth. Quickly, charges against were dismissed. Even so, once blamed the guilt is established regardless of the truth. This tactic effectively destroys a person's credibility. In fact, it is used as a tactic to distract people from the real culprits. Yet, who disseminated these charges against him to the media? This would lead directly to the culprits.

In contrast, Bush and Blair are proven liars. Their lies are common knowledge. Then, why would anyone even remotely believe anything they say? Bush and Blair based the invasions of entire nations on mere lies. Their minions purposely fabricated intelligence to facilitate support for the criminal wars. This is the truth that the entire world realizes. Yet, they did this exclusively to serve their Israeli masters.

The official line is laced with lies. Analysts are disturbed at the scope of the disinformation. Many of these investigators fear for their safety and wish to remain anonymous. One such investigator has wisely observed the following (note: some of the wording has been upgraded for easier reading):

> Of all the coverage of the London bombings, it is extremely upsetting to me, but not surprising, that one detail is being left out of every mainstream media article: *Visor Consultants*. On July 7th, 2005, four days prior to the bombing, this security firm was conducting a "terror drill" in the London Underground at the exact same time in the exact same locations that the actual bombs went off. Just after the bombings on BBC Radio and ITV News Visor's Managing Director, Peter Power, discussed this amazing coincidence. This…is made even more eerie due to the fact, reported by the Associated Press, that U.S. government intelligence agencies were conducting drills that featured planes crashing into buildings at 8:30 on the morning of September 11, 2001." He further notes that despite this stream of facts the "mainstream media (are)…eager to pin the attacks on Al Qaeda and Islaamic extremists almost immediately, even before any real evidence was discovered."

This is no coincidence. Rather, it is a deliberate and wicked plot by Western governments. The goal is the complete conquest of Islaamic lands.

CHAPTER 10
9/11 and the Real Terrorists

The statement that the Muslims attacked the United States is a lie. Even the FBI knows this. The following section proves that rather than the Muslims there were other people responsible for the attack. These perpetrators operated largely internally.

Here, the focus is on the 19 men accused of destroying the World Trade Center. Of course, this attack resulted in thousands of deaths and injuries. Furthermore, people are continuously becoming sickened due to residual damage from this crime. Yet, while the Muslims are blamed they were never involved.

The image of the accused Muslim hijackers will forever be imprinted upon the minds of Americans. Thus, it is important that Americans, as well as people globally, clearly realize the true culprits. What's more, it is critical to bring this issue to closure by finding the perpetrators and bringing them to justice. This is the normal and expected course of action, dictated to humans ages ago, for instance, in the ancient scriptures. It is the means of justice. Yet, it is the way of any just civilization.

No crime of such a magnitude must go unanswered. To falsely attribute it to others is itself a crime. This is precisely the crime committed by the Zionist entity.

The 9/11 disaster is the greatest crime ever committed on American soil. What follows is a critical analysis of the accused to determine any culpability. First, the accused must either be proven or excluded as the culprits before any further investigation can be performed.

After the disaster the Muslims stood accused. Supposedly, these Muslims attacked the West because they hate it. They struck America, because of what it stands for. No one bothered to investigate the accusations to determine if they are true. Rather, it was merely proclaimed so in the media. Also, the FBI listed the Muslims as the culprits—19 of them, along with bin Laden. People presume that this is the case because the government, as well as media, proclaim it. Yet, most people have never independently verified these claims. What's more, for many Americans the dictates of the government are to be trusted—without question. The FBI, a respected American authority, said the Muslims did it, and the vast majority of the public accepts this. Without facts, a judgement was made. What follows is a thorough analysis of each of the accused Muslims. The purpose is to determine if these men really attacked America.

The conclusion is that the Muslims did not strike America. This is confirmed by the latest research by top American scholars. For instance, Brigham Young University's Steven Jones, Ph.D., published a report demonstrating the official story as fraudulent. His conclusion was that there was no Islaamic attack on New York City. Rather, he demonstrated that the buildings were brought down by explosives. He even concluded that the charges were pre-set. Thus, said the professor, rather than the planes themselves it was bombs which ultimately destroyed the buildings. This statement is supported by other evidence such as the fact that FEMA had already set up a crisis site the night previously. Jones is a Brigham Young University physics professor and expert in passive fire protection systems. Now, this man has been muzzled by the federal government, which threatened his university with sanctions. Regarding 9/11 the official story is fraudulent. Even so, it is appropriate to analyze this to determine if the Muslims have culpability. The various Muslims accused of destroying American landmarks are as follows.

The supposed hijacking of American Airlines 77

The first five men listed as follows were accused of hijacking American Airlines 77, which supposedly hit the Pentagon. The accused Muslims are described as follows:

#1 Khalid al-Midhar

The FBI said that this man was a hijacker and that he may have lived in Los Angeles as well as New York City. To this day he is criminally referred in the press as a hijacker. Yet, as reported by a number of Middle Eastern newspapers *he is alive.*

Apparently, al-Midhar is a victim of identity theft. He had nothing to do with 9/11 and has never committed a crime. He is a rather mild mannered individual. Any careful review of his nature and physique reveals that he is a poor candidate for a hijacking. Yet, in the minds of many Americans his crime is sealed, since he was/is irresponsibly portrayed in the media, for instance, the *Washington Post*, as a 'terrorist and hijacker.' These are mere lies.

However, al-Midhar apparently lived for a time in San Diego. Early in 2001 he and another Muslim or, perhaps, men using their identities visited Montgomery Field, a community airport. They spoke to instructors at Sorbi's Flying Club. There, along with friend and fellow accused Muslim Nawaq al-Hamzi, he attempted to learn how to fly.

This is presented as evidence of a plot. Yet, there are tens of thousands of Middle Eastern men who learn to fly every year, because the schooling in America is premier. Here is what his instructor said about furthering their flight training:

> ...after only two lessons they advised them to quit. "Their English was horrible, and their mechanical skills were even worse," said an instructor... "It was like they had hardly even ever driven a car." "They seemed like nice guys," the instructor said, "but in the plane, they were dumb and dumber."

Yet, it does appear that these men were truly there. Eyewitnesses, in fact, friends roomed with them and confirmed their presence. Even so, it is of no consequence. Al-Midhar is alive and well. Thus, he was not a 9/11 hijacker. People in the media can say what they will. Yet, the fact is this man was simply not there.

All derogatory statements about him are lies. Yet, the statements have been continuously repeated in the media. The fact is during 9/11 he was not even in the United States.

There is another crucial issue, which may explain the use of this man's name. When he was in the United States (2000), he rented a room from a man he thought was a fellow Muslim. Instead, he was an FBI informant masquerading as a Muslim. As reported by *CBS News* this undercover agent helped open a bank account for al-Midhar and even prayed with him. This could explain the theft of his ID.

2 Majed Moqed

It is difficult to find any information about this man. Most of what is available is from the government posting. A Saudi national, he is apparently from a wealthy Saudi family.

No one knows Moqed's status. Friends say that he and his father went to Afghanistan to join the fighting there. Again, this is of little consequence. In 2001 Moqed is not listed as entering the United States. The jet he supposedly hijacked reportedly struck the Pentagon. However, no remains of this man were found there. Nor were any remains of a jet found there. What's more, there is no evidence that this man boarded any flight in the United States on that day. Nor is there any proof that he was even in this country at that time.

Moqed most likely died in warfare in Afghanistan. There, his ID was confiscated. Thus, he was not involved in the 9/11 atrocity. What's more, as documented by detailed reports of flight instructors this man had no capacity to fly a commercial jet. Since there is no evidence that during 9/11 this man was in the United States or had boarded any jetliners, this rules him out as a hijacker.

3 Nawaf al-Hamzi

Official information regarding this man is scanty. He or, perhaps, someone using his identity, is listed as living possibly in Fort Lee, New Jersey, Wayne, New Jersey, and/or Los Angeles.

The government says this man helped commandeer Flight 77, crashing it into the Pentagon, for instance, calling him "The terrorist." People have been led to believe through media reports that he, along with Hani Hanjour, overpowered the entire flight crew, and, then, successfully flew the plane.

Yet, pictures show the man as frail. He could easily be overpowered by the martial arts-capable flight attendants and pilots. What's more, no one can explain how completely inexperienced pilots could, in fact, successfully fly such a complicated jet, let alone perfectly strike the planned target.

His purported guilt was based entirely on vague information, for instance, that he may have undergone flight training (or perhaps someone using his name did so). Yet, there is no evidence that al-Hamzi boarded this flight. Nor is there any evidence that he was even at the airport at the time. Nor is there any proof that he could fly such a plane.

Yet, all this is irrelevant. This is because the plane didn't even hit the Pentagon.

With a major airplane crash there is always wreckage. At the Pentagon there was no such wreckage, that is from a Boeing 757. This means that there was no plane crash. It also means that the official story is a lie.

There were no jetliner engines found in the Pentagon crash site. Nor was there any baggage. Nor were there any parts to wings. Seats and cushions were essentially non-existent.

It is repeatedly mentioned that al-Hamzi, as well as Hanjour, purchased tickets for Flight 77. Yet, there is not a single eyewitness who recalls seeing them nor are there any video images. What's more, according to the official registry posted on the CNN Web site neither of these men were on the flight. Thus, al-Hamzi has been falsely accused of the commission of a terror act.

Al-Hamzi had no ability to commandeer and fly a 757. Although his whereabouts are unknown it is implausible that he was a perpetrator of the 9/11 crimes. What's more, he had no history of violent acts of any kind. Rather, he was known as both frail and docile. Like al-Midhar he was directly under the scrutiny of an FBI informant, who had 'infiltrated' his life disguised as a Muslim.

4 Salem al-Hamzi

This person is described by the FBI as living possibly in Fort Lee, New Jersey and/or Wayne, New Jersey. He was also infamously described as one of the Muslims who worked out in Gold's Gym in Greenbelt, Maryland in the weeks prior to the hijacking. The implication was that he was performing strength training for the the brutal acts which were attributed to him on the jetliner. The dilemma is that the real Salem al-Hamzi had never been in the Greenbelt area gym, nor for that matter had he ever been in Maryland.

The media is criminally responsible for these lies. This is libel. Al-Hamzi wasn't even in the United States at the time. He too is alive. He is a worker at a petrochemical plant in Yanbou, Saudi Arabia. It is interesting to note that Maryland houses a great number of espionage agencies. This explains the Greenbelt, Maryland connection.

Dozens of eyewitnesses report the fraud regarding the news reports. This man, accused of hijacking Flight 77 and killing Americans—striking an American symbol of power, the Pentagon—wasn't even in the United States at the time. What's more, he never trained in Gold's Gym. The *Orlando Sentinel* confirms according to the Saudi Consulate that al-Hamzi is "not dead and had nothing to do with the heinous terror attacks in New York and Washington."

Al-Hamzi lives happily in his native country of Saudi Arabia. There is no way he could have been on any of the 9/11 flights. Nor did he attack anyone with a box cutter. He is another victim of Mossad's (and/or the CIA's) tyranny as well as much blundering by federal agencies.

According to the UK's *Telegraph*:

> Mr. Al-Hazmi is 26 and had just returned to work at a petrochemical complex in the industrial eastern city of Yanbo after a holiday in Saudi Arabia when the hijackers struck. He was accused of hijacking the American Airlines Flight 77 that hit the Pentagon.

Here again, the Mossad and/or other secretive government agencies proved incompetent. Their use of fabricated IDs led the trail back to them. Yet, this had to be at least to a degree an Israeli act. Surely, the U.S. government wouldn't embarrass itself to such a degree by making such astronomical errors. That would be truly unAmerican. Even so, secretive government agencies were obviously involved in planning this diabolical act.

Americans pride themselves on doing excellent work. This grand country is the greatest source of productivity in the world. It is the vast 'engine' which drives the world. It is truly the greatest place on this earth to live and to conduct a good, decent, enterprising life. Here, much of the finest work in the world is produced. Thus, it would be unfathomable that this was strictly an American coup. There were too many blunders, too many omissions. Incredibly, America's top law enforcement agency posted a list of 19 men, all of it wrong.

In the past in their brazen acts the Mossad has blundered. Thus, this organization must be largely the source of this fabricated list. The supposedly invincible Mossad is little more than a group of rabid, arrogant liars, who will commit any crime to further their wicked goals. Yet, neither the American authorities nor the Israelis have issued an apology for this slanderous enterprise. No such sources have taken responsibility for the grief, agony, in fact, utter bloodshed, which they have caused.

Yet, during the 9/11 crisis the media continuously marked the Muslims as the culprits, including the fully alive al-Hamzi. As reported in the news wires a car *registered in the accused's name* was found abandoned at the Dulles Airport, the airport of origin for this flight. This was promoted as evidence of culpability. Yet, this man was on another continent at the time and had, what's more, never been to Dulles Airport nor anywhere near it. This means that no Muslims were involved and that, rather, men posing as Muslims had placed this car as 'evidence.' Someone using al-Hamzi's ID rented the car and left it there purposely to create a false trail. It would not have been another Muslim. Rather, it would have strictly been the enemies of Islaam.

Again, the teachings within the Qur'an, as well as the teachings of the Prophet Muhammad, are pure. This is a threat to the establishment. Yet, there is another reason for this attack. It is to detract from the trail of the true perpetrators.

Regarding any tickets purchased in their names the same people with the fabricated or stolen identities could easily purchase such tickets as well as food, motel rooms, or any other potentially incriminating devices. Again, this was all to leave a trail incriminating Muslims. What's more, all this was done to confuse law enforcement, that is from determining the actual culprits. Yet, the tickets were of no consequence, because:

a) they were purchased using stolen identities: the men whose names were on the tickets were living overseas at the time.

b) they were used as evidence that the Muslims bombed New York City, this being based upon a Muslim who was not even in the United States at the time.

c) they were never used. It was a false trail. For instance, no one bearing al-Hamzi's name used the ticket on any flight on September 11. In the United States there were no people with this name on any of the flights originating from the East Coast.

e) they were used as evidence, even though the FBI knew they were never used. However, all the general public was told was that there were tickets purchased in the names of the accused Muslim men. Then, if the purchasers had fake IDs, this would be easy to do.

5 Hani Hanjour

"Believed to be a pilot," Hanjour is listed as living in Phoenix and/or San Diego. There is definite evidence that at one time he lived and studied in the latter. The government claims he piloted the plane, which slammed into the Pentagon. Somehow, we are to believe, he came all the way from San Diego to do so. Thus, the government deliberately made this appear as an Islaamic attack. This creates a warring mentality, making the Muslims the enemy. Of course, global wars greedily benefit certain industries, particularly the defense, espionage, and drug industries.

Yet, is this true? Have the Muslims really attacked America's infrastructure? Muslims benefit by living in this great nation, and foreign nationals benefit from its superb educational system. Could students, who were here in this country to learn various skills, have, suddenly, attacked and destroyed a part of it? The fact is regarding this even government sources leave much doubt. For instance, according to the *Washington Post* and confirmed by CBS News and ABC News regarding the strike on the Pentagon:

The unidentified pilot executed a pivot so tight that it reminded observers of a fighter jet maneuver.

The hijackers-pilots were then forced to execute a difficult high-speed descending turn. Radar shows 'Flight 77' did a downward spiral, turning almost a complete circle and dropping the last 8,000 feet in two-and-a-half minutes.

All of us experienced air traffic controllers know that that was as military plane...you don't fly a 757 in that manner. It's unsafe. On the latter point it must be realized that, when moving close to the ground, they must greatly slow down. They cannot safely fly at top speed.

Russ Wittenburg, one of Americas top pilots and an expert on all realms of commercial flying, agrees. He says that it would be impossible at that speed to crash a 757 into the Pentagon. The maneuvers would be, he continued, 95% impossible for even the most experienced pilot and 'impossible' for an amateur. He notes that Hanjour could never have achieved this feat and that even if he was super-skilled and somehow could have done so, still, the mechanics of the plane would have failed him. Such a huge plane simply could not have achieved the recorded flight pattern. What's more, Wittenburg has far greater credibility than any government official. His words are more reliable than, for instance, those of proven liars such as George Bush, Dick Cheney, Douglas Feith, Richard Perle, Dov Zakheim, and/or Paul Wolfowitz. The latter all told blatant lies to the American public and continue to do so.

The major networks agree that the feat was impossible, even while the government continues to fallaciously tout the Hanjour (and Muslim) connection. Again, Muslim pilots are constantly taking flight training in this country as are Christian, Hindu, Oriental, and Jewish pilots. This has never previously been evidence for criminal or suspicious activity, that is until the standard government story of diabolical "simulator trainees," who, somehow, became expert pilots through training on video screens. This created a vivid image of supposed ruthless Arab terrorists, who had planned and achieved this crime.

Yet, can anyone learn how to drive a car only on a simulator? Everyone knows that first hand experience is required to do so. The same is true even more so with flying.

Even so, CBS News quoted instructors as saying Hanjour was incapable of maintaining the most basic skills for flying, "I couldn't believe he had a commercial license of any kind with the skills that he (was touted as having)." Or, quoted Hanjour's chief instructor, "He had trouble controlling and landing the single-engine Cessna 172," and, incredibly, "I'm still to this day amazed that he could have flown into the Pentagon (or)…that he could fly at all." What's more, Wittenburg, a true expert in the field, says that the idea that Hanjour could commandeer this plane successfully, making extreme maneuvers in the midst of a plethora of obstacles and at more than top speed, is "ludicrous." Only the most gullible person would believe it. Thus, the highly credible Wittenburg made it clear that no such plane could have been flown in that fashion. This means that rather than a 757 the Pentagon was struck by a different object. What's more, since there was no 'hijacked' plane, then, there were no Muslims. This is supported by the fact that within the Pentagon there were no remains of Muslims or Arabs.

Even if these men could have flown this plane, still, there is no evidence of their presence. Ohlmstead has shown through the recovery of the original autopsy reports through the Freedom of Information Act that Hanjour's remains were not found in the Pentagon. While he is accused of being the ringleader of the hijacking team there is no proof of his involvement. In fact, there is vast proof to the contrary. For instance, the official flight registry shows that there is no Hani Hanjour. There is also no forensic evidence of his body. Therefore, the claims against him are false. In other words, he did not attack the Pentagon.

The effort exerted at the Pentagon to find bodies was thorough. Some experts noted that this may have been "the most comprehensive forensic investigation in U.S. history." So, when forensic experts ruled out any evidence of Hanjour, it meant just that: he was not involved.

As reported on *Wing TV* Wittenburg analyzed the government claim. He said that it would be impossible for an inexperienced pilot, such as Hanjour, to have flown the aircraft as tracked by the FAA. This was due to both technical reasons and a lack of experience. To make that flight massive G-maneuvers were necessary, difficult even for a crack jet fighter pilot. Said Wittenburg about the accused pilot's ability, which bears repeating:

> (According to the government) there is a pilot named Hani Hanjour. Now from all the…flight schools he attended…every single instructor said this guy, his…capabilities were feeble. He was basically inept.

His conclusion was even more telling:

> So what I'm asking you is that according to the official story: Flight 77 dropped 7,000 feet in about two and a half minutes. It did a 270 degree bank, swooped in only inches above the ground and struck the Pentagon. Now, 95 percent of all top rate pilots couldn't even pull this maneuver off. So, would (a nervous, inexperienced, and tiny) Hani Hanjour (about to die) be able to do this?

In the entire history of modern flight virtually no hijackers fly planes. Rather than killing them hijackers are dependent upon pilots. At all costs they attempt to keep these pilots alive. If anyone is killed, it is usually the passengers. There are essentially no cases on record in the United States of hijackers successfully piloting major commercial airliners to their targets (or destinations). Now, people are to believe that this happened on 9/11, even though it has never been previously achieved? People are to believe that these huge jets were piloted by amateurs, three of which struck precisely their targets, all through inexperienced pilots, some of whom had never even flown a mere Cessna? None of these men had ever flown a plane solo. So, they could never have flown such huge jetliners. This is a wicked joke played on the entire human race.

In a chilling testimony provided by his family Hanjour was last heard of some eight hours before the September 11th attack, when he called his parents to check on their health. They recalled, "he was very normal." Thus, this man was defintely murdered. This was to prevent the real truth from being revealed, that is that Hanjour had nothing to do with this crime.

The supposed hijacking of American Airlines 11

The following five men are accused of hijacking American Airlines 11, which supposedly struck the north tower of the World Trade Center:

6 Satam al-Suqami

All that is said by the FBI is that this man was born in 1976 and was last known to live in the United Arab Emirates. An official report from the FAA is as follows:

...an on board flight attendant contacted American Airlines Operations Center and informed that a passenger location in seat 10B shot and killed a passenger in seat 9B at 9:20 a.m.

She did not say who it was. The news media then reported that the passenger killed was Daniel Lewin, a decorated Jewish commando. Officially, he was supposedly shot and killed by passenger Satam al Suqami.

It would be very difficult for this man to achieve this. He had no experience in combat, and, what's more, Lewin was from the infamous Israeli elite commando regimen, Sayeret Maktal, the latter being extensively trained in hostage-taking and rescuing skills. What's more, a gunshot on a plane causes decompression, destabilizing the entire flight. There was no evidence of any such destabilization or decompression on any of the September 11 flights.

Incredibly, this official FAA document, called Executive Summary, September 11, 2001, charges this frail-appearing man with murder—the killing of a fit, experienced Zionist commando by a relatively weak supposedly fledgling pilot. This makes no sense. Nor does it make sense that, coincidently, amidst a supposed Islaamic hijacking there is on board seated next to the accused Muslim a crack highly muscled Zionist commando.

This portrayal is based upon a phone call, apparently from a flight attendant. This call was reportedly from a cell phone. However, no one has confirmed that this was for certain the flight attendant's voice. What's more, cell phones typically are dysfunctional during flight. At the time of the disaster the technology did not exist to make in flight reliable cell phone calls. It would be presumed, then, a living Satam al-Suqami would be a vital component of solving this mystery. However, it is unlikely that this man is still alive.

There is little no evidence that he was killed on the plane. It was merely reported in an FAA memo, saying a man in seat 10B hijacked the plane and killed the person in 9B. Thus, obviously, since al-Suqami was not on this flight, someone within the agency attempted to pin this on Muslims. Even so, the attendant did not specify the names of these people.

There is another suspicious report which lends to a conspiracy. A passport attributed to al-Suqami was discovered lying essentially untarnished outside World Trade Center Building #5. How this passport alone survived the inferno within the World Trade Center caused by jet fuel and how it could have possibly floated so conveniently onto the ground is never explained. The perfect crime is not perfect.

A critical question is: What evidence exists that this man was on board? In the official flight registry Lewin is listed as a passenger but not al-Suqami. The government says he was a culprit, and the FAA lists him as seated on 10B. However, as published on CNN the American Airlines registry lists no such man. The airline says one thing and the government says another. This dichotomy is highly bizarre and is proof of a plot. The fact is the government is unable to prove to any degree that this man was involved. There isn't even any proof that he boarded the plane. Yet, since an Operation Northwoods-like plan was surely in place, then, there would not have been an occupied plane. In other words, the object which struck the north tower was an unmanned drone. This is confirmed by various eyewitnesses in New York City, who observed that no regular jetliner struck these towers. Rather, according to these eyewitnesses the towers were struck by non-commercial planes "without windows," which were "gray" in color. The fact is these could only have been military drones. It is now believed that these drones were rigged with explosive devices to maximize their destructive effects.

7 Waleed M. al-Shehri

The FBI gives several different dates of birth for a person of this name. Apparently, this man was being impersonated, complete with fabricated IDs, and the culprits were sloppy, leaving a trail. This man was listed as living possibly in Florida, that is in Hollywood, Orlando, and/or Daytona Beach. Again, the FBI document says, "He was believed to be a pilot." The FBI also said he attended flight school there under the sponsorship of Saudi Airlines.

Al-Shehri, the same one pictured on the FBI list, is very much alive. He is a victim of stolen identity. As documented by the FBI the person impersonating him moved frequently. Incredibly, internationally, the real al-Shehri was marked as a terrorist, when he had nothing to do with this act. For several years someone masqueraded as him, all to create a trail that would be used to target Islaam. Yet, here, obviously the espionage agencies which attempted to target the Muslims did a sloppy job. They left al-Shehri and at least nine other patsies alive.

Al-Shehri lives in Morocco, where he is finishing his flight training. He is a pilot with Saudi Airlines. He had nothing to do with this vile act. Saudi authorities have proven categorically that he was not in Florida, nor was he sponsored to train there through the airline. Thus, it is obvious that the claim of an Islaamic attack on the United States, is a lie.

It was popularly reported that the FBI raided a hotel room, claiming that on September 10, 2001, al-Shehri stayed there. Yet, al-Shehri wasn't even in the United States at that time, let alone Florida. According to his father the al-Shehri posted on the FBI's list is surely his son. However, he said, the FBI's claim that his son was in Hollywood, Florida just (one month) prior to 9/11 is false. The fact is as fully documented by flight records in 2000 al-Shehri had left the United States for Morocco. This is also confirmed by stamps in his passport.

It is unfathomable that the people behind this would make so many mistakes. Did they fail to consider the consequences of these revelations? How arrogant it is for them to believe that such a plot would remain hidden, that is that the truth would never be known. Lies are easy to reveal, because they beget further lies.

8 Wail al-Shehri

This man is also alive. He is the brother of Waleed al-Shehri. Both are sons of a prominent Saudi diplomat. The fact that he is alive has been confirmed on video. The FBI listed him as living possibly in Hollywood, Florida. Again, this is where the Mossad operated a massive and now-broken spy ring. Here again, his name was misspelled.

Do the Zionists think that Americans are so gullible that they would never learn the truth? Are they unable to realize the intelligence of Americans and their constant search for the truth? This is yet another blunder of the Mossad, because, here again, it has been fully confirmed that this man is not only alive but that, in fact, he had nothing to do with this horrific act.

In the U.S. media all statements regarding this man are lies. On the news wires claims that he clandestinely attacked America are baseless. Employed by Saudi Airlines

Wail al-Shehri is a pilot. His presence in this country, that is prior to 9/11, was fully approved by the U.S. government. There was nothing suspicious about his activities. Rather, suspicion against him has been created by Islaam's enemies.

When interviewed by the *LA Times,* Gaafar Allagany, the head of the Saudi Embassy's information center, reported that he is in personal touch with al-Shehri in his workplace and that he is alive and well. What's more, he confirmed that he had never trained as a pilot in south Florida.

Three of the five accused Muslims of Flight 11 are confirmed alive. Then, did the remaining two solely overpower all resistance—all flight attendants, passengers, and pilots—and crash this plane on a virtually perfect mission of destruction? The fact is since the majority of the accused Muslims are still alive and were in other countries at the time of the disaster, and since the FBI's official story regarding them is wrong, the entire theory that the Muslims attacked America is now debunked. Any claim otherwise is an outright lie. For instance, Larry King, Wolf Blitzer, Aaron Brown, and others still erroneously refer to the 19 as killers. Regarding those who perpetrate such lies, obviously, they have their own wicked agenda, which they pursue.

The people who posed as the al-Sheri brothers performed evil acts. They posed as Muslims to mar this faith. With malice they listed as their sponsor Saudi Airlines. This was to leave a trail pointing to the Muslims as the culprits. In contrast, neither of these men attended the flight schools in question. Thus, the people there who used their names and attended the flight schools were imposters, most likely Israeli Jews.

9 Muhammad Atta

Regarding this man the most compelling information relates to eye- or ear-witness accounts. This is of greater relevance than mere videos released through the media. This is corroborated by the fact that the videos of other Muslims are bogus. Thus, any video clips of Atta are insufficient proof of a criminal act. Such videos are merely create the impression of Islaamic terror.

Atta's father is under siege. In the media he has been vilified. Yet, he is a prominent Egyptian lawyer. So, the relevance of his statements must be assessed.

Prior to the accusations against his son the elder Atta was never regarded in a derogatory fashion. Yet, now he is under siege. He had raised a loving family of highly educated sons and daughters. It has only been since 9/11 that, suddenly, he is regarded as virtually insane. Until news reporters descended upon him there were no reports of him being a "loose cannon." What's more, agents of both the CIA and FBI have approached him disguised as reporters. Their purpose was to "get the dirt" on him.

Yet, since he is the accused's father his words are critical. The fact is of all people a father is the least likely to tell lies about his son.

Western reporters visited the elder Atta. Then, they attempted to discredit him. Atta simply said that his son called him a day or two after the attacks and was "normal." Thus, his son could not have been involved in the attack. The fact is there is no reason to presume that the elder Atta was lying. His son, he said, did not talk about the incidents related to the explosions. He also stressed that he has been living in Germany, where he is completing his research on urban improvement and that he did not leave this country. What's more, he had no American Visa for 2001, a fact confirmed by congressional investigation.

When the global powers are afraid of the consequences of certain revelations, they have a standard procedure. They vilify the involved person(s) in an attempt to weaken their credibility. In other words, they make them appear as if they are irresponsible, even insane.

As reported in the news journal ArabicNews.com the elder Atta insisted that his son was a victim of identity theft. When pressed regarding the whereabouts of his son now, he responded, "Ask Mossad."

Regarding the accusation of ramming Flight #11 into the World Trade Center Atta reiterated that he knows his son well, saying that he has no idea how to fly a plane and, in fact, fears flying. What's more, he reported, he regularly vomits and gets sick from jet travel.

This is from a known source, the man's father. The rest is mere speculation. Muhammad Atta's close friends also dispute the claims of a split personality or violent tendency. True, a father could lie. Yet, he is a more reliable source that media aggressors, who spread the agenda of hate, particularly those who make it their mission to vilify Muslims.

The second important issue is that Atta was modest. Obviously not a womanizer his friends reported that he was shy among women. He never drank alcohol or visited bars, nor would he attempt to do so as a 'disguise.' He was deeply religious and, what's more, showed no tendency towards violence. Rather, he abhorred violence and complained deeply about those who would bomb public buildings for political gain.

Contrary to popular claims Muslims don't have split personalities, one for a public persona and, then, a secret one. If people are to believe media reports, somehow, Muslims are allowed to violate all decency for political gain. Rather, such a propensity is promoted in Judaism, while it is banned in Islaam.

There is no history of Muslims doing so. The claim that Atta would transform himself from a sheepish person who kept his distance from women to a raucous and drunken philanderer, groping strippers at an adult club: this is completely untenable. The man had no such vile tendencies. Rather, he is serious about life. In fact, he is a city planner. His job is to improve the infrastructure of city center. His entire life is focused upon improving a city's infrastructure. Such a person would be an exceedingly poor candidate for destroying the World Trade Center.

Reporters have done all that they can to find evidence for radicalization. They were unsuccessful. Regarding politics Atta was uninvolved.

Here is what the FBI said: Atta was born 1968 and possibly lived in Hollywood or Coral Springs, Florida. He is also listed as possibly living in Hamburg, Germany. He was described by the government as a possible pilot. However, this could not be true, because Atta was, rather, an architect. He took no flight training.

The Atta family is known for strong facial features. This is the typical Egyptian face. The Mossad, as well as the powerful ones in the U.S. Government, knew that the photo of Muhammad Atta would be the ideal one to convince people of a sinister element. This is why he was selected as the 'ringleader.' Without doubt, this man is being judged exclusively based upon his photo. There is no evidence that he harmed or killed Americans—or anyone else.

Muhammad Atta has been blatantly accused. Yet, clearly, from his history this man was the least likely type of person to be involved in any aggression. A paraphrased news report is as follows:

Atta graduated from Cairo University with a degree in architecture (a most unlikely candidate to destroy buildings). Since the mid-1990s he spent most of his time studying urban planning in Hamburg, Germany. Colleagues described him as "decent, quietly religious, and soft-spoken to the point of shyness."

His father said his son was raised to be solidly apolitical and to focus on "work, home and family." Atta maintained that the evidence against the accused hijacker, including the Arabic flight manual in a car in the Logan airport parking lot and his son's United Arab Emirates passport, had been faked and planted in order to create a rush to judgement against the Muslim world.

"They found a flight manual in the car," he said. "Is he going to be studying on the way?"

Also, consider his son's views on global events. He demonstrated, reported his father and friends, a disgust for the destruction of public buildings and the killing of the innocent. Thus, there is no possibility that he would be involved in such destruction. The fact is Atta was a decoy concocted by Zionist elements, all to divert attention from the real culprits.

It must be noted here that Atta's stolen passport was found in perfect condition with a slightly burnt edge a few blocks from the collapsed towers. It had to be match-burnt and, then, planted. It is implausible that if Atta was in the plane that any of his belongings would have survived the fireball. What's more, this was a domestic flight, and there was no need for a passport. How convenient it is that of all passengers only items belonging to the accused Muslims were found. No passports for any other passengers on Flights 11 and 175 were found. Nor were any other known IDs or personal affects discovered. The fact that his passport was stolen would surely indicate that this was planted to create a false trail.

The spies had in hand the passports, which they conveiniently dropped in those areas. This was to purposely mislead law enforcement. Supposedly, uninformed Americans would immediately presume guilt. A false picture of Islaamic terror was memorialized, yet, it was all the act of spies. In real life no Muslims were involved. Investigators have also made note of the discrepancy between the behavior of a God-fearing person versus the deviant actions of his look-alike, the man falsely claiming to be Atta in the bar *the night before the event.*

Atta was selected as the ringleader not by the 19 supposed hijackers but, rather, by the media or, more correctly, those who run the it. He was selected by the FBI or, rather, those who dictate to it. It was intended that this would perpetuate the image of sinister Middle Easterners. This is because in his photo he had a serious appearance. This would, it was believed, be interpreted as sinister.

Yet, why rely upon unsubstantiated and, in fact, erroneous claims in the media? Rather than news reports, which can be biased, direct sources are more reliable. This would be people who knew Muhammad Atta, for instance, his father, relatives, or friends. From these it can be determined what he was really like. The fact is there were two people using the name Muhammad Atta and also his passport. One of these men was real, and the other was a an imposter. The conclusion is in the United States someone was surely posing as him. What's more, this imposter wasn't a Muslim. The fact is Muslims have no history of posing as fellow Muslims for espionage purposes. The exceptions are the occasional paid informants for the FBI or Mossad, people who have Muslim-appearing names but are not true to their faith.

In 1999 in Germany Atta's passport was stolen. He reported this to police. This passport, then, miraculously survived the fireball of an exploding jetliner? Everyone saw this fireball. Can anyone fathom how such an ID could survive?

The 5 foot 7 inch, 150 pound architecture student had no history of violent acts. He was shy, particularly around women. What's more, he had never taken flying lessons, nor had he ever flown a plane. Obviously, he had nothing to do with this atrocity.

His devotion to his faith is well known. Friends in Germany refrained from drinking or cursing in front of him. In contrast, eyewitnesses confirm that a man using Muhammad Atta's name acted precisely the opposite. This means that there was a person masquerading as him. What's more, in the United States or elsewhere religious Muslims do not purposely transform themselves into boozers and womanizers as a disguise, that is merely to attack Westerners. As again reported by Pastore:

> …someone using Atta's identity had enrolled in a Florida flight school in 2001 and then broke off his training, making it a point to tell his instructor he was leaving for Boston. In an October 2001 interview with an ABC affiliate in Florida, flight school president Rudi Dekkers said that his course does not qualify pilots to fly commercial jumbo jets. He also described Atta as "an asshole." Part of the reason for Dekker's dislike for Atta stems from a highly unusual incident that occurred at the beginning of the course. Here's the exchange between ABC producer Quentin McDermott and Dekkers:
>
> MCDERMOTT: "Why do you say Atta was an asshole?"

DEKKERS: "Well, when Atta was here and I saw his face on several occasions in the building, then I know that they're regular students and then I try to talk to them, it's kind of a PR—where are you from? I tried to communicate with him. I found out from my people that he lived in Hamburg and he spoke German so one of the days that I saw him, I speak German myself, I'm a Dutch citizen, and I started in the morning telling him in German, "Good morning. How are you? How do you like the coffee? Are you happy here?," and he looked at me with cold eyes, didn't react at all and walked away. That was one of my first meetings I had."

It is curious that among the remnants supposedly left behind by the accused hijackers or, rather, Israeli 'illegal' aliens at Boston''s Logan airport is a English-German dictionary. Obviously, this Mossad agent was attempting to compensate for his ignorance of German words, since the real Muhammad Atta, the one that the Florida flight instructor thought he was conversing with, knew German fluently. The real Muhammad Atta would have spoken with the instructor in excellent German. The hostile reaction tells of a spy caught in the game. The real Atta might need an Arabic-English dictionary but not an English-German one. Only a person attempting to learn German would need it.

This was obviously not the Muhammad Atta described by various German friends and colleagues as well as family members. This flight school student was impersonating Atta. He lived in the same area as the nest of Israeli spies caught by U.S. law enforcement agents. This masquerading was in preparation for 9/11. Thus, this person was clearly attempting to make 9/11 appear Islaamic.

10 Abdul 'Aziz al-Omari

The official FBI statement lists this man as having a probable residence in Hollywood, Florida. The FBI also said he is "believed to be a pilot."

As reported on *ABC News* he is still alive. He lives in Saudi Arabia. In fact, there are two men with this name in this country, and both have come forward to the authorities. The *New York Times* reported that "al-Omari is…apparently cleared in the case." There is nothing apparent about it. The FBI said he was a dead suicide bomber, who slaughtered Americans as well as hundreds of foreign nationals. This was broadcast all over the world. The FBI and Justice Department have vastly blundered. Al-Omari is alive and, what's more, had nothing to do with this crime. This is why the government refuses to pursue him. Even so, Larry King still erroneously refers to the 19 as real hijackers and killers.

The FBI, rather, the U.S. government, told lies. This is yet another Muslim who is vindicated. One of the two al-Omari namesakes who have come forward is a pilot with Saudi Airlines. According to the *Independent* he said he was "astonished to be accused of hijacking a plane and accused of being dead." On September, 23, 2001, he visited the U.S. consulate in Jeddah to demand an explantation.

Perhaps his name was used as the result of identity theft. In 1995 the other man who has come forward, again, Abdul Aziz al-Omari, reported to the police his passport was stolen. In Denver, Colorado he studied electrical engineering. However, while it was reported otherwise he had *never been to Hollywood, Florida*. In contrast, this is where the notorious Mossad spy wing operated, which was discovered in 2001 by U. S. agents—the same year as 9/11.

The 'other' al-Omari was equally astonished and told British reporters (London *Telegraph*, September, 2001): "I couldn't believe it when the FBI put me on their list. They (correctly) gave my name and my date of birth, but I am not a suicide bomber. I am here. I am alive. *I have no idea how to fly a plane.* I had nothing to do with this (italics mine)." It was this al-Omari who while studying in the United States had his passport stolen.

According to numerous reports in the news media, as well as official statements from the FBI, al-Omari was a definite hijacker. He was the one, they claimed, who was caught on a surveillance camera accompanying Muhammad Atta to board the plane. This is a surveillance camera that supposedly shows both men going through security. Then, according to a signed affidavit in court the FBI says that it found al-Omari's, as well as Atta's, luggage, which, somehow, failed to make the flight. Says the affidavit, signed under oath by both the agent and the presiding judge, David M. Cohen, al-Omari drove, along with Atta, a blue Nissan to the Portland, Maine airport, making their early morning flight. Of note, the address and phone number listed on the rental car form was in Florida. The luggage, they said, failed to make it and was searched.

Yet, while all this was being investigated and reported and while this man stood accused, al-Omari was going about his normal life in Saudi Arabia. He left no luggage in the United States. What's more, this luggage bears none of his fingerprints. Furthermore, on 9/11 he was no where near Portland, Maine. Nor had he ever been to Maine. Nor was he anywhere near the United States at that time. Nor did he even know where Maine is. This means that the 'evidence,' that is the often broadcasted surveillance film depicting Muhammad Atta and al-Omari, has no relevance. What's more, the fact that al-Omari had nothing to do with it also absolves Atta. Furthermore, this brings into question any supposed video evidence incriminating Muslims. The fact is it is all faked.

In this luggage was found, incredibly, a Qur'an and a will. This was broadcasted in the media as evidence of an Islaamic attack. Both the will and the Qur'an were purposely planted, in fact, by Islaam's adversaries.

The supposed hijacking of United Airlines 175

The next five men were accused of hijacking United Airlines 175, which, it is attested, hit the south tower of the World Trade Center:

11 Marwan al-Shehhi

According to the FBI he is listed as having a possible residence in Hollywood, Florida and was "believed to be a pilot." This man, or someone posing as him, supposedly visited Muhammad Atta at Airman Flight School in Norman, Oklahoma. Yet, Norman, Oklahoma is home of ex-CIA chief David Boren. The fact is al-Shehhi has never been to this city. Nor had Muhammad Atta. Thus, the visitor was an imposter, who was disguised as a Muslim.

It was this man who the FBI reported was 'spotted' in the United States the weekend before the bombing. Said the report, "he (Atta) and al-Shehhi were spotted partying… playing video games and drinking."

Here, the FBI is grossly in error. This is because Marwan al-Shehhi is still alive. He does not know Atta and has never met him. Thus, it is obvious that instead of the real man someone using al-Shehhi's identity was seen. Thus, what the FBI was referring to was a non-Muslim, who was in disguise. This non-Muslim used a forged identity and posed as al-Shehhi. This was in order to create the trail for terrorism, so that the act, which was fully planned in advance, would be falsely attributed to the followers of Islaam. The purpose is to demonize them in order to perpetrate the war effort, all in the name of corporate profits and Israeli expansionism. It is also to distract world attention from the Israelis for their murderous acts and, instead, keep the focus on Islaamic terror.

Can anyone fathom how erroneous this is? This man is the son of a Muslim scholar, the latter of whom had died recently. His mother lives in the United Arab Emirates, and he lives in Morocco. He is a quiet and religious man, who is very much alive. He had nothing to do with the bombing and, what's more, he was not even in the United States at the time.

Even more ludicrous are the early media statements about him. All these statements are baseless. Originally, on national news he was listed as a hijacker on Flight 11, the same jet Muhammad Atta was wrongly accused of hijacking. Al-Shehhi was probably placed on this flight due to the fact that the media reported these men as associates, even though in "real life" the two had never met. Later, the official story was altered; Al-Shehhi was suddenly placed on Flight 175, presumably because the FBI needed a Muslim name for a pilot on this flight. All these names arose from the so-called Justice Department.

It would be expected that the names were drawn from actual passenger lists. So, how can this Department justify moving these men's names about like chess pawns? This proves a conspiracy to create a specific image, that is to convince the public of an Islaamic attack, all to disguise the real motives for this murderous act.

12 Fayez Ahmad Banihammad

Regarding this Muslim all that is mentioned is a possible residence in Del Ray Beach, Florida. Again, this was the area of Zionist intrigue. He is said to have entered the United States a few months prior to 9/11. This was through a VISA issued through, apparently, Saudi Arabia. Later, in June 2001 he is mentioned as opening a bank account in Dubai (United Arab Emirates) with another man. Here, according to U.S. officials he supposedly set up the facility to fund the terrorist attacks. Yet, none of the accused Muslims received any funds from this country. His current status is unknown. He has most likely died in warfare, while his identity is being used fallaciously.

13 Ahmad al-Ghamdi

All that is mentioned by the FBI is a possible residence in Del Ray Beach, Florida. In Saudi Arabia al-Ghamdi is a common last name, much like 'Smith' or 'Jones' in America. Ahmad al-Ghamdi was an engineering student in Saudi Arabia. In 2000 he left the country to join, apparently, the jihaad in Chechnya. He has not been heard from since.

Even so, regarding this man the FBI's information is faulty. The man listed as Ahmad al-Ghamdi is a real person but is not the man pictured. Nor does any of the FBI's information correspond to him. The fact is the real Ahmad al-Ghamdi has never been in the United States. Thus, all the information regarding about him listed by the government is of no consequence.

14 Hamza al-Ghamdi

This man is merely listed as a possible resident of Del Ray Beach, Florida. Yet, according to his father the picture provided by the FBI bears no resemblance to him.

There is other suspicious evidence related to the claims
against this man. The father said that he never lived in Del
Ray Beach. Yet, according to the *Washington Post* a man
using al-Ghamdi's ID opened a post office box there, along
with a man using al-Shehri's ID. However, incredibly, al-
Shehri, who is still alive, was also not in this city at that
time. This clearly proves that these men were imposters. Of
note this is the city where in 2001 the Israeli spy ring was
busted. In contrast, not a single Muslim was arrested for
'spying' in this region. Thus, the two people who opened
this P. O. box were non-Muslims. The fact is these were
Israeli operatives.

15 Mohand al-Shehri

The FBI misspelled this man's name. The name is actually
Muhammad al-Shahri. Mohand is a derogatory spelling
commonly used by medieval authors to denigrate the Prophet
Muhammad. Like many of the aforementioned, he is merely
listed as a possible resident of Del Ray Beach, Florida. Yet,
here again the FBI is in error, since al-Shahri is alive and,
what's more, has never lived in any of the residences
attributed to him.

The Saudi Embassy adamantly reported that al-Shahri is
alive and well and was not in the United States during this
time and had "nothing to do with the heinous terror attacks in
New York and Washington." Furthermore, the Saudis have
proven that "he was not in the United States at the time of the
disaster." This man was known by his teachers as a regular
student of a quiet nature. Thus, any association of him with
terror is bogus, in fact, his picture was used on forged IDs.
The FBI listing of him as a hijacker is baseless, false, and
discriminatory. Like the other accused Muslims, he had

nothing to do the murderous acts at the World Trade Center and/or Pentagon.

The supposed hijacking of United Airlines 93

The final four men are accused of hijacking United Airlines 93, which, it is attested, crashed in rural Pennsylvania:

16 Saeed al-Ghamdi

The FBI merely lists al-Ghamdi as a possible resident of the former Zionist den, Del Ray Beach, Florida. It also claims he was part of a group who overpowered the crew of Flight 93 and took control of it.

This man is alive. He overpowered and fought no one. Nor did he in any way attack America. Thus, he had nothing to do with 9/11. During the years 2001 through 2002 he lived in Tunisia. Yet, early in this crisis the supposedly thorough and credible BBC said he was "linked to al-Qaeda network" and "part of a terrorist network:" all lies. As reported in the *Daily Telegraph* (London) al-Ghamdi said, "I was completely shocked—for the past 10 months I have been based in Tunis, the capital of Tunisia, *with 22 other pilots.*" Thus, he has dozens of corroborative witnesses to prove that he was nowhere near the the supposed hijacker cells during this time. There, he was learning to fly an Airbus 320. He continued, "The FBI provided no evidence of my personal involvement in the attack." Yet, again, he stands accused of being in the 'bin Laden' network. These accusations are continuous, even though he has been thoroughly exonerated. To quote the Saudi Embassy he is "not dead and had nothing to do with the heinous terror attacks in New York and Washington."

It has already been established that Jews disguise themselves as Muslims. They even go to mosques, attend prayers, and engage in the community. They even marry Muslim women. Then, they create strife. This is in order to incriminate the followers of Islaam. Adus Isaac is a most recent example. Another example is the notorious criminal Abu Nidal. Rather than a Muslim he was instead a Jew in disguise. The Shah of Iran was another example. As mentioned previously Indian authorities caught 11 Jews posing as Muslim preachers who they detained as suspects for a hijacking. So, regarding 9/11 why wouldn't the same be true?

Incredibly, the U.S. government has reported that this man or, rather, a man using his name, lived from 1988 to 1991 in New Jersey. There, with a family and children he worked for a drug company. His landlord confirmed that a man with the same name as the accused Muslim lived there at that time. He left, said the landlord, because "he was transferred to the Midwest." Yet, the real Saeed al-Ghamdi, the one whose picture the whole world saw and who was part of the focus of world-wide contempt for Islaam—this man would have been at that time only about 15 years old. Thus, again, a man posing as a Muslim was attempting to established an Islaamic connection.

The fake al-Ghamdi, a Mossad operative, is seemingly connected to an anthrax death. The realtor who found this Mossad agent's apartment was the wife of the editor of the *Sun Tabloid* of Boca Raton, Florida, it was these offices which were contaminated by an anthrax letter. The reporter to whom the letter was addressed, Bob Stevens, died. He had previously reported on the hypocrisy of the Bush administration. It is likely that, here, an exposé was being developed about 9/11-related lies. Thus, this facility was effectively destroyed, and the lead reporter was killed.

Al-Ghamdi was previously in the United States for flight training. This was pre-approved by the U.S. government. He schooled at the Embry-Riddle Aeronautical University.

Numerous Middle Eastern newspapers have interviewed al-Ghamdi, proving he is alive and that, what's more, he was during the 9/11 crisis in Tunisia. The accuracy of this was confirmed by the Arabic paper *Asharq al-Aswat* as well as the *Telegraph* and BBC. Saeed al-Ghamdi is yet another Muslim who is wrongly blamed.

17 Ahmad al-Haznawi

This man is listed merely as born in 1980 and possibly being a resident of Del Ray Beach, Florida. He is accused by the Justice Department of vile acts, that is of overpowering and perhaps killing the crew of Flight 93. Then, according to the government he commandeered the flight. However, this is a mere accusation, utterly baseless. There is no proof that this man hijacked a plane. Nor is there any proof that he died on this flight. Nor is there any documentation that during 9/11 he was even in the United States. It appears that even the identity of this man as represented by the FBI is fraudulent.

As reported in *Arab News*, September 22, 2001, al-Haznawi's brother disputed the accuracy of the FBI's photo. He said, "There is no similarity between the photo published and my brother." Thus, the FBI's information is false.

18 Ahmad al-Nami

All that is mentioned is that he had a possible residence in Del Ray Beach, Florida. He or, rather, his imposter lived there "with two other hijackers" for several years. Yet, none of this is of any consequence, because, incredibly, al-Nami is alive. Thus, statements calling him a hijacker are lies. Located in Riyadh, he is an administrative supervisor with Saudi Arabian Airlines.

As reported by the *Telegraph*, September 23, 2001, "I'm still alive, as you can see. I was shocked to see my name mentioned by the American Justice Department. I had *never even heard of Pennsylvania* (where the site of the crash is) the plane I was supposed to have hijacked." He had never lost his passport and found it "very worrying" that his identity appeared to have been "stolen" and published by the FBI without any checks.

His statement proves a vile attitude, a rush to judgement. It is as if there is a thirst to pin any violent deed on an Arab or, rather, Muslim. It is a judgement against a people merely for wicked gains: the pursuit of wealth and power.

Yet, what was the Mossad (or CIA) thinking? Did they merely presume all people as fools and that no one would realize that the accused are still alive and would come forward to refute all? A living patsy would be a nightmare. This espionage effort was poorly planned. Dead people tell no stories. People could readily presume the guilt of a dead man. There is no one to raise a defense.

19 Ziyad Jarrah, Lebanese national

This is very odd. Virtually all the accused Muslims were Saudi Arabians, while there is a lone Lebanese man. This was Ziyad Jarrah, a happy and peaceful Lebanese national from a respected family.

At the Pennsylvania crash site another 'miracle passport' was found. Like the passport found at Ground Zero it was singed on the edges. This passport belonged reportedly to Jarrah, who was accused of piloting Flight 93 to its destruction. Yet, there has been no independent confirmation that this was truly his passport, and the photo recovered looks decidedly different than his.

The official FBI posting only mentions that Jarrah is 'believed to be a pilot' and that he may have spelled his last name 'Jarrahi.' However, his family has stated that he never spelled his name in such a manner.

This was planted evidence. One researcher noted, "Why were all these Muslims, Ziyad Jarrah and Mohammad Atta, whose passports were found as evidence, "Why were they carrying passports for internal domestic flights…?" Even more telling is the fact that no airport employee recalls seeing these men or their passports.

The likelihood that the Lebanese national Ziyad Jarrah is a terrorist is nil. There is no history of Lebanese nationals terrorizing American people or institutions. Lebanese are notoriously life-loving and, what's more, they rarely if ever kill themselves. This is particularly true of young Lebanese. They love their country and pride themselves on their ancestry.

The nature of Jarrah is documented by those who knew him best, his loved ones and fiancee. As reported in Beirut by Zohair Majid of the respected Saudi newspaper *Al-Watan*, October 1, 2001:

> Relatives of Ziyad Jarrah, the Lebanese on the list of suspects the FBI has finally released, still believe there has been some mix-up or error in identities.
>
> This was made clear by Ziyad's father, in Maraj, the small Lebanese town where the family lives—in an interview published yesterday by the Saudi newspaper, Al-Watan.
>
> Ziyad's relatives believe that his passport was forged as his original passport has been missing since last year.

According to Ziyad's father, the young man had gone to the United States for pilot training which would help him get a good job in Lebanon. "Ziyad was about to return to Lebanon as he completed his studies in the U.S," his father said.

Ziyad told his family that he would arrive in Lebanon on Sept. 22 the day of his cousin's wedding. He said that he would stop over in Germany to try and persuade his German girlfriend to accompany him home to Lebanon (he was intending to marry her). In addition, he informed his father that he had bought a wedding dress in the U.S. His girlfriend stated that Ziyad talked to her on the day of the attacks...but the conversation was cut off suddenly, Ziyad's father said. His relatives also learned from the girl that she had never heard of Muhammad Atta or Marwan al-Shaihi or any of the other names of the suspects, which have appeared in the press.

Ziyad's father quoted the girl as saying, "I have lived with him since 1996 but he never mentioned those names nor did anyone with those names ever call him." She denied that Ziyad had an Afghan wife. Seven months ago, she visited Ziyad's village and met his relatives.

They were told that Ziyad would marry her in the summer and were asked if they could accept her as his wife. Some of the foreign media met Ziyad's dentist in his village.

The dentist said Ziyad was moderate in his religion and had never seemed to be a zealot or fundamentalist.

All of his friends and acquaintances said that he did not hold extreme religious views. Along the same lines, his classmates and friends saw him as a broad-minded Muslim. Neither did he ever appear to be an enemy of the United States; those who knew him found him jovial and possessed of a pleasant easily likeable personality.

Ziyad's uncle, Sameer Jarrah, a bank manager, said Ziyad was born in 1975 and educated in Beirut. He did not visit his village except during vacations.

> Another uncle, Jamal, said the family was not politically active. They are all proud of their country but are, at the same time, deeply disturbed and concerned about the repression and Israeli occupation in Palestine. He continued, "We cared but we were also concerned about our children's education and their future."

On September 11 Jarrah was one of the few accused Muslims who was actually in the United States. He was to remain in the United States through mid-September. Then, he was to depart to Hamburg, Germany to pick-up his girlfriend. He has not been heard from since that day, when his phone conversation with his girlfriend was cut short. As his girlfriend then did not hear from him for several days—his routine was to call her at least once per day—she called the police and filed a missing persons report.

What happened to Ziyad Jarrah? His remains were not found at the crash site. He was most likely murdered by the Zionists. His family has requested his remains numerous times, but the government refuses to acknowledge it. This is because the government has no such remains.

Again, the conversation with the girlfriend ended suddenly. He said "I love you" three times, which she regarded as unusual. The media speculated that this was because he was about to die in the hijacking. Regardless this man was not on any such flight. Thus, the only other explanation is that he was assassinated. His captors, in fact, may have allowed him perhaps one more call before killing him.

Had Jarrah survived he would have seen his face on national TV. Then, he would have gone straight to the authorities. This would have decimated the plot. Thus, he was eliminated.

There is another compelling fact which disputes the official story. Ziyad Jarrah had no contact with any of the other 19 men. Thus, media reports that he was part of a 'terrorist cell' are fabricated. Yet, why not? The list itself is bogus.

Victims

None of the accused Muslims of the September 11th attack appeared on the original manifests of the passenger list. Media reports of these various men as passengers are fabricated. These fabrications were made as if true by postings through the Justice Department. Of note, this department is now under control of a noted Zionist, Michael Chertoff. Previously, it was under the auspices of the extreme fundamentalist Christian, John Ashcroft. Both these men played a direct role in the slaughter of the innocent.

People still refer to the hijackers as "those Muslim fanatics and terrorists" who "hate us." They speak wildly about revenge and invasion, that is against the various Muslim peoples. This hate is based upon mere lies: a supposed Islaamic attack on the U.S. which never occurred. Ten of the accused are alive and well. All have full time jobs. Many are commercial airline pilots. The majority are Saudis. Courtesy of the United States government many of these men were previously in this country in flight training, largely for commercial jets. The government well knew they were here, strictly for peaceful purposes. Many of the flight schools were in southern Florida, the very region which was a hotbed for Zionist espionage. What's more, no one in this government is interested in prosecuting the Zionists.

In 2001 mainly in south Florida 200 Israeli spies were arrested by the FBI. In contrast, no a single Muslim spy in the entire United States was found. These spies had fully infiltrated U. S government facilities, including flight training schools, military bases, and nuclear power facilities. Again, it is notable that a number of the accused are victims of identity theft, many of them, including Muhammad Atta, reporting their identities stolen.

In the media Muslims, particularly Usama bin Laden, are vilified. Emphasis on bin Laden was apparently in hope that the focus would be on him instead of the other accused Muslims, many of whom, in contrast to bin Laden, had no history of military activity. What's more, like Lee Harvey Oswald, bin Laden was used as a scapegoat to justify the global agenda. This is because the culprits knew that any scientific investigation of this issue would demonstrate the official story a lie, rather, fraud. This fraud is the basis of a brutal war. This has led to the deaths of tens of thousands of people, including some 3,000 U.S. service-people. Diabolically, this also includes the destruction of entire countries.

Evidence of fraud: German analysis

German investigators found the 9/11 data to be specious. It was the renowned and former German cabinet member, Andreas von Bülow, who made some fascinating observations regarding the bogus nature of the claims. In his interview in a prominent Berlin journal he said, "For 60 decisive minutes the military and intelligence agencies let the fighter planes stay on the ground (yet) 48 hours later the FBI presented a list of suicide attackers. Within ten days, it emerged that…seven of them were still alive."

The destruction of the World Trade Center was an enormous catastrophe. Afterwards, there was only chaos. It was an absolute shock to law enforcement. Then, how could, magically, within a day or two, the FBI know the answer? Even so, many of the accused are dead or in hiding, unable to defend themselves. What's more, none of them were American citizens, who might defend themselves vigorously. This was all too convenient. Without proof, the enemy was proclaimed, and the war was finalized. Yet, the FBI failed to even achieve this correctly, since virtually immediately after the list was publicized a number of the accused Muslims were proven alive.

A massacre was perpetrated. Within a few months thousands of the innocent were killed and injured. Other countless thousands were tormented and tortured. What's more, Islaam stood accused. Now it is known that these accusations are false.

It is also known that the war itself is bogus. Therefore, the killings of the Iraqi and Afgani people is purely murder. People were purposely misled to believe in an Islaamic attack. How great an atrocity this is: to lay false blame for this massacre and do so purposely. The Muslims are blamed to create patriotic fervor, all to support a wicked war—all to perpetrate global control. Thus, the entire war is based upon lies. Now, due to these lies nearly 3000 Americans have been directly killed, with thousands of others maimed and wounded. The fact is even regarding American soldiers no one knows for certain the degree of the carnage. Thousands more, Iraqis, Iranians, Europeans, and Americans, have been poisoned due to toxic chemicals, uranium residues, vaccine intoxication, and stress. What's more, tens of thousands of American veterans will endure yet further agony—the emotional trauma of living with the fact of the torture and killing of the innocent. This is highly stressful to the individual, a permanent stigma, which can never be shed.

It was the FBI's Robert Muller who reported that his agency was "fairly confident" that the names of the hijackers were not aliases. Yet, as von Bülow notes, when it was absolutely revealed that at least four of the men were victims of identity theft, the FBI did nothing, but according to German standards, he noted, they "should have been removed from the list. All four had reported their passports stolen, and none of them were in the United States at the time of the hijacking." Yet, the question is who stole their passports, because, then, the true culprits can be found. This is because whoever used these passports, while disguising themselves as Muslims, are the true culprits of the World Trade Center crime.

These spies used Muslim passports, that is they posed as Muslims. They stole these passports and, then, even attempted to hijack an entire religion. In addition, these spies forged other passports and attributed them to Muslims. This is the crime that the Muslims have endured, all at the hands of Western powers.

It was not only passports but also social security numbers which were stolen. These were used by operatives as they prepared for this war. Using forged documents bank accounts were established. Money was mobilized; tens of thousands of dollars were spent on airline tickets, rental cars, hotels, pilot training, and more. This set the scenario for the major event. It also created a confused array of evidence, all to distract sincere law enforcement. All this was processed through forged documents, and this is how innocent Muslims all over the world are implicated.

Von Bülow has observed numerous contradictions that weaken, in fact, debunk the official story. Westerners condemned the Muslims and spewed out vitriolic messages while, notes Von Bülow, at least five of the accused weren't even in the United States at the time of the disaster. In other words, it can be proven that while 9/11 was being perpetrated these men were overseas. Ahmad-al Nami, manager at Saudi Airlines, was in Riyadh. Abdul-Aziz al-Omari and Salem al-Hazmi were also in Saudi Arabia. Waleed al-Shehri was in Morocco, and in Tunisia Saeed al-Ghamdi was taking flying lessons.

What is this attempt to incriminate Muslims for taking flying lessons? Jews and Christians take such lessons. So do blacks and hispanics. This is mere racism, a crime in this country.

Fake documents: proof of a conspiracy

The suicide note is un-Islaamic. Thus, this, too, is bogus. In the entire history of Islaam no such note has been produced. This is a gross violation. No true Muslim nor any Muslim scholar nor even any ignorant Muslim would produce it. Rather, it was synthesized by Islaam's enemies. In fact, this is a Mossad concoction. It was created to destabilize Islaam as well as to cause fear and hate.

Since the time of the Prophet Muhammad the Jews have belittled the Muslims. They were jealous due to the fact that the latter received the latest divine revelation. During the Prophet's time they constantly attacked him. Today, they still do so. The Zionists are well known for their slanderous campaigns against him. This note is of that calibre.

Through such a forgery the Zionists attempt to serve several objectives. This is to portray Islaam as diabolical, even demonic. This makes no sense. Why would nearly one fifth the world's population follow a demonic cult? It is also to divert attention from the real culprits and to portray the Muslims as mad-men. This is to incite patriotic or warring fervor in order to justify a prolonged conflict. It is also to create the potential precedent for a third world war. This is known as the 'clash of civilizations.' It is a clash Islaam wants nothing to do with. However, the suicide note is an attempt to create such a clash.

The note opens with a mistake no Muslim would ever make. As noted by veteran Middle East correspondent Robert Fisk it begins with a commandment which is unknown. All official Islaamic correspondence opens with the Qur'anic phrase, *In the name of the most merciful and compassionate God.* In contrast, the supposed suicide note opens with, "In the name of God, myself, and my family." This is blasphemous. It is a complete bastardization of Islaamic teachings. What's more, it is deliberate. This is a definite attack on Islaam. Thus, the note is a perpetration of Islaam's enemies.

For Muslims this statement is a kind of association of other powers or elements with God: raw blasphemy. It is as if to elevate the authority of family ties, even the self, on par with God. In Islaam this is a crime. The very purpose of this way of life is to end the worship of the ancestors. This is by making almighty God the source of adoration. It specifically warns all believers to hold only Him in awe and to never focus on pride of ancestry. Thus, the Islaamic view is diametrically opposed to this writing. Any Muslim who would promote it would be essentially godless.

Again, the very purpose of Islaam is to end the holding of ancestry as high. It is to curb selfishness. This is further proof that this is a Western document. No Muslim would do it. This also proves that the entire 9/11 plot was conceived by Western powers deliberately to target Islaam. Fisk researched this with a number of scholars and was told such a statement is "extremely erroneous and unheard of."

The fact is the only other name a Muslim might add next to God's is the Prophet Muhammad's. This is because this man established this religion, and, so, Muslims are indebted to him. Rather than any family member it is the Prophet Muhammad whom they ask God to bless. This is how it has been for 1400 years. Why change now?

The Jews refuse to accept this man's prophethood. This is true, *even though he is predicted in their scriptures*. In contrast, consider the Muslims' point of view. It is that any rejection of the prophets revered by the Jews, Moses, Abraham, and/or Isaac, would lead to hellfire. Yet, when the Prophet first arrived, the Jews recognized him as true, because, again, their very scriptures predicted him. Only later did they reject him when they regarded his mission a threat to their power base. It was their tendency in any contact with him to purposely refuse to recognize him as true. In the suicide note the mention of the Prophet is marginalized, and, what's more, when he is mentioned, it is usually in ways unknown in Islaam.

A copy of this note issued by the FBI was found in luggage attributed to Muhammad Atta. How incredible: of all people flying that day only the supposed ringleader's luggage was preserved. The likelihood for this is exceedingly remote. Regardless, the note is bogus. This means it was planted. This also means there was a premeditated effort to portray Muslims as diabolical. It is also a classic ploy to distract attention from the real culprits. Another copy was apparently found in the rubble of the crash site, that of 'Flight 93' in Pennsylvania. This too was planted. Yet, regarding this flight there are numerous bizarre issues. Numerous eyewitnesses, including the local mayor, reported that there was no jetliner which crashed in the region.

The possibility of both these notes, with their chilling and incriminating language, surviving intact, one at Ground Zero and the other in Pennsylvania, is nonexistent. This proves they were planted. What's more, these are the same sites where the slightly singed passports attributed to Muhammad Atta and Ziyad Jarrah were found. Jarrah was accused of being the pilot who drove Flight 93 into the ground. Atta was accused of piloting Flight 11 into the north tower. These accusations were not based upon any proof but, rather, were merely 'reported' by the government.

Regardless, two of the supposed hijackers, that is those who were supposed to be on Flight 93, are alive and were in another country at the time, while another is believed to have died in fighting in Afghanistan. That leaves only one as the potential owner of the suicide note: Ziyad Jarrah. Yet, this man had no motive to either kill Westerners or himself. The fact is he was pro-Western. He had no history of anti-Western sentiment. Nor was he in any respect militant, hostile, or suicidal.

Before making it public the FBI did no investigation regarding the validity of the suicide note. Any true Islaamic scholar would have debunked it. The fact is they didn't even bother to check it for fingerprints.

People find it easy to believe that the attack was from outsiders. Muslims are the convenient scapegoats. Or, perhaps they desire a simplistic model for their world view that they can easily comprehend. In contrast, regarding the possibility that this country was attacked from within: people find this unfathomable, truly chilling. That Americans or the Westerners would deliberate kill their fellow people—and that this would, particularly, be done by people who are in power—is difficult for most people to comprehend. Yet, this is precisely what occurred.

There are numerous other factors which call into question Jarrah's role. How could an obviously Arab-appearing person get on a plane without a ticket? As mentioned previously

Jarrah was a poor candidate for a hijacking. Even if he were a good candidate he is the only possible one of the four mentioned that could have been on that plane, even though forensic reports show no Arab remains. Also, he is not on the manifest. Even with all this there is that possibility that he 'snuck' on the plane or that he was disguised as someone else. Yet, even this remote possibility is debunked by a simple fact: on September 11th while in New York he had talked to his girlfriend. What's more, he had just announced that he was going to get married and even bought a *Western-style white wedding gown* to take back with him. Also, as confirmed by his land-lady on September 9th in preparation for his wedding he bought a brand-new suit. This is proof that this man, the real Ziyad Jarrah, knew nothing of any terrorist attack and, surely, had no intent in participating in such a deadly operation. No one has ever before killed himself while doing this: why now?

Even so, in particular regarding this Lebanese national there is no way that a man of his history and personality would have attacked America. Incredibly, he would have been the first Lebanese national to have ever done so, despite the fact that tens of thousands of such individuals either reside in this country or have attended studies here. Thus, the second 'Ziyad Jarrah,' that is his imposter, is the only culprit here, the only one worth investigating.

His girlfriend was adamant that she had never seen nor heard of any of the accused. Then, she reported something ominous: after talking to him a second time the conversation was suddenly cut off, and she hasn't heard from him since.

Prior to his disappearance it was his routine to call his girlfriend every day. He busied himself in preparation for their wedding. No suicidal person would do so. In the entire history of the human race no man has after announcing his wedding turned himself into a suicide bomber. Thus, it is obvious that rather than a suicide bomber he was a regular person. Based upon his behavior there is not even an iota of evidence that he was about to commit a crime. This plus the fact that there was a non-Muslim, who was impersonating him, eliminates him as a possible culprit. In fact, it proves an ominous fact, that is that to hide the truth he was murdered.

Two of the supposed Flight 93 hijackers have been found alive. This nullifies the hijacking theory. Since Saeed al-Ghamdi and Ahmad al-Nami are alive, then, obviously, they were not on the jet. This means that they were falsely accused—by supposedly the most credible government sources and media outlets in the world. Since the FBI was wrong about two of the men, then, it is also assuredly wrong about the remaining ones.

The conversation of Jarrah with his girlfriend has been confirmed by German police. The time-line is worth re-emphasizing. On the morning of September 11th his girlfriend talked to him. It is unlikely that he could have casually talked to his girlfriend, saying nothing about impending doom, and, then, rush out and hijack a plane. He talked to her at around 7:15 a.m. Departure time was an hour and a half later. Regulation requires check-in at least an hour prior to take-off. When he called, he was not in an airport. This means he had a maximum of thirty minutes to arrive at the airport prior for check-in. An obviously Arabic-appearing man with an accent would have found such a timeline difficult. Then, apparently, he made a second call to his girlfriend telling her that he loved her three times. She found this call unusual. As of September 11th he disappeared, never to be found.

Jarrah was murdered. Possibly, the murderers allowed him one final call before killing him. He was perhaps the sole accused Muslim who was in the United States at the time of the disasters. Bin Laden, al-Hamzi, al-Omari, Atta, al-Shehri, and al-Nami were all overseas. Surely, he had to be disposed of prior to the FBI announcement. Had he been alive to absolve himself he would have immediately went to the authorities. A living Jarrah, this well-respected student from a dignified Lebanese family, surely would have unraveled the plot.

A man posing as Ziyad Jarrah, who was not a Muslim but who, like Adus Isaac, was a mere imposter, was well known to the FBI. The man operated largely from New York City. He used the spelling 'Jarrahi.' Had this information been revealed, that is that the Muslims who were blamed were mere patsies and that non-Muslims were acting as them under disguise, then, the entire basis of an Islaamic 9/11 would have been debunked. Plans for the war of Shock and Awe would have been neutralized, and the war and all its horror would have been prevented.

Of course, the 9/11 commission in general disputes these findings. Then, originally, it was the noted war criminal and mass murderer Henry Kissinger who was to head that commission. This was halted by protests, noting Kissinger's ties to the armaments industry. Rather than allow anyone to review his files Kissinger voluntarily resigned.

Rather than death this man was preparing exclusively for life. Yet, the dichotomy is explained by the fact that there were two Ziyad Jarrahs, the real one and the imposter. The fake Jarrah left a paper trail to implicate Muslims. Truly, the existence of a fake Jarrah completely absolves this Muslim of any crime. In fact, it brings into dispute the entire claim of an Islaamic attack.

Even so, there is no proof that Jarrah was on the plane. The voice recording of a man with an accent on the black box is not Jarrah's. This has been consistently confirmed by family members. The fact is this recording was obviously staged. Nor is there any possibility that he could have flown one of these complicated jets. Like the thousands of people in the World Trade Center this man was most likely murdered, and, what's more, his body will never be found.

A copy of a passport bearing Jarrah's name was found at the 'crash' site. This passport was partially singed on the edges, while the face was intact. It was quite opportune to find this, considering that this was the only passport discovered at this site. The singing on the photo's edge makes it appear as if it was match- or lighter-burned.

Yet, what would be the purpose of carrying a passport on a domestic flight, and what would be the purpose of doing so for a suicide bomber? Did the bomber want the world to know who was responsible? Did he desire to create a black mark for his religion? Did he want the atrocity to be associated with Muslims or Arabs? Surely, this is what was achieved. What's more, if he would have used this passport as an ID, surely his check-in agent would have come forward, remembering seeing him and/or creating his ticket.

Regardless, the man wasn't on the flight. He had called his girlfriend an hour or so before take-off, apparently from New York City. The flight left from Newark. This city is four hours from New York. He called his girlfriend at around 7:15. The flight departed at 8:45. There is no way he could have made this flight.

Yet, the 911 commission firmly maintained that Jarrah was the culprit, placing him squarely behind the controls in the cockpit. It was he, they proclaimed, who drove this plane into the ground at over 450 mph, blasting it to shreds. Then, they said, DNA evidence would confirm it, since bits of "all the hijackers were found." The government says the DNA for this flight is known. Even so, despite numerous requests by his family none of Jarrah's DNA has been provided.

The suicide note is a fake. No Muslim wrote it. Thus, the singed passport and suicide note were obviously planted. This proves that the entire basis for the claim against this man is fraudulent. It also means that the government only tells lies.

The number of absolved Muslims now stands at 10. These men were simply not there, that is they were not on these planes. Nor were they accounted for in any airport that day. Nor is there even the slightest evidence that they boarded any of the planes in question: there are no confirmed/used tickets, CCTV video images, or eyewitness accounts. What's more, many of the accused were not even in the United States at the time. This means that the perpetrators of these violent acts were non-Muslims.

Muhammad Atta's imposter

Regarding Muhammad Atta there are new revelations. In addition to reiterating that he had talked to his son a day after the explosions Muhammad Atta, Sr. has recently (2005) reported that his son is "alive and well." He said he is in a secret place, so that he won't be assassinated by the U. S. (or Jewish) secret services, he told the German newspaper *Bild on Sonntag*. He also categorically "denied that his son had taken a part in the atrocities…" Of note, both the CIA and FBI visited him and attempted to determine Atta's whereabouts prior to 9/11. Yet, it is White House insiders who have reported that during 9/11 investigators were unable to place Atta in this country.

The elder Atta learned about the World Trade Center disaster a day or two after the event when he turned on the TV after coming home from vacation. There, he saw the jets striking the towers and also his son's passport. This is likely the same passport, Atta has noted, that was previously stolen, most likely by Mossad agents.

This raises an interesting point. Why would the real Atta be in possession of his stolen passport? From an investigative point of view it would be important to determine who is the passport thief. This would lead directly to the culprit(s). Yet, rather than the perpetrators they concentrate on the victims. Atta said, "As I saw the picture of my son, I knew that he hadn't done it. My son called me the day after the attacks (September 12), and we chatted about this and that…at that time neither of us knew about the attacks."

It is important to note the elder Atta's views about terrorism. Despite the difficulties faced by Muslims in the Middle East and despite popular reports that he has called for hate against the West he said he "did not condone" terrorism.

Mr Atta described his son a "gentle and tender boy," who enjoyed reading history and geography books. His parents nicknamed him "Bolbol," which is Arabic for nightingale. In other words, he was a son like all others. That was 2002. Except for his father's statement, his exact status is unknown.

The media has attacked Atta for this descriptions of his son. Yet, who would know his child better, the father or the media?

The fact is it is the media itself which proves that father knows best. Compare the father's description to that of the diabolical 'Muhammad Atta,' who lived in Florida. Mentioned previously, this is a report by a restaurateur (CBS News, September 14, 2001) of the Atta he encountered:

> Tony Amos, the manager of Shuckums Oyster Bar and Restaurant in Hollywood (Florida) just north of Miami, was interviewed by the FBI, and he and his barman and a waitress all identified Atta and his cousin as some hard drinkers who propped up the bar last Friday.

> *Atta's bill for three hours of vodka drinking came to $48. When he drunkenly disputed the charge, Mr. Amos intervened. "Of course I can pay the bill," Atta told him. "I'm an airline pilot."*

This makes no sense. Atta was a non-drinker. He never went into bars, nor did he despite any pressures visibly become 'rowdy.' This was not the Muhammad Atta of real life. Rather, this was an imposter.

Atta is an engineer specializing in urban planning. He had never taken any flight training. He hated flying. The person who blared that he was a pilot was doing so to make a scene in order to mislead law inforcement. This was to purposely portray Islaam as wicked, since with IDs and credit cards in Muhammad Atta's name he represented himself as Muslim. This was a set-up to create a false trail.

Regarding the man in the bar what was the purpose of boasting about his profession? A pilot bragging in a bar? Commercial pilots are notoriously subdued about their skills. They rarely brag. People respect their credentials without any need for boasting. Even so, does it make sense to get drunk the night or weekend before a hijacking, an act which would require the utmost concentration and flying skills? These facts further prove the extent of the conspiracy.

Muhammad Atta cannot fly a plane and has never attempted to do so. Atta had absolutely no training in this field. Only Atta's imposter attempted to do so. An individual posing as this man had trained at a Florida flight school. In contrast, the real Atta spent his whole adult life in the field of public engineering, with an emphasis upon improving the infrastructure of the inner city. He loathed terrorists and, particularly, those who bomb public buildings. Rather than destroy them his entire purpose was to upgrade the infrastructure of cities. This has been confirmed by dozens of eyewitnesses.

The FBI proclaims as evidence the so-called suicide note as well as will. Surely, these are evidence but rather than of an Islaamic act of a conspiracy against Islaam. Both were attributed to Atta, that is when found in a rental car and luggage left in Portland, Maine. He remains accused despite the fact that his father said he lives in Germany. At the time of the disaster Atta was obviously in Europe.

The suicide note and the supposed will, as well as the planted luggage, were conveniently available. The supposed ringleader left a trail of evidence for all to see. Obviously, Atta is a mere patsy, who was set up for this fall.

Proof in the details: the bogus suicide note

Fisk's analysis has already been mentioned. The following is an analysis from the point of view of Islaam itself:

The note begins with the statement, "The Last Night." There is no use of such Islaamic wording. The note continues with a request that the person give allegiance and/or agree to die for whatever cause. However, there is no mention of God's cause, the only possible reason a Muslim could give his life. This refusal to mention God's name is demonstrative of a secular movement, for instance, Zionism.

This vague 'giving of allegiance' is proof of a non-Islaamic source. The fact is Islaam means allegiance exclusively to God. This is true even over family ties. Such vague statements have no relevance to this faith. In fact, they are its antithesis.

Then, says the note, the person must "know the plan well—in fact, very well and know also all military aspects of the enemy well." This is also bogus: there is no Islaamic use of such terms. Then, the follower is told to 'shave the excess hair and perfume.' No Muslim who is fighting an enemy is going to waste time shaving the body, what's more, before death there is no requirement anywhere in Islaam to shave hair. Wearing perfume is recommended in general, as it is in Western culture.

Before war no Muslim general or leader has ever recommended such recitations. Rather than in any Islaamic writings these are *found only in this letter, an obvious Western creation.* Then, the prediction in advance of martyrhood is made with the statement that the person should "reflect over the meaning" of these Qur'anic sections to "prepare for martyrhood." This again has no Islaamic basis. It was the Prophet Muhammad who said, "Do not seek your own death, any of you, neither the person who does good, in case he might add to his quota through a longer life nor the offender, in case he might obtain God's forgiveness…" So, this plotting one's death is a direct violation of the Prophet's words. Next, says the note, is to 'remind the self to listen and obey (but to whom he should obey is not specified), especially during the night,' and it continues "because you are going to face a serious situation where it is very necessary for listening and obeying 100%." No Muslim has ever used such terminology. Muslims have no organization which plots such strategies. Rather, this is Israeli jargon.

This obeying the superiors is typical of the Mossad. In contrast, Muslims rely exclusively upon the words and inspiration from God and the teachings of the Prophet Muhammad. In this note these are not mentioned as the source for struggle. Rather, only the man-made planning and obeying of the superiors is emphasized. Thus, rather than a Islaamic notation this is its antithesis, diametrically opposed.

The supposed believer is then told to "pray during the late night and insist on demanding and requesting victory—also to gain a clear conquest—to also make the effort easy. Then, in what is unprecedented for a Muslim resistance fighter it recommends a prayer to "conceal our activities." The fact is rather than an Islaamic group these are words of spies.

The use of the word 'conceal' fully reveals that this note is a forgery. Or, perhaps, it is derived from an actual document for secret societies. The breadth of the evidence points, however, to the Israelis. The idea of prayer late at night is definitely a part of Islaamic ritual for those who choose to do so. However, "prayer for concealment" and "deceit" has no Islaamic basis. Rather, this way of life prohibits it.

The person is then told to have "much remembrance." There is no such Islaamic prayer. Then, it says that the best of remembrance is the recitation of the Qur'an. This also has no Islaamic basis. What's more, it says that this is in accordance with those who are knowledgeable from the person's contacts. Such a method is banned in Islaam. For a true Muslim the Qur'an is not merely for recitation. Rather, it is the source of guidance. What's more, rather than 'contacts' God alone is the One to rely upon. In Islaam, there is no vague 'remembrance and recitation.' This is the garbled, deceptive language of a spy agency.

The note then claims the need for a consensus regarding the Qur'an. The Qur'an was precisely established 1400 years ago. There is no need for a 'consensus.' Someone is trying to appear 'smart.' Then, it says that 'the Qur'an is sufficient for us, because it is the speech of the creator, the one you are going to meet.' While this is true, again, no Muslim uses such a phrase. In contrast, the Islaamic phrase is "God is sufficient for us, and so are the ways of His messenger." If the authors would have written this, then, there could have been some validity in it. Yet, instead, they created their own statements that no Muslim has ever before written.

Without doubt, this note was written by someone other than a Muslim. Its authors know nothing about Islaam. This means that it was written by someone other than Muhammad Atta. It ultimately means that the note was planted to frame him. Regardless, how could the note have survived? The plane exploded in a fireball. Any paper within it would have been immediately incinerated. Everyone saw how the planes disintegrated into nothing. The impact of those planes against steel and concrete was massive: all was obliterated.

From the towers the suicide note could never have fallen down intact. Then, this is the only piece of paper from the entire plane which survived? Too, the only ID which survived was also his and another accused Muslim? This is absurd. How convenient: the odds for this are trillions upon trillions to one. Rather, it is impossible. What's more, the fact that it was planted fully exonerates him as a culprit.

Next, the 'agent' is told to clear the heart and purify it from any impurities—to forget a thing called the world. This is equally bizarre. It is as if this material world is unclean and that there is a need to purge all materialism. Islaam disassociates itself from such "Judeo-Christian" thinking. Then, it continues with 'the time for play has passed.' Regarding these words perhaps this is the most revealing of all. A dedicated Muslim doesn't talk flippantly about playing. There is no need to remind the Muslim of this, because he has already rejected the idea that life is merely fun and games, that is per the Qur'an, essentially, 'We have made this life more than mere play and jest.' What's more, the terminology of this entire section is fraudulent, again, unknown in Islaamic literature. Yet, in contrast, Jewish scholars make it clear that in Judaism it is the pleasure of this life which is the focus.

Then, it says something no Muslim has ever recited previously: '...the time of truth has come and how much of our lives have been wasted, so shouldn't we invest these hours to offer offerings of closeness and obedience.' Closeness and obedience to whom, the authorities of the state and racial pride, which are banned in Islaam? Rather, it is Judaism which promotes such an approach. The fact is the Muslim does all he can to work for the sake of God. What's more, it was the Prophet Muhammad who said, categorically, "Do not look back, do not live in the past—never be one of those who say, 'If I only would have done so and so.'" He stressed that a person should never think this way—not even for a moment. This is the opposite of the content of the note.

In what is truly a bizarre statement it continues, 'Let your heart be at ease regarding your marital relationship, except for a few light moments. In it you will start your happy, content life with everlasting bounty with the Prophet, confirmers of the prophets, and the martyrs. What's more, the righteous are the best of companions.' Again, this is non-Muslim lingo. Islaam has a distinct language, and this violates it. There is no wording in it of being with "the confirmers of the Prophets," nor is the statement "everlasting bounty with the Prophet" found anywhere in Islaam. The fact is this is sacrilegious. Rather than any human the bounty is with God. This shows that whoever wrote this note has no knowledge of Islaamic and, rather, has an incredibly distorted view. The fact is this note is fiction.

It continues with incomprehensible statements about trials and tribulation and what might befall a person: all of it nonsense. Islaam has clear rules that are rather simplistic. Again, there is no Islaamic basis for such distorted, secretive statements. What's more, this religion does not focus on tribulation. All it proclaims is that if a person encounters difficulty to be patient and to keep God in mind. It only says that, ultimately, the difficulty will be eased, that is per the Qur'an "surely, with difficulty there will be ease."

In all the years of Islaamic warfare no such words have ever been spoken. Why now? Woodward and others call these words "chilling." This is true, but rather than Muslims the Zionists are the culprits. So, they are the ones who are truly chilling. They slaughtered the war protester Rachel Corrie with buldozer. Is there anything more gruesome than that? In contrast, the association with of this term Islaam is erroneous.

In the corrupt minds of those who wrote this there is a revelation. It is the fact that the adherent is told to *Prepare the Weapons*. Yet, is this anything other than the very box-cutters and bomb-laden vehicles that on September 11 in New York City only one group possessed: the Mossad? There were no Muslims in New York City or Washington, D.C. or anywhere else in the United States found to possess these 'weapons.' Only Zionists were arrested due to their aggression near the World Trade Center. Recall the note, that is the supposed 'necessary preparations': "clothing, *luggage*, knife, tools, *identity cards*, and *passport* (italics mine)." It was only the Zionists who possessed all such materials, plus box cutters. All these devices were found in the hands of Israeli aliens. Yet, no such materials were found with Muslims. This alone is absolute proof of Zionist involvement as well as the innocence of the Muslims. Then, the note culminates with a barbaric statement, "sharpen your razor, his (tool of) slaughter." Yet, the Zionists know Arabic relatively well. Thus, they exclusively created this document.

Why would a killer need to say this or, rather, write it down? Then, why would he carry it with him to incriminate himself? The fact is this is to foment fear. This note was planted. The mild mannered Atta, who has no history of violent acts and had never even been involved in a fist fight, could hardly be responsible. Rather, these are the words exclusively of professional killers, who have no remorse.

In what is a most unheard of proclamation the writer says, "Make your clothes taught—this is the path/example of the early righteous community. Then, tighten your shoes very well, and wear firm socks that hold firmly onto the shoe and will not come out of it." This is diametrically opposed to the truth. The Prophet Muhammad and his people were Islaam's only early righteous community. They never wore tight clothes. They never tightened their clothes for any purpose. Rather, as do all desert dwellers they wore loose clothes—the clothes of the bedouin.

There is no record in Islaamic literature of such a statement. So, since this doesn't refer to the Muslims' righteous community, which community does it refer to? Regardless, no Muslim warrior or fighter, and, surely, no potential martyr, adheres to any ritualistic tightening of clothes. Everyone knows this simple fact: Middle Easterners wear loose clothes. Yet, after 9/11 there were pictures available of the Israeli commando Daniel Lewin, who, it is attested, died on Flight 11 (or was at least listed as a passenger). In such pictures he is in commando gear and is wearing *very tight clothes*.

Incredibly, this suicide note even describes what to do on the plane. It reprehensibly deems it a, God forbid, "Raid in the path of Allah." There are no 'raids' in Islaam. There is only "fighting against oppression." It also *actively promotes* the idea of the virgins of paradise, which contrary to popular belief is an uncommon focus of Muslim scholars.

The call to "Ask God to reward you with martyrdom" is yet another violation. In contrast, according to the Prophet:

"Do not actively seek your own death." Thus, the fact is rather than Islaamic this is anti-Islaamic jargon.

Obviously, this is a vilification of Islaam. This is proven by commentators' use of words such as "chilling, ruthless, and barbaric." This note was written by Islaam's enemies. This proves that there is a specific effort to portray it as diabolical. Even so, one individual, a self-styled scholar, said the opposite, that is that, incredibly, this is "Islaamic jargon." The only person who could say such a thing is a person who is unfamiliar with Islaamic teachings or, rather, a hostile individual, whose purpose is to destabilize Islaam. This is Imad-ad Dean Ahmad from Bethesda, Maryland. So, there may be on the media the occasional person who attempts to validate the claims against Muslims. Yet, who are such persons?

Bethesda, Maryland is the headquarters of American's spy, as well as armament, agencies. The basis of Ahmad's organization, a supposed Islaamic think-tank, is revealing. It is affiliated with the U. S. Department of Defense. Thus, it can hardly be regarded as independent. The group promotes the United States' Middle East agenda. What's more, it does so strictly for economic gain. Ahmad, who purports to be an Islaamic scholar, is directly tied to the armaments industry. In other words, this group has a specific economic agenda that molds its views. In contrast, the view in this book is based exclusively on the teachings of Islaam. There is no economic agenda which is attached.

Thus, the suicide note is fake. It has nothing to do with Islaam. Rather, this is a PR stunt to target this religion. It is a brainwashing tactic. No sound Muslim agrees to it. In fact, as has already been demonstrated it grossly violates Islaamic law.

A Muslim would never commit to a statement 'In the name of God, self, and family,' nor would any Muslim repeat such a corruption. Nor would any Muslim teach this blasphemy. Rather, he would regard it as sacrilegious and fear repeating it, let alone teaching it to others. The fact is from the Islaamic point of view such a statement is an avenue directly to hell.

The implications are clear. Muhammad Atta is a decoy. He had nothing to do with this note nor any suicidal acts. Rather, he would find it frightening, in fact, appalling. This means that the note was planted as evidence against him. It means that all evidence found in the United States related to him is fabricated. It also means that this man was not a hijacker. This means that there were other powers behind the destruction of the World Trade Center and the Pentagon. These powers deliberately plotted these acts to make them appear Islaamic. Such powers sought to disguise their involvement by fabricating information, all to deceive the public. As stated by former CIA chief William Casey, "We'll know (our plan) is complete when everything the American public believes is false." Thus, these powers, Zionist and/or otherwise, merely created the note to portray the Muslims as cruel and diabolical as well as to distract attention from the real perpetrators.

Bob Woodward, a prominent columnist from the *Washington Post*, wrote a review of the suicide, rather, aggression, note, using the following ominous heading: *Chilling Advice for Hijackers*. He was sure to pin this as an Islaamic creation.

A supposedly 'seasoned' Washington veteran he should know better than to rigorously attribute this to Islaam. He provided no confirmation of its source. His article capitalizes on the theme of 'bloodthirsty Arabs or Muslims,' who supposedly kill Westerners arbitrarily. Said Woodward (the Post, September 28/01):

> Mohammad Atta, one of the key organizers among the 19 hijackers...carried out the September 11 terrorist attacks..."

Woodward then goes on to implicate al-Omari as a hijacker. Yet, his statements about both of these men are false. For instance, Atta has never flown a plane nor taken flight lessons. Neither had al-Omari. Here, Woodward acts as both judge and jury. Has he left any doubt regarding who burned the victims alive? What's more, with his inflammatory title he directly and maliciously attacks Islaam, all based upon lies.

Woodward is a correspondent for one of the top news firms in the world. Was he unaware of the compelling statement of this man's father, where he clearly stated that he talked to his son *after 9/11*? This alone is sufficient cause for reservation.

He furthers these lies, describing how Atta and al-Omari spent the night together in Room 232 of Portland's South Portland Comfort Inn. Everyone remembers this representation: it was repeated constantly in the media, supported by video footage of what appeared to be these men in an airport. This was purposely done to make the terror act appear Islaamic. Woodward emphasizes these men as the culprits. Yet, doesn't he monitor the news wires? This is supposedly his job. Here, he failed intolerably. This is because these news wires have clearly shown that al-Omari is alive and well. On that day he was nowhere near the Portland Comfort Inn, nor was he even in the United States. This, again, is proof of a plot. The fact is he had nothing to do with the hijacking.

There are two al-Omari namesakes who as early as September 17, less than a week after the disaster, came forward, including one who had suffered a stolen passport. On such prestigious news wires as ABC and the BBC their innocence and health status was confirmed, well prior to the posting of Woodward's article. Woodward is spreading mere propaganda. London's *Independent* and *Telegraph* also reported this. Just after 9/11 both these men, who Woodward slanders as murderous, were proven alive. Thus, he is guilty of libel. Yet, rather than for the sake of legitimate news he writes strictly for financial gain.

Yet, if it wasn't Atta or al-Omari, then who was it? Actually, there were no Muslim hijackers. The planes were remote controlled. What is certain is that there was an elaborate attempt to blame the Muslims. What's more, it was premeditated. This was largely through the use of planted evidence, including the fabricated suicide note. Now, there is no further speculation. The official story is packed with lies. Woodward's lies are proven by the fact that al-Omari is still alive. Even in the orthodox media there is suspicion, for instance, as reported in the *Sunday Herald*, that evidence was planted deliberately. The Muslims were set up. There is no doubt about it.

It is realized that this is difficult for most people to believe. It is typical for people to believe the 'authorities.' Yet, the information in this book is real. None of it has been confabulated. Without doubt, lies are being told. This book proves that. What's more, the lies are aimed directly at Islaam. Every effort is made to portray it as a source of violence. Yet, again, can anyone name a single global war caused and maintained by a Muslim nation, a war where tens of thousands, even millions, were/are killed? Rather, the fact is in the past 200 years it is mainly Muslim blood which has been spilled. In the Iran-Iraq War, a conflict created by Zionist agents, some three million people were slaughtered and/or maimed. Yet, this war against Islaam is a prolonged one. For instance, during the 1920s when the Muslims of the Middle East, Cairo and Baghdad, rebelled against colonial rule, they were bombed by the British and French, incredibly, with mustard gas: thousands were slaughtered. Thus, rather than the perpetrators of terror they are its victims. What's more, the culprits are exclusively Western powers.

Conclusion

Islaam is the truth from almighty God. This is why it is attacked. The Qur'an is unaltered divine revelation. Regarding this there is no doubt. Islaam means to surrender. The surrendering is to the will of God. It is the same system which was revealed to the previous prophets. The only difference is it is unaltered. Thus, it is purely divine.

It is also just. This is because it is based on the laws of God. It is also because it is the most pure revelation available, sent by God for human benefit.

Islaam is diametrically opposed to terror. The fact is, historically, it is the most liberal of all faiths.

The barrage against the Muslims is continuous. Every vile aggression is perpetrated against them. Islaam is associated with terrorism, extremism, fanaticism, and fundamentalism. This is all based upon lies. Likewise, no one deems the various Zionist agents or their Christian lackeys who murder anyone they choose, as terrorists.

There was no Islaamic attack on the United States. Rather, as proven by the capture of numerous nests of spies it was the Zionists who attacked it. What's more, through the plots of Zionist thugs—Wolfowitz, Sharon, Netanyahu, Zakheim, Perle, Pipes, Abrams, Kristol,

Bremer, Feith, and others—the U.S. government routinely attacks Islaamic lands. Can any such men prove that they did not deliberate defraud the public and purposely lie, for instance, about 9/11 and Islaamic terror? Was this not all so they could uphold the agenda of a foreign entity, that is Israel? Who can prove that this was not so?

German investigators have proven that the Muslims had nothing to do with these crimes. Rather, they have deemed the crime as exclusively Western. As noted by Helmut Schmidt, 25 year cabinet member of the German parliament, the attack was operated by "the highest levels of the U.S. intelligence," along with a vast number of Zionist agents. The Zionist agents were involved at every conceivable level of the operation. In fact, they were the perpetrators. The act was conceived, as well as enacted, largely by individuals such as Paul Wolfowitz, Donald Rumsfeld, Richard Perle, Daniel Pipes, Douglas Feith, and Dov Zakheim, the majority of whom are Israeli nationals. In contrast, there was no Muslim or 'al-Qaeda' involvement. Thus, attributions in film, press, TV, and in various government/FBI channels of these acts to the Muslims are complete lies. For instance, intelligence expert Andreas von Bülow has confirmed that building 7 of the complex was used as the local command and control center for the operations, while Cheney conducted master operations from his bunker in Washington, D. C. On the evening of September 11 building 7 was purposely demolished through set charges. Thus, these wicked ones perpetrated a well orchestrated and premeditated crime against American citizens as well as foreign nationals.

The crime continues in the form of pain and agony for the victims' families as well as fulminant disease in workers, firemen, and locals. Von Bülow also reiterates that, for certain, the insider trading, which occurred a week prior to the attacks, is proof of "an inside job." Thus, the plan was fully plotted and achieved internally. In contrast, there were no foreign invaders and, particularly, no Muslims. Building 7, he says, was the "optimal place" from which to use remote control technology to guide the jets into the buildings and, then, destroy the crime scene by blowing up the towers. It is well known that no one was allowed to inspect or investigate these scenes. Regarding the remote control technology needed to fly the jets Zakheim is the specialist in this regard. To coordinate this crime he joined the Pentagon *just prior to the strikes.*

Again, it was William Rodriguez, eyewitness and former maintenance director of the north tower, who gives the absolute proof. He was in the basement of the tower when bombs went off. Here is the critical point. As witnessed by Rodriguez the bombs went off well *before the plane strike.* Categorically, he said, before the plane strikes bombs had already exploded. During these explosions, which occurred in the basement of the tower, he aided several colleagues, who were severely injured and/or burned. He has proven that there were explosions in the building nearly one-half hour before the jetliner impact. These bombs, he noted, were planted.

His testimony is confirmed by a recent article by C. Bollyn of the *American Free Press,* which shows photographs of the remnants of the massive steal beams still standing, which supported the towers (picture available at Rense.com). As anyone can see these beams had been clearly blown by specifically set explosives. The most likely explosive was thermite. When it explodes, the latter burns so hot that it cuts through steel. In contrast, it is impossible for the fire from an exploding jet airliner to do so. This focus on jet fuel is a hoax. All physicists and architects know this is impossible. Yet, still, people are led to believe that this was an Islaamic attack, with Muslim hijackers. This is obviously wrong. Rather, incredibly, the perpetrators are exclusively non-Muslims. Yet, as a result of such false beliefs people are wrongly killed. Entire countries are invaded and conquered based upon such lies.

People are also led to believe that London was bombed by Muslims. Yet, for over 200 years the British Empire routinely bombed—and still bombs—Islaamic countries. Despite this no one calls the British terrorists, even though such acts are purely terror. Even so, the entire claim of an Islaamic attack on London is false.

Muslims are called radicals. They are deemed 'zealots.' Yet, what could be more radical, more completely zealous, than to invade and bomb entire countries based upon lies?

Muhammad Atta and Sidique Khan are accused of being ringleaders. Supposedly, they radicalized their presumed followers. This is said, even though, for instance, Atta had no contact with the persons he supposedly radicalized. Nor was Khan ever involved with 'radicalization.' Thus, these are inventions of Western governments. Whether 9/11 or the London bombings these lies are spread to cause wars. What's more, the wars are strictly for corporate profits.

Much of this hate originates through Washington, D. C.-based newspapers. For instance, the *Washington Post* disseminates a relentless barrage which is antagonistic to Islaam. Other sources which foment hate include the major global newspapers and TV networks, CNN, Fox News, even al-Jazeera. The fact is none of the commercial networks tell the real truth about global events. This is because each of these networks has its own 'corporate' agenda.

The fabrications are readily proven. Consider the

numerous alleged videos, which implicate Muslims. These messages are attributed to supposed extremist Muslims. One such video specifically was attributed to Abdul Aziz al-Omari. Like the bin Laden video it is a fake. Al-Omari had nothing to do with the bombings. In fact, he was on *another continent at the time*. Thus, the video representing him was part of the plot. Even so, says the Post in yet another fabrication regarding September 11 these Muslims, specifically "Saudi volunteers," knew "exactly what they were doing." Furthermore, the editors report:

> "al-Omari said on the video, 'I am writing this with my full conscience and I am writing this in expectation of the end, which is near, an end that is really a beginning.'" It continues, "We will get you. We will humiliate you. We will never stop following you,"..."God praise everybody who trained and helped me, namely the leader Sheik Osama bin Laden: may God bless him. May God accept our deeds."

These are vile lies. The al-Omari video is a complete fraud. The question is who produced this and other fabricated videos? The secretive agents of Zionism will stoop to any level to mar Islaam. Yet, as demonstrated previously it was bin Laden who categorically denied in an official interview with *Ummat Magazine* any foreknowledge of 9/11. Nor did he commit it. It was also this man who virtually immediately after the attacks released a video denying responsibility. It is also the U. S. government, which recently (2005) stated that it has no proof of bin Laden's involvement. Thus, the video of a supposed admission by this man is a fraud. Furthermore, this proves that any such videos, which are released claiming Islaamic responsibility, are false. Again, without doubt, the aforementioned al-Omari video is a fake. Then, surely, the video of Sidique Khan is also bogus. Yet, no one saw Khan or any other accused Muslims setting any bombs. The fact is other than accusations—mere judgements in the media—there is no evidence against them.

Regarding 9/11 the ATM photograph was another fraudulent item posted by the government. Here, there is a man accompanying what appears to be Muhammad Atta. This is reportedly al-Omari. Yet, the man in the video bears no resemblance to al-Omari. He didn't even live here at the time. This proves that espionage agencies purposely use videos to falsely incriminate Muslims.

Then, says the Post, "only three members of the Hamburg cell—Atta, Jarrah, and al-Shehhi (or al-Shehri)—*died on September 11*. (Other members): Essabar, Bahaji, and Binalshibh, *fled* Germany…all three are sought on an *international arrest* warrant…" Yet, as has been made clear on page 11 al-Shehhi is alive and well, living in Morocco. What's more, he had never been in Germany. Nor had he ever met Muhammad Atta. Nor had Jarrah and Atta ever met. This proves that there was no Islaamic Hamburg 'cell.' Thus, here, the Post spreads lies.

The agenda against Islaam is obvious. This is perpetrated by the Zionist cartel. This cartel owns the media, which makes this possible. The fact is someone was 'paid' to write this article, because it is all lies.

The majority of the accused Muslims, men who were proclaimed as global terrorists and mass murderers, are alive. Furthermore, they are not terrorists. What's more, they had nothing to do with the destruction and devastation of 9/11. Rather, America was attacked by a secretive, in fact, Western, organization. This organization used the cover of Islaamic terror to avoid incrimination. The same occurred in London.

In both these disasters only the Israelis admittedly had foreknowledge. Since the Muslims were framed for 9/11 it also makes sense that they were framed for the London bombings. BYU's Professor Steven Jones says the Muslims had nothing to do with 9/11 and that rather than due to suicide bombings the buildings were destroyed via controlled demolition. World Trade Center architects also confirmed that a plane crash could never alone have caused the collapse. Within these towers, they noted, there was a massive steel-reinforced concrete core, impossible to destroy through jetliner crashes or even fires. Then, there is no possibility that the Muslims killed the victims. Regardless, there were no Muslim hijackers on that day. Rather, it was Western individuals who were the culprits. Wolfowitz had already made clear the plot of Western elements to create a terror act, that is a "new Pearl Harbor." Thus, these terror attacks were planned, as well as achieved, by non-Muslim powers.

This demonstrates the fraud of the 9/11-related convictions of various Muslims, for instance, in Germany of the Moroccan Mounir Motassadeq. He, too, had nothing to do with this crime. How could he? The Muslims had no involvement in 9/11. Thus, his role as a supposed accomplice/coordinator was fabricated. The fact is Motassadeq is wrongfully imprisoned. It is impossible for him to have had any role. The fact is he must be released immediately.

Zacharias Moussaoui is also wrongfully blamed as well as imprisoned. How could he be guilty? He committed no crime. Like Lee Harvey Oswald he is a scapegoat. His trial was a mere sham, a means to distract attention from the real criminals: the powerful ones of the Israeli entity and the U.S. government. Said Moussaoui (2006) while he was being falsely prosecuted for murder, "All of this is an American creation. This has nothing to do with me." He has also made it clear that he was under complete FBI surveillance. So, obviously, the claim that he "knew something that would have saved lives" is ludicrous. Furthermore, in his court pleadings Moussaoui himself makes a highly valid point. It is that if he was really a part of this plot and if he knew anything, then, his arrest alone would have alerted any 'hijackers' and, as a result, the plot would have been aborted.

He also repeatedly emphasizes that he was continuously under FBI surveillance prior to being arrested. Therefore, he notes, the government claim against him 'knowing information that could have saved lives' is further disproved. Even so, he has been sentenced to life in prison. In contrast, illegal aliens from Israel were caught at the scene. These illegal aliens were in the process of committing criminal acts. The Israelis were caught with massive amounts of explosives, wads of cash, and box cutters, plus, again, they were in the country illegally. No such evidence has been found against Moussaoui—not even remotely so. Plus, in contrast to the Israelis the imprisoned Muslim, Moussaoui, had an actual Visa. Yet, even so, if he confessed, one issue must be remembered. This man, held in solitary confinement, had been tormented. Surely, he was tortured. This torture was to cause him, essentially, to lose his mind. Lights have been kept on him 24 hours per day. He has not been allowed to sleep or even rest. Thus, he was brainwashed or at a minimum tormented. This means that any statements issued by him have been done so under duress.

Even so, the government case against him is bogus. Says the government, "He will be convicted of murder only if it can be proved that he indirectly caused an American to die. This is through lying about what he really knew about 9/11. Because he lied, we will prove, we were unable to *hunt down the 19 hijackers* in order to stop the attacks." This is the entire government case. The fact is there is no case, because there were no 19 Muslim hijackers. The man must be released. The government bases its entire case on lies, and, what's more, Moussaoui is telling only the truth by stating that he had no information regarding the hijackers. This is because there were no such hijackers.

In no way could he have caused American deaths. The government is on a witch hunt. This is because there were no Muslim hijackers on September 11, 2001. Thus, if Moussaoui would have said what the government expected of him—to admit foreknowledge—no doubt, he would be lying. The government case now stands refuted. On September 11 there were no Muslim plots against the United States. Not a single foreign or domestic Muslim attacked any American building, nor did any such person kill even a single person.

Yet, ultimately, under the duress of torment a person may relinquish his rights. Such a person may say anything in an attempt to ease his burden. This is the result of torture. It can never be regarded as evidence, that is if justice is the basis of any decision. Yet, if the purpose is to create a scapegoat to maintain the status quo, then, the eliciting of through torment self-incrimination would be expected. Moussaoui killed no one. He committed no crime. Yet, he is being tried for execution and at a minimum is given life in a maximum security prison reserved only for the most dire of criminals— a man who has never harmed anyone or stolen so much as a piece of bubble gum? Yet, incredibly, it cannot be proven that he had even the intent to commit a crime. The reason for this torment is obvious. He is innocent, and the government knows that if he gains contact with the outsider world he will find absolute proof of the conspiracy against him. Even so, before him no other person in this country has been imprisoned merely for thinking of or intending to commit a crime. Incredibly, this man, accused, imprisoned, and threatened with execution, has harmed or killed no one. In contrast, Dick Cheney, George Bush, Paul Wolfowitz, Dov Zakheim, Donald Rumsfeld, Condolezza Rice, Henry Kissinger, Paul Bremer, Douglas Feith, Elliot Abrams, Daniel Pipes, and Richard Perle, among others, including the powerful entities/persons, who finance them, are directly responsible for the deaths of hundreds of thousands of individuals, including some 4000 American service-people. Yet, due to their aggression countless other Americans, especially service-people, have been maimed and/or sickened. Plus, these agents of death are also responsible for the destruction of both the World Trade Center and the Pentagon. Given the public trust they abuse it, even causing the massive loss of life: how vile.

These are irrefutable murderers. Yet, Moussaoui, who has killed no one, is under the threat of the death penalty and is serving at a minimum life in prison? Surely, he is nothing but a patsy. Furthermore, the penalty is held without a single witness to any crime. In contrast, the entire world, let alone millions of Iraqis and Afghanis, as well as Pakistanis and Palestinians, have witnessed *first hand* the utter murder committed by such aforementioned individuals as well as the Israeli outlaws Netanyahu, Perez, and Sharon.

In the Middle East there are tens of thousands of eyewitnesses to the murders committed by Western tyrants. In contrast, Moussaoui harmed no one. Yet, the acts committed by the non-Muslim perpetrators, including the Vice President and the President of the United States, have led to countless thousands of deaths. Thus, Moussaoui, as well as Lindh, must be released immediately. So should all other Muslims or any other individuals held without cause on the fabricated basis of an Islaamic 9/11. There was no Islaamic action against the United States. These are mere lies to distract attention from the real criminals. What's more, as this book is going to press Moussaoui is being assessed for execution., although that conviction was dismissed. In this respect a report of the court's activities was posted (April 2006) by Michael Sniffen on AOL News. The report is filled with wicked lies. Here is a list of the points made by the article:

- That according to prosecutor David Novak Moussaoui showed "no remorse" for the deaths of various Americans, who died in the attacks. Yet, since Moussaoui was never involved in the attacks, whether or not he showed remorse is irrelevant. This is a mere hate campaign to pin the crime on the wrong man and, therefore, by insinuation all Muslims. It is also so the true criminals behind this can remain disguised.

- That he should be given the death penalty, because this would show that "we are the United States of America, and we are not going to put up with a bunch of thugs who invoke God's name to kill nearly 3,000 Americans." Here there are two lies. There were no 3,000 Americans killed, but, rather, half the fatalities were foreign nationals. What's more, there were no Muslims who attacked it Rather, it was destroyed by Western individuals using Muslims as scapegoats. So, then, there are three lies told by the prosecution. This is prosecutory misconduct. It is a vilification campaign to distract attention from the real killers. Like Moussaoui said, the trial is "a circus, a charade." So, all the points made by the prosecutors are lies. For Moussaoui's own view of his arrest and incrimination in the form of his own hand written (now typed) and signed pleadings see Appendix B.

Regarding the Muslims arrested in the United States after 9/11, many of whom are still held, none are murderers. Nor are any of them rapists. Nor have any such people bombed other nations or stolen their wealth. Nor have any legitimate charges been brought against them. Yet, in contrast, all such crimes are committed by Western powers against the Muslim peoples. These are the real criminal acts which must be held culpable as well as punished.

In England transit authority insiders reported that the Muslims were wrongly blamed for the bombings and that it was, in fact, government/secretive operatives who were responsible. What's more, eyewitnesses dispute the possibility of Muslim bombers. Bruce Lait, passenger on one of the carriages, said, essentially, that the accused Muslim, in this case Shehzad Tanweer, set no bomb. Nor was this man even on the carriage.

Regarding terror it suits the global and corporate agenda to blame the Muslims. For instance, as a result of the war against Islaam Western companies have earned hundreds of billions of dollars. For certain powerful corporations war is highly profitable. It is a sure way to earn massive profits.

As demonstrated by the U.S. government's Operation Northwoods to create a fabricated war—a war of false terror—a scapegoat is required. The areas in Florida where the supposed Muslim terrorists operated, Del Ray Beach, Hollywood, and Coral Springs, are precisely where the Israeli spies, who were impersonating Muslims, were caught. Rather, incredibly, with the exception of perhaps Ziyad Jarrah none of the accused Muslims can be placed in the area. Instead, here, in 2001 nearly 200 Israeli spies were arrested. One nest of such spies was located within blocks of the fabricated address for Muhammad Atta. Many of these spies were held in solitary confinement and deported. These included Israeli military officers. All were illegal aliens. In contrast, during this time not a single Muslim immigrant was caught in the act, either spying or committing terror. Nor were any Muslims legitimately deported for these reasons.

Regarding 9/11 the majority of the accused Muslims are alive. What's more, they had nothing to do with the heinous crimes in New York City and the Pentagon. These men, now proven innocent, include Khalid al-Midhar, Salem al-Hamzi, Waleed M. al-Shehri, Abdul Aziz al-Omari, Wail al-Shehri (Waleed's brother), Marwan al-Shehhi, Muhammad al-Shahri, Saeed al-Ghamdi, and Ahmad al-Nami. Also, according to family members Muhammad Atta is still alive. This finalizes the list of the absolved at 10, all very much alive.

During 9/11 congressional members placed Atta as "not in the country." The claim that Atta trained at flight schools in Norman, Oklahoma is a lie. The fact is over half the accused are alive and, surely, had nothing to do with this catastrophe. This fully refutes the entire claim against the Muslims. What's more, clearly, this demonstrates that no Muslim hijackers flew jetliners into American buildings. Likewise, it proves that the Muslims accused as accomplices, such as Zacharias Moussaoui and Munir Motasaddeq, are purely scapegoats, fully innocent. How can anyone be an accomplice to an act that never happened?

The fact is the the entire act was fabricated. This was to serve a brutal agenda: to further the greedy desires of the war mongering rulers. Thus, in 9/11 thousands of Americans, as well as foreign nationals, were killed, merely for financial gain. It is also for the lust of power and control.

Regarding the 9/11 and London terror acts there is no evidence of Islaamic involvement. On the contrary Islaam's enemies are responsible. Incredibly, in September/October 2001 only Israelis—in fact, illegal aliens—were arrested attempting to bomb public buildings. These Israelis were caught with explosives, grenades, and guns. In contrast, during that time no Muslims were found attempting to bomb public buildings.

The wars in Iraq and Afghanistan are based upon lies. The authorities in the White House purposely misled the American people. Thus, the wars are merely corporate murder, where people reap vast riches on the death and misery of others. In a vile consequence due to radiation poisoning thousands of innocent babies and children—the vast majority being Muslims—are brutally dying. Other thousands are born defective. Still others die at birth from grotesque defects, some even being born without a brain. This increased incidence of birth defects, as well as cancer, is occurring in Iraq, Kuwait, Saudi Arabia, Afghanistan, Syria, Turkey, and Iran but also other Mediterranean countries, such as Italy and Spain, and even as far away as England and the United States. Israelis, This is due to the vile, as well as illegal, use of, essentially, nuclear-tipped weapons—the true weapons of mass destruction. George Bush lied about those weapons, all to create a synthetic war. Furthermore, Palestinians, Lebanese, Israelis, Turks, Italians, Greeks, and Africans are also vulnerable to this toxicity. Thus, just as in Vietnam American countless lives are being lost needlessly.

This is because the war is illegitimate. What's more, these are Western crimes: true terror.

The same is true of Palestine. Here, the Israelis are the oppressors. The fact is as documented by Christopher Sykes in *Crossroads to Israel* Palestine was conquered exclusively through terror. Thus, it is the Israelis, the conquerors of Iraq and Palestine, who are the true terrorists. In the entire history of Islaam no similar acts have been committed.

The Israelis commit vast terror. They do so flagrantly but also clandestinely. They bomb infrastructure, even religious centers: all to create strife. They even bomb mosques, masquerading as 'sectarian Muslims.' Then, they heap blame on the Muslims. This is so that they can continue to commit vile terror. The Zionists are parasites, who live on stolen land. For human beings all they cause is harm. What's more, they specialize in blaming others for their crimes. Thus, rather than the Muslims it is the Zionists who are the true harbingers of terror. The fact is the Zionist entity is the primary destabilizing factor on this earth. It serves no productive purpose. Rather, all it causes is loss, in every conceivable way. Without doubt, the Zionists will even destroy there own people if it promotes a wicked agenda.

Regarding 9/11 Zionist involvement is obvious. It was they who exclusively profited from this act. They plotted it and, then, enacted it. They raised spies, who imitated Muslims. In the stock market they placed bets, *before and on September 11*, earning tens of millions of dollars. Incredibly, much of this trading occurred from the World Trade Center itself, as proven by the contents of recovered hard drives. Let the Israelis dispute this fact. Then, let them prove otherwise. In 1991 the avowed Zionist, Paul Wolfowitz, stated categorically that in order to justify global conquests there was a need for a major terror act. This was to serve as a cover for war. The fact is the war had already been planned. Thus, rather than a 'catalyst' 9/11 was an excuse, that is to perpetrate murderous wars. Yet, not a single Muslim in this entire world knew about this. Nor did any Muslim commit it. Rather, in Islaam any such act is condemned.

Wolfowitz' proclamation is available for all to see in his document, Project for a New American Century. Here, he calls for a "catalyzing event" to justify Israeli expansionism. This is the entire purpose of his dictum. What's more, this organization is funded directly by huge armaments corporations, which are Israeli-infested. Thus, rather than the Muslims it is these who are the perpetrators of mass crimes.

The slander that is heaped upon Islaam is also evidence of a plot. For instance, consider the internationally broadcast media clip of Palestinian Muslims, who were purportedly celebrating the 9/11 carnage. This was shown within hours of the disaster: how readily it was shown. Yet, the analysis of Mark Crispin Miller, Professor of Media Studies, New York University, is telling. He clearly proved that the footage was filmed years prior. The event, incredibly, was a funeral of nine Palestinians who, in fact, were murdered by the Israelis. Said Miller:

> ...to show it without explaining the background and to show it (repeatedly) is to make propaganda for the war machine...

The question is who showed this and, rather, who ordered its showing? This will lead directly to the perpetrators. Yet, such representations by the media are no minor issue. The fact is this led to the slaughter of the innocent. In the aftermath of 9/11 a Pakistani Muslim, a convenience store operator, was murdered because he looked 'Arab.' A Sikh was slaughtered because he appeared

'Muslim.' A Christian Arab was murdered because he looked Islaamic. Hundreds of people were fired from their jobs because they appeared 'Muslim.' These are the crimes instigated by the media and other criminal elements, which foment lies for selfish gains. The victims were killed because people in the West are told that a certain people attacked them, Muslims and dark-skinned people. Yet, if they only realized who the true culprits were, because, surely, the FBI tell lies. Surely, the government did evil, because what it taught was purely false. What's more, these lies led to the murder of the innocent.

Aren't the hijackings the entire basis of the attacks against Afghanistan and Iraq? Aren't they the basis of the imprisonment in Western countries of thousands of Muslims, including John Walker Lindh, Zacharias Moussaoui, and Munir Motasaddeq? Is it not also the basis of a supposed war of civilizations? Yet, here, it has been proven that there was no Islaamic attack. Obviously, the Muslims were/are maliciously blamed, accused of mass slaughter. As a result, there was/is international indignation against them. This led to brutal warfare. Yet, it is all fabricated. Thus, obviously, any wars based upon these lies are true crimes against humanity, in fact, genocidal.The same will be true of any future attack against Iran.

Then, for those who dispute this who can give even the slightest evidence that the Muslims did this? The fact is the evidence is precisely to the contrary, that is that the Muslims were framed and, what's more, that they are free of any blame.

The Israelis control the press. So, they spread every conceivable vileness. They purge the American public of their money through so-called aid. Then, they use these funds to spread corruption. One such corruption is their constant attack against Islaam. The following is proof of their lies. It is also proof that they truly control the media and that their objective is to target Islaam, as per this front page article in the *Chicago Tribune* (January 02/2006):

> Derby, England—Lina, a wide-eyed 18-year-old, is still trying to get the hang of freedom in 3-inch heels.
>
> Until a month ago, Lina had never worn Western clothing. Her parents, immigrants form Pakistan, insisted she wear the jilbab, a head-to-toe covering, favored by conservative Muslims.
>
> When she turned 16, her parents informed her that she was "engaged" to her first cousin, (who) she detested. When she balked, she said, her parents withdrew her from school and locked her in her room, where they told her she would remain until she consented.
>
> "They put two padlocks on the door and they locked the windows," she said. they also installed spikes along the top of the backyard fence so she couldn't climb over.
>
> Lina's imprisonment lasted nearly two years. The only time she was allowed of of her room was to do housework. There were frequent beatings, she said, and endless mental cruelties.
>
> "My mom threatened me with a knife. They also cut my hair off."

This is obviously an attack against Islaam. Who can now deny that there is a war against it? For instance, would anyone knowingly associate with a way of life that promoted this? If this were truly Islaamic, no one would associate with this faith. This is the aim of the article. True, what she endured was vile, however, there is no Islaamic basis for it. The fact is rather than a Muslim *this women is a Sikh*. Her full name, Lina Sanghera, is entirely Sikh and/or Hindu. Her parents are exclusively Sikh, that is non-

Muslim. This custom is an Indian one and has nothing to do with Islaam. Thus, the Tribune has acted maliciously by blaming Islaam for a custom of non-Muslims. Are the Zionists so desperate that they must attribute any vile act to Islaam, including pagan traditions, the very traditions which Islaam refutes?

On the back page of the Tribune article the fact that Ms. Sanghera was Sikh was subtly admitted. Thus, by broadcasting this on the front page the objective was achieved. Notice the insinuation in the second paragraph, that is *favored by conservative Muslims*. This was purely to make these acts appear Islaamic. Thus, the attack is registered, and the damage is done: pure lies. These are the same lies told regarding the 19 accused Muslims, the four accused British youths, and, most dramatically, the wrongfully accused Usama bin Laden.

A direct set-up, an actual attempt to frame Muslims, is even more revealing. This relates to the September 11 atrocity. It demonstrates the extent to which the enemies of Islaam will plot to achieve their objectives. This is in regard to the planned bombing in New York City of, incredibly, its primary bridges. An 'anonymous' caller told a 9-1-1 dispatcher that, a "group of Palestinians" were "mixing a bomb" inside a white van. Then, the caller even told the dispatcher where the van was headed, that is to the Holland Tunnel. This was obviously a decoy. Yet, how could an anonymous caller know precisely where the van was headed or even what they were doing? What's more, no one who would do this would make this so obvious, that is "mixing junk in a van." This was an Israeli plot: there is no doubt about it. However, the plot was foiled due to shrewd law enforcement individuals, who closed all tunnels and bridges. On one of the bridges they surely found a white van "filled with explosives." However, rather than Muslim it was the Israelis who were the culprits.

Here, the Israelis directly plotted to pin a terror act upon the Muslims, even though the former were the perpetrators. These Israelis, as dictated from the highest level of the Zionist entity, had planned and plotted the destruction of a U. S. landmark. It was just barely foiled. Here, the Israelis intended to kill. What's more, proof of the plot against the Muslims is found in this transcript (NBC News):

> Dispatcher: Jersey City police
> Caller: Yes, we have a white van, 2 or 3 guys in there; they look like Palestinians and going around a building. There is a minivan heading toward the Holland Tunnel, I see the guy by Newark Airport mixing some junk, and he has those sheikh uniform.
> Dispatcher: He has what?
> Caller: He's dressed like an Arab.

This is obviously a set-up, proven by the transcript. The caller was an Israeli secret service agent. His purpose was to seed disinformation. This was to falsely create hate and blame. Then, after establishing the false trail these Israeli agents plotted to destroy a major bridge, most likely the George Washington Bridge. Then, obviously, the police dispatcher would contact the media, and the blame would have been registered against the Palestinians, as well as, in fact, Muslims. Yet, there is another obvious proof of this fraud. It is the insinuation of 'Arab' dress. This is because in the United States Palestinians usually wear Western-style clothes. This is true even in their own country.

People hate Muslims because they have been told vast lies. They hate them because they believe they are associated with acts of horror. Yet, all this hate is misplaced. This is because, incredibly, the acts for which the Muslims are accused were committed by others, notably malicious Zionists as well as powerful people within the Western system. What's more, these lies originate from the Zionist-controlled press. Thus, if there is to be any hate or, rather, investigation, it must be against the Zionists.

Regarding these crimes—the crimes of 9/11 and other modern terror acts—justice must be served. Thus, the true culprits of these catastrophes must be revealed as well as prosecuted. Regarding 9/11 this was no bin Laden attack. This man was merely used as a distraction. He had nothing to do with it.

It is realized that people have a difficult time believing this. Yet, this book has provided definite facts. It is the fact that there was no Islaamic 9/11. It is also the proof that the official story of the London bombings is a fraud. Ultimately, it is proof of high crimes by the Zionist entity. After all, it is this entity which plotted through its operatives the attempted bombing of the George Washington Bridge, the attempted decimation of the Mexican Congress, the tank shelling of the Church of Nativity, along with the slaughter of its Christian bell-keeper, and, most dramatically, the destruction of the World Trade Center. Thus, rather than only Muslims the targets are largely Christian.

On 9/11 there were no Muslim hijackers. Rather, the airplanes were most likely military drones. These drones were guided by remote control. Existence of two drones is virtually confirmed: those which hit the twin towers. There is no confirmatory evidence regarding the Pentagon strike or the crash in Pennsylvania, that is that any commercial jetliners or drones were involved. Rather, as confirmed by Cincinnati's WCPO-TV, Channel 9, the supposed crashed jet in Pennsylvania, Flight 93, never did so. Instead, it landed safely in Cleveland's Hopkin's International Airport. Due to the terror attacks and the reported concern of a possible bomb on-board it had been diverted there. This has been fully confirmed, even by United Airlines. It has also been confirmed by the city's mayor. Regarding the Pentagon it was struck by a much smaller projectile, either a missile or small jet or, perhaps, a combination thereof. Dulles Airport flight controllers have made it clear that it was a military jet.

Regardless, the World Trade Center plane strikes alone could not destroy it. Nor could a fire do so. In fact, never before in history has a fire caused the collapse of a sky scraper.

The proprietor of the trade center complex, Larry Silverstein, admits to the real cause of its destruction. He said on PBS that regarding at least one of the buildings in the complex, number 7, it was purposely destroyed. He admitted that set charges were the cause and that *he placed the order*. Then, people are caused to focus on Islaamic terror: how vile. Building 7 was the command and control center for the entire complex. It also housed the offices of the CIA and FBI.

It was Silverstein and colleagues, who were the primary beneficiaries. Some three months before the attack his Israeli-owned consortium took out a hefty multi-billion dollar insurance policy on the towers, with just such an act in mind. In other words, he was specifically insured for a violent terror act. Silverstein sued the insurance company in an attempt to gain twice the insured value on the basis of two terror attacks—two jets. However, the insurance company prevailed and only paid out the required amount, some 2.2 billion dollars. Yet, this is, in fact, ill gotten gains, because this was no accident. Rather, this was a deliberate act perpetrated by the buildings' owners.

The Israelis were directly involved in these acts (see Appendix A). They, along with certain powerful ones in the U.S. government, including Dick Cheney, Donald Rumsfeld, and Condolezza Rice, and even the President himself, were the only ones who knew in advance. No Muslim knew anything about the plot. What's more, on 9/11 the Israelis were exclusively arrested, virtually at the scene. In contrast, no Muslims were seen or arrested there. What's more, it is a Muslim's duty if having foreknowledge of such potential crimes to report it to the authorities. Thus, if any true Muslims would have known about these acts, they would have given due warning.

Obviously, instead of the Muslims there were other forces responsible for these catastrophes. Yet, then, who is responsible? As proven by the capture of hundreds of spies Israeli involvement is certain. The espionage, including the impersonating of Muslims and the attempting bombings of American landmarks, was ordered at the highest levels. Thus, the plot was ordered by the likes of Sharon, Netanyahu, and Perez. To reiterate in the months leading to the terrorist attacks Israeli aliens, actual Mossad agents, posed as Muslims. They held forged IDs in Muslims' names and created false paper trails. Even so, as confirmed by Robert Muller, head of the FBI, not a single shred of evidence—not even a signature or receipt—places any Muslim as a perpetrator.

Even so, no Muslims posed as Jews. What's more, historically, there has never been any public terror in the Islaamic world. Rather, Islaam has served as a wedge against such tyranny. For true terror consider the campaigns of Alexander the Great, Atilla the Hun, Ghengiz Khan, Joseph

Stalin, and Adolf Hitler. Yet, American and British authorities have committed even more ghastly terror than these: the Vietnam War, Hiroshima, Nagasaki, the slaughter of the Native Americans, the Iran-Iaq war, the invasion of Iraq, and the invasion of Afghanistan. All such acts of terror were perpetrated by non-Muslims. Even so, today, when terror does occur, particularly in Islaamic lands, it is a consequence of interference by Western powers. This is indisputable. Consider the capture in Iraq of British and Israeli men "dressed as Arabs." These spies packed enough explosives to destroy entire city blocks and were fully plotting to kill the innocent, while blaming it on 'insurgents.' Then, there is the vile case of the rape and murder of a 20-year-old Iraqi girl by an American soldier, fully confirmed by the U.S. authorities. This degree of vileness wasn't sufficient. To disguise the crime he and his colleagues also killed her mother and younger sister. Thus, rather than in a mosque or a poor Middle Eastern country the culprits will be found instead within the Western system itself. Thus, Islaamic terror is an illusion.

This book is based upon extensive research. There is nothing which is speculative. What's more, anyone can confirm its contents. There is proof beyond any doubt that the atrocities of September 11 were non-Muslim acts. So, will anyone give thought to the implications of this? The fact is those implications are obvious. It is that there is a vicious global war against Islaam and its followers. Yet, it is a war based exclusively upon lies. It is the powerful ones within the United States and Israel who are responsible for these lies. Then, it is also these powerful ones who are the perpetrators of terror. Islaam stands for peace, which is proven by its history. No one can deny it. Thus, regarding 9/11 and the

London bombing the Muslims are blameless. Rather, like the souls lost on 9/11 they are victims. Even so, the very purpose of Islaam is to prevent such horrors. This is why it is the most elegant, sophisticated system in existence.

Appendix A

List of Zionists directly involved and even perpetrating the September 11th atrocities

The following is a list of known Zionist agents, who have infiltrated the U.S. hierarchy. These agents serve exclusively the Israeli entity, as well as their own personal gain. They offer nothing substantive to the American public. All the listed individuals demonstrate at least circumstantial involvement in the 9/11 atrocities. What's more, the evidence for involvement is far greater for the Zionists than any accused Muslims. Furthermore, Pentagon insiders are well aware that the Zionists are the perpetrators of major aggression and that they are the logical plotters of the September 11th attacks. It is known definitely that they were plotting to attack the Alaska Pipeline and that they had nearly blown up the George Washington Bridge. What's more, Zionists were the only people in the United States ,who brazenly celebrated the destruction of the World Trade Center. This alone gives evidence of their involvement.

Dov Zakheim

Role/Position: This man began in the Bush administration as an advisor during the 2000 presidential campaign. He was under instructions from the Israelis to infiltrate the Bush campaign to gain power over the presidency. Thus, after the election he became the Undersecretary of Defense, remaining in this position from 2001 to 2005.

An avowed Zionist Zakheim's goal is the maintenance and expansion of the Israeli entity. He arises from a family with a history of terrorism. His father belonged to a division of the Irgun and Stern gangs. These gangs had a proven history of murderous acts. In the document *Rebuilding America's Defenses: Strategy, Forces and Resources for a New Century* published by The American Enterprise's *Project for a New American Century,* in order to justify invasions of Muslim countries Zakheim called for a "catastrophic and catalyzing event…like a new Pearl Harbor." This proclamation must be emphasized, because it was published one year prior to the attacks. The purpose of the internal terror attack was to justify expansion of the Israeli entity and, ultimately, to control all events in the Middle East in Israel's favor. The terror act would, it was predicted, create the necessary frame of mind for Americans, so they would support invasions of other countries—so they would willingly send their sons and daughters to slaughter.

The war, it was believed, would be 'good for Israel' and would bolster the Israelis' wealth and power. To gain complete control over the U.S. military, however, as well as to overpower opponents in the State Department, who were resistant to another Middle East War, Zakheim determined that a terror act of 'massive scope' was necessary. He received instructions from high level Israelis to proceed.

Upon infiltrating the Pentagon he took control of the finances. Then, after plotting the act and perpetrating it—after purging the treasury, of which he had full control of untold billions of dollars—Zakheim resigned. Of course, any terror act would be immediately blamed on Muslims. This is despite the fact that the Muslims could never have afforded to do so, nor did they have strategic access to the necessary facilities. Andreas von Bülow has confirmed that, clearly, the 9/11 attacks were exceedingly costly and could only have been achieved by well-financed intelligence operatives. Zakheim is an Israeli spy, who perpetrated vile acts to serve his masters.

Incredibly, before joining the Pentagon, Zakheim was the CEO of Systems Planning Corporation. Of note, an SPC subsidiary, Triada Corporation, was precisely the group which oversaw the investigation into the original (1993) terrorist attack on the World Trade Center, also blamed exclusively on Muslims. This act too must be revisited for the Zionist connection.

According to its Web site Zakheim's corporation makes its money in militarism. Thus, he uses his insider position to increase his wealth. The money he gains is from government contracts, for military spending. This money derives from the American public. The monies are collected by the IRS, which is also headed by a Zionist. Obviously, Zakheim lobbies for his own company and has no patriotic function.

His company, which has operated within the Pentagon for some 25 years, specializes in a unique technology for *remote control flight of planes*. This is known as Flight Termination System or FTS. This is used to destroy target planes, known as drones. The technology allows for remote explosions in the event of a test that goes awry. The method is highly elaborate, a kind of sophisticated technology for war games. This technology is so advanced that it allows for the control of numerous remotely flown planes, all from a distant location. The range is several hundred miles. In other words, Zakheim represents a technology for total remote control of planes, even large planes such as military tankers. These systems allow for the taking over of the flight of any such airplanes, which are used in war games. This technology is effective for numerous types of aircraft, including passenger jets.

His Web site confirms that near the time of the 9/11 disasters the airforce was a significant customer. That year the technology was delivered to the Eglin Air Force Base in Eglin, Florida. He has also admitted in his own materials to have provided another airforce base, Florida's MacDill Airforce Base, with 32 Boeing 767 aircraft. These aircraft were provided as part of a Boeing/Pentagon tanker lease agreement.

Zakheim's activities are highly suspicious. They demonstrate that this man is one of the few with the capability to inflict an internal terror act upon the American people. He surely had the access, plus, he had the motive. In contrast, bin Laden had no such technology and/or access.

Again, he had full access. Through his investigations of the original World Trade Center disaster he had all the necessary information about the building structure and any blueprints. Surely he had access to various Boeing craft, the very type that struck the World Trade Center. It was also Zakheim, along with Wolfowitz and Feith, who made clear that a massive terror act will likely be needed to gain the American public's acceptance for militant acts. Thus, Zakheim is the likely perpetrator of this disastrous attack. The Muslims had nothing to do with it.

The evidence against Zakheim is significant. His father was a member of Betar, a known terrorist organization. This organization was formed by European Zionists to attack the power base in various countries, who appeared hostile to the Jewish agenda. Betar members were cohorts with the notorious Irgun and Stern gangs, the ones responsible for the bombing of the King David Hotel and the numerous massacres at various Palestinian villages. Their campaigns led to the deaths of hundreds of British soldiers and civil servants. Thus, Zakheim has a family history of terrorism. The notorious terrorist Menachem Begin was a personal friend of the Zakheims.

Zakheim's avowed goal is the control of the Middle East. This is no surprise, since the published goal of his father's terrorist organization was the control of Middle Eastern oil. Yet, since they are Polish in origin the Zakheims are non-Semites. They surely have no historical right to this oil. Thus, is it any surprise that part of the so-called coalition force is Polish nationals?

As final proof of Zakheim's involvement, he published a paper detailing his ultimate goals. They are the creation of a Pearl Harbor-like terrorist attack in order to force the U.S. into war and, then, the application of the resulting war status to launch a coup *against any non-Jewish forces in the government.* Thus, rather than an attempted conquest against the Middle East or Iraq, the ultimate goal of Zakheim's acts is the conquest of the United States.

To reiterate it is necessary to review Zakheim's achievements: he is the creator of *The Project for a New American Century.* This was published in September 2000, *precisely a year before 9/11.* In this article, page 51, he, along with fellow Zionists Paul Wolfowitz and Douglas Feith, states that the "process of transformation, even if it brings revolutionary change, is likely to be a long one, *absent some catastrophic and catalyzing event—like a new Pearl Harbor."* Then Bin Laden surely wouldn't do this to satisfy these Zionists. Rather, obviously, the September 11 atrocities were Zionist acts. This is confirmed by the Pentagon itself through the respected Army School of Advanced Military Studies, which published that regarding any internal terror act the Zionists are the "wild card, ruthless and cunning with the *capability* to target U.S. forces and make it look like a Palestinian/Arab act." This precisely describes the capacity of Zakheim and his cohorts. In contrast, the U.S. government has been unable to provide even to the slightest degree any supposed 'Arab' hijackers. Rather, the photographs provided by the government of the so-called perpetrators are fraudulent. Then, while bin Laden denies any involement is there any precise denial from Zakhein, Wolfowitz, Feith, Perle, or their likes?

Paul Wolfowitz

Role/Position: Directly under Rumsfeld from 2001 through 2005, the entire time of the initiation and 'completion' of the Iraq war, this man was the Deputy Secretary of the Department of Defense. He was second in command under Donald Rumsfeld. His position was a civilian one created by the Zionists themselves. From here he was appointed by George Bush to run the World Bank. According to a number of Jewish observers he is a "primary architect of the Iraq war." Along with Zakheim, Wolfowitz helped create a Project for a New American Century, where he described the need for a massive terror act, leading to thousands of American deaths, in order to justify invasions. In particular he desired justification for the invasion of Iraq and Iran. In this document he clearly stated that a massive terror act in the United States would facilitate his goal. This goal was to orchestrate U.S. aggression. Wolfowitz is an avowed Zionist, whose entire objective is the preservation of the Israeli entity, along with personal gain. The entire approach for the invasion of Iraq was largely based upon Wolfowitz' dictums, a man with no military or combat history.

Irve Lewis 'Scooter' Libby

Role/Position: This man was the Chief of Staff for Dick Cheney. He was also Assistant for National Security Affairs to the same. He resigned after being indicted for obstruction of justice and perjury, a mere fall guy, regarding the leak of the identity of CIA agent Valerie Plame.

Douglas Feith

Role/Position: A main architect of the war against Iraq from 2001 through 2004, this man was the Undersecretary for Defense Policy. An avowed and vicious Zionist, his ancestors are strictly European, mainly German. He is a non-Semite. Thus, regarding any investigation of him, he surely cannot complain of anti-Semitism, again, because he himself is not only non-Semitic but is also decidedly anti-Semitic, since the victims of his violent policies are primarily Semites.

Feith bears direct responsibility for creating the so-called post-Iraq invasion rulership, which includes, among others, Ahmed Chalabi, a known thief, as well as General Jay Garner and Paul Bremer. Feith is the man who bypassed the normal channels in Washington, D.C., the CIA and other intelligence agencies, and set up his own agency. From here he fed the president false information. He disseminated "blatant lies" to the administration in order to achieve Zionist aims.

It is well known that Feith is exclusively loyal to the Israeli entity. In contrast, he has no loyalty to the American republic. He has direct relationships with the rulership of this entity and throughout the plotting of this attack communicated with both Binyamin Netanyahu and Ariel Sharon.

Feith's hostile Zionist intentions are obvious and are, therefore, easy to document. For instance, his former law partner, Marc Zell, is precisely the lawyer for the "fanatical Israeli settlers movement," which is usurping the deeded land of Palestinians. He is currently embroiled in a potential criminal prosecution. This relates to Pentagon spy Larry Franklin. Yet, it was Feith who brought Franklin into the Pentagon.

Feith's former law firm, Feith & Zell, was originally Israeli-based. Its clients include defense contractors who have paid Feith, through this firm, tens of thousands of dollars. Even before the war on Iraq Feith developed a company, Fandz International Law, to 'assist in reconstruction and coalition force activities' in Iraq. One of the goals of Feith & Zell was the re-establishment of a lucrative oil pipeline from the Iraqi fields to the Israeli port of Haifa, a long-time Zionist objective. Thus, his motives for causing war were largely profit-oriented, because such an achievement would reap him potentially billions of dollars. The objective was to use the U.S. military apparatus to achieve this, purely selfish. For his own personal gain he placed American, as well as Iraqi, lives at risk.

In his attempts to further his own personal interests Feith helped create and control two fabricated entities: the Defense Policy Board and the Office of Special Plans. Both are corrupt entities, the entire purpose of which is self-gain and Israeli expansionism. The former head of the Defense Policy Board, Richard Perle, resigned due to corruption, notably using the office of the presidency to further his own financial gain. Regarding the Office of Special Plans this was responsible for disseminating to the president false information about Iraq in order to create the 'justification' for war. As noted by Tom Barry of AntiWar.com, Feith's office "housed the Office of Special Plans as well as the Office of Northern Gulf Affairs," both of which were lobbying agencies for the Israeli entity. They both also served as channels for the creation of business opportunities, pure profiteering, from the war. His office also housed, says Barry, the so-called Undersecretary for Defense Intelligence, another fabricated group, headed by Stephen Cambone. It was Cambone who established the policies for interrogating, as well as torturing, the men imprisoned in both Guantanamo and Abu Ghraib. This was based upon the Israeli act against the Palestinians. This office also is responsible for the types of tactics used in Abu Ghraib, which have been the cause of international condemnation. Therefore, this black mark against the United States is exclusively Israeli, or Zionist, in origin.

Feith is a lobbyist for armaments makers and other war-related industries. Thus, he directly profits by causing war. This was his main motivation for calling for war against the various Muslim countries. It had nothing to do with national defense or security. Thus, incredibly, U.S. service people are risking their lives for the vile machinations of bloodthirsty Zionists, including the arch-Zionist Douglas Feith, a man who General Tommy Franks deemed "one of the stupidest (expletive deleted) guys on the face of the earth." Of course, this refers to the false intelligence he fed to the U.S. military, which was done to counter State Department resistance to the war agenda. Thus, the acts of Feith have been murderous. The fact is, there is infinitely more evidence proving murderous acts by this man than any of the accused or imprisoned Muslims, including the imprisoned Zacharias Moussaoui and John Lindh—including all those imprisoned in Guantanamo and/or Abu Ghraib. The 3,000 or more Americans killed in combat, as well as the 11,000 or more who have died of disease or accidents—Feith is directly responsible for all such deaths, since he maliciously lied in order to cause this war, horrendous violence based exclusively upon lies. Again, the lies are largely Feith's in origin.

Feith has also been directly involved in torture. His law firm has recruited Israeli firms for providing torturers, paid for by the U.S. government. Due to the vile acts of Feith, some 50 Israeli torturers, that is 'interrogators,' were placed in Iraq. These Israelis were paid to commit their acts through U.S. monies. Yet, the Iraqis have never harmed any Americans. Nor have they attacked the United States. Thus, they are victims of Zionist hate crimes. Feith has repeatedly brought business to Israeli companies that have received contracts under homeland security and the Defense Department. Thus, he gained personally from his policies. This is a conflict of interest, purely corrupt.

Michael Chertoff

Role/Position: He is the so-called Secretary of Homeland Security. His first loyalty is the Israeli entity, and technically, he is an Israeli citizen. He is fully aware that there was no Islaamic connection with the September 11 atrocities. Here, he has fomented only lies. He has come under fire recently for knowing in advance about the degree of damage from Hurricane Katrina—that the levees would likely fail—and doing nothing about it. His response to Katrina is regarded as incompetent.

Richard Perle

Role/Position: Playing a key, if not the key, role in the creation of this war, until 2003 Perle was the Chairman of the Department of Defense Policy Board. This is a fabricated organization. It has nothing to do with the needs of the United States. Rather, its entire purpose is to serve the Israeli entity. Perle remains a consultant for military 'policy' to the war criminal Donald Rumsfeld.

During the Reagan Administration he was widely criticized for corruption after it was reported that he had recommended that the Army purchase an armaments system from an Israeli company that a year earlier had paid him $50,000 in consulting fees. He was also accused in a report submitted to the U.S. Securities and Exchange Commission of having breached his fiduciary responsibilities as a director of Hollinger International by authorizing several controversial transactions, which diverted the company's net profit from the shareholders to the accounts of various executives. At Hollinger Perle received over $3 million in bonuses in addition to his salary. The total earned was approximately $5.5 million, and the investigating committee mandated that the money be returned. This was essentially a 'discipline' for corruption.

Ariel Sharon

Role/Position: This man was instrumental in assisting numerous Zionists in the infiltration of the White House. He also controlled the infiltration of Mossad and Haganah agents throughout the United States. This includes the agents who were responsible for the attempted destruction of the George Washington Bridge and the bombing of the Alaska Pipeline. This also includes the various Mossad agents found behaving suspiciously near U.S. nuclear facilities. All such activities were coordinated and approved by Sharon's authority.

Benjamin Netanyahu

Role/Position: A known spy, he has formerly worked within both U.S. and Israeli spy agencies. He helped coordinate the infiltration of Zionist agents into the Defense Department. Netanyahu is a known spy and murderer, who is responsible for infiltrating the leadership of the United States with various Israeli agents. These agents are responsible for the theft of state secrets. He, along with the insiders he helped place in Washington, is a chief architect of the U.S. invasion of Iraq. Netanyahu, as well as Sharon, admittedly knew in advance about the September 11 attacks. What's more, this man had complete knowledge of the operations in the United States of various Israeli spies, including those who attempted to destroy the George Washington Bridge. The fact is Netanyahu has called for the terror strikes in the United States and is one of the few individuals who had admitted knowledge of the September 11 attacks. What's more, Zakheim, Feith, Abrams, and Perle are merely his frontmen.

Elliot Abrams

Role/Position: A convicted man, of purposely withholding information from Congress, Abrams is the Deputy National Security Advisor. He is less than trustworthy, since in regards to the Iran-Contra affair he pled guilty to two counts of a misdemeanor, essentially of lying to Congress.

For those who might deem these comments to be racist or 'anti-Semitic,' consider the words of two of the world's top political scientists. These are John J. Mearsheimer, professor of political science and a co-director of the University of Chicago's Program on International Security Policy, and Stephen M. Walt, academic dean of the Kennedy School. Their paper, "The Israeli Lobby and U.S. Foreign Policy," demonstrates the truth of the aforementioned assessments. For instance, in summarizing the authors Tom Regan notes that the Bush administration is hopelessly infested with "fervent advocates of the Israeli cause as Elliot Abrams, John Bolton, Douglas Feith, I. Lewis 'Scooter' Libby, Richard Perle, Paul Wolfowitz and David Wurmser." What's more, the authors make clear, U.S. interests are never helped by such Israeli agents and are, rather, compromised. Furthermore, due to their acts there is no improvement in security but, rather, a decline in global safety.

Government insiders offer even more damning evidence. Ray McGovern, a former intelligence analyst for the CIA, declared that the United States went to war in Iraq for oil, Israel, and military bases craved by administration 'Zionists' so "the United States and Israel could dominate that part of the world." He said that Israel should not be considered an ally and that Bush was doing the bidding of (then) Israeli Prime Minister Ariel Sharon, a known mass murderer.

Israeli foreknowledge confirmed

On September 11th, 2001, the Israelis issued definite warnings to their fellows. No other people from any other country received such warnings. These warnings came in the form of text messages, which are received instantaneously. These warnings were from Israelis to fellow Israelis to prevent their deaths or harm. According to the Washington Post the messages were received by the Israeli firm

Odigo, which confirmed that two employees received text messages warning of an attack on the World Trade Center two hours before the attacks. In addition, Alex Diamandis, Odigo's vice president of sales and marketing, confirmed that workers in its research/development office in Israel received a warning from another Odigo user some two hours prior the first attack. The point is that only the Israelis knew in advance. Only they gained the benefit of this by protecting fellow Israelis. In contrast, no Muslims were issued advance warnings. As a result, a significant number of Muslims died in the carnage. This is compelling evidence of Israeli culpability in the attack. The fact that only Israelis received the warning is an important clue. This means that they are the only ones proven to know about the disaster in advance. It also means that they bear complicity to the crime, since they knowingly allowed others to die. Thus, all further investigation related to this criminal event must be focused upon them.

Muslims who were WRONGLY ACCUSED and had no role in the September 11 attacks:

The people and citizens of Afghanistan

The so-called Taliban leadership of Afghanistan

Usama bin Laden (or any of his colleagues)

The people and citizens of Iraq

The people and citizens of Saudi Arabia

The people and citizens of Yemen

The people and citizens of Pakistan

The people and citizens of Iran (including any and all clergy)

Zacharias Moussaoui

Mounir Motassadeq

Khaled Shaikh Muhammad

Ramzi bin al-Shib

The Muslims of the United States of America

Appendix B

The Written Pleadings of Zacarias Moussaoui

The following are the word-for-word pleadings of Zacarias Moussaoui. They are available on the internet hand-written. The wording has been slightly upgraded to correct grammatical errors. These are his exact words, with upgraded English. Information in parenthesis helps explain the meaning. There are numerous revelations here. It can only be imagined how much more information would be procured without the redactions. Yet, even so these writings serve as proof that the entire claim of an Islaamic attack against the United States is bogus and that, particularly, Zacarias Moussaoui is entirely innocent of all charges. At most he is a prisoner of war—the war against Islaam. Incredibly, the pleadings are completely opposite of the representations of this man by the media. In particular, Zionist elements have sought to use him as a scapegoat to avoid their own prosecution.

In the Name of God

Super Redacted   September 19/02

Zacarias Moussaoui v. US   Muslim v. Crusader

*Keep your mouth shut, Dunham**

Motion to stop Dunham playing the superstar

God is Great

It is about time that Leonie Brinkema shut the mouth of her wannabe superstar Dunham. In January I requested Dunham and McMahon (and the rest) to sign a confidentiality agreement that they will not discuss the case around me to the outside world. I specifically insisted on a *no* book deal on Moussaoui. At first Dunham said it was no problem and that regardless he was bound by professional ethic. That was before he went on holiday [REDACTED STATEMENT]. When he came back he said when I pressed him to give a written agreement. "I write what I want about my life and even if I mention you in my book it does not mean people will buy this book because of you."

No doubt that Americans are interested in the life of Dunham before he got my case.

Everthemore, Dunham has been trying to be on every TV or radio (show) he could grab. In around March he told me that he went to a lawyer conference and discuss my case publicly to raise "awareness."

Leonie Brinkema must order Dunham to keep his mouth shut and to stop misrepresenting (himself)as my lawyer. Dunham is not my lawyer (and, rather) he is my main enemy—without him the government will not even go to trial.

Leonie Berinkema must order that Dunham is not allow to discuss my case publicly (on) TV, media, conference, books, news article, internet, etc. At least they could wait until I am dead to make money out of me.

Slave of God

*This refers to Frank Dunham, a standby lawyer appointed by the U.S. Government for Moussaoui. However, during the trial Dunham repeatedly compromised Moussaoui's defense. In 2005 Moussaoui asked for Dunham's withdrawal.

In the Name of God

In the US District Court of the 14th District of Virginia, Alexandria

Zacarias Moussaoui v. US
Motion to compel the government to withdraw the charge against me,
because the FBI was conducting an undercover surveillance operation.
Testimony of the FBI agent Coleen Rawley, a lawyer in the Bureau of
Minneapolis, and her expert knowledge on FBI investigation will establish
the FBI cover up. Hearing must convene to hear Coleen Rawley.

God is Great

The US government must withdraw all charges, because it knows that I
was *under FBI surveillance and (fully knows) what was my activity in
US and abroad.*

FBI agent Coleen Rawley is a first class witness and expert on how
Senior FBI officials were and are trying to prevent a deep investigation
of my background before September 11 (and now) in order to avoid to
have to charge me and go to court (and be given a lawyer) and,
therefore, potentially running the risk to have a leak that will have made
headlines before September 11 and alert the (supposed) 19 hijackers on
the fact the FBI had arrested a Muslim Arab at PanAm, the same school
where (the United States government) believed the hijacker trained a
few weeks before.

I am sure that Coleen Rawley did not know the full extent of the
information that was in the (possesion) of FBI…on and about my arrest
August 16, 2001. The government and Leonie Brinkema have placed
all documents under seal to prevent even their own agent to understand
the corruption and cynical (plots) of senior FBI agents.

Leonie Brinkema will most probably try to pretend that Coleen Rawley
is not relevant for the investigation on September 11. Coleen Rawley's
testimony under my examination will call the Americans to know how
their own government cynically allowed September 11 in order to
destroy Afghanistan.

Slave of God

In the Name of God

In the US District for the Eastern District of Virginia Alexandria Division

Zacarias Moussaoui v. US

Motion to appear in front of the Grand Jury converse on September 11 attack to testify.

God is Great

I, slave of God, Zacarias Moussaoui must be allowed to testify under oath under penalty of perjury in front of the Grand Jury to converse on the September 11. I have extensive and relevant information on how did this operation happen.

The prosecution has denied me the right to appear in front of a Grand Jury in New York and is falsely claiming that I refused. I challenge the US government to produce any court transcript any document where I refused to appear in front of the Grand Jury.

In fact, days before I was due to appear in court in New York to give my response on whether or not I will testify the US government indicted me. This is another example of their manipulation of the US legal system to gag me and prevent me to expose the cover up of the FBI.

As it has been said by the government that the threat of slave Usama Bin Laden (may God protect him) and Al Qaeda and associates is on going. I must be allowed to testify about my knowledge of the activity of these "terrorists" and on the September 11 attack.

As I was forbidden to have access to any kind of national security information (in fact almost any kind of information) no security reason can be falsely claim by this Court. I will stipulate to be chained, handcuffed, leg cuffed, stun belted, (and managed by) 20 or so marshals—as long as I can say what I know about Sept 11 attack.

An immediate hearing and response must be given by Leonie Brinkema

Slave of God

In the Name of God
In the US District Court for the Eastern District of Virginia Alexandria
Division

Zacarias Moussaoui v. US   No. 01-4SSA

Motion to give me a chance to defend myself by seeing Brother Freeman
to receive out of court legal assistance on Federal Law.

God is Great

In almost 10 months I have seen only Brother Freeman to help me
against the full forces of the Federal US Government. Every
conceivable trick has been played on me—*they cheat, lie, and threaten
all the time.*

Leonie Brinkema is not only the general to organize my killing she is
the executioner. The FBI cannot win the case without her stopping me
to speak in court. She wants to remove me from my defense. They
know the agenda of my defense. They know that I can prove beyond
reasonable doubt that this case is an FBI government cover up.

There is enough circumstantial proof, as well as direct evidence, to show
that the US Government and FBI, etc. were conducting a surveillance
operation on me and the (supposed) 19 hijackers. They arrested me and
not (accused hijacker Hani Hanjour) who was (supposedly) a few weeks
before me at PanAm Flight School (and has been reported as a danger),
because they knew that I was not with (the) 19 hijackers and, therefore,
they will not be alerted or scared by my arrest. (To have arrested Hani
Hanjour or his imposter) [REDACTED] will have alerted (the supposed)
19 hijackers (and stopped the plot).

Brother Freeman must be allowed to see me and help me, for out of
court legal assistance.

Leonie Brinkema is constantly looking for any excuse to remove me
from court. She knows that I must be killed to close their case—once
and for all. They know that, God willing, one day somebody will speak
out in the FBI or government, therefore, I must be killed before. Even
life in prison sentence is not good for them because one day people will

continued on next page

come to understand that their Judge Leonie Brinkema is orchestrating a conspiracy to murder Zacarias Moussaoui.

If the US Government and FBI has a strong case, they claim for the last 6 months, why do they use every dirty trick to prevent me defending my life? (Note: it is this same government, which spread lies that he wanted to kill himself as a martyr by setting himself up for the death penalty)

Brother Freeman was allowed to see me, but when he refuse to join their conspiracy to kill me, they kicked him out of the jail and Leonie Brinkema threatened him by lying in court (as usual). Deception is the way of Leonie Brinkema.

At the moment I have nobody to investigate the case for me outside (no one) to contact witnesses in my favor abroad to identify witness for subpoena. *I have no access at all to news.* No right to TV, to newspaper, to radio, even the prayer timetable. I have to calculate it now. No phone, no printer.

That the only way for them to win this case is to have *no* opposition.

Slave of God

[REDACTED STATEMENT]

Sensured by [REDACTED] States March 18, 03

No more Game: Top (warrior in the name of God) Khalid Shiek Mohammed and Mustafa Hawsawi must speak out freely.

To the court of 'appall' of 9th 'Circus:'

Motion to force Leonie to "rule" on (supposed) 9/11 mastermind Sheik Mohammed and chief financial officer Brother Mustafa for their appearance and testimony at the trial of the sworn enemy of the United (States of America), namely Zacarias Moussaoui.
[REDACTED STATEMENT]

In her endless, vicious plot to kill me Leonie is refusing to rule on Sheik Mohammed, (supposed) 9/11 Mastermind and Brother Mustafa [REDACTED] are essential for my (own defense) on the conspiracy to kill me [REDACTED] So I must have access to them well before trial to prepare my [REDACTED STATEMENT] and they must be at trial to humiliate Ashcroft.

Leonie must rule now as the issue of access to Sheik Mohammed and Brother Mustafa is even more important that the one of Ramzi.

Therefore, the court of 'Appall' should expose in a consolidated manner the access of Sheik Mohammed, Brother Mustafa, and Ramzi.

I cannot want to have a trial without Sheik Mohammed, Brother Mustafa, and Ramzi.

[REDACTED STATEMENT] otherwise you will have deny him as a material witness

[REDACTED STATEMENT] and nobody will be with any doubt that the United (States government has lied) [REDACTED STATEMENT] and that their "judges" are no more than Mafia Boss, entrusted with day to day running of their gigantic criminal organization.

(Regarding) you, criminal(s) of the Court of Appall, of the 9th Circus (aka Court of Appeal of 9th Circuit), you must immediately force Leonie to give a ruling on my brother.

Her latest vicious trick is that I cannot even have the order where she vomit her lie; it is secret

[REDACTED STATEMENT]

[REDACTED STATEMENT]

Sensored by (Soviet) States of America or USSA
March 31, 03

Zacarias Moussaoui

(Supposed) 9/11 Mastermind Must be Heard

Emergency motion to destroy the order of Leonie Brinkema that denies
access to Mohammed statements, so they be included into the brief to
the court of Appall of the 9th Circus (aka court of appeal)

[REDACTED STATEMENT]

As her continued effort to kill me Leonie Brinkema has denied Zacarias
Moussaoui access to "leaked" Mohammed statements on his *no* role in
9/11

This court of appeal must immediately force her to order the United
(States government) [REDACTED] to hand over Mohammed statements.

As you pretend to be deciding whether or not Ramzi should be at
Moussaoui trial (aka circus)

You will understand that statements of the (supposed) mastermind of
9/11 are relevant to decide what exactly Ramzi knew (or didn't know).

Take (into) account that the United (States government) [REDACTED]
has falsely claimed that Ramzi implicated me in 9/11 its obvious that
(these) statements of Mohammed (which) contradict this Ashcroft lie are
essential in deciding whether I should cross examine Ramzi to establish
my no 9/11 status. The indictment claimed that Ramzi sent me money
from Mustafa to be trained like the (other) 9/11 hijackers. (The)
statements of Mohammed and Mustafa will force this court to admit that
the United (States government) [REDACTED] brief on why they refuse
access to Ramzi is a pack of lies. Ashcroft knows that Ramzi,
Mohammed and Mustafa will all say that I was not the 20th hijacker.

PS [REDACTED]

continued on next page

Action: this court must reverse the March 28/03 order of Lieonie Brinkema, where she "denied" without prejudice access to Mohammed.

This court shall halt current proceedings until this Mohammed statement (is turned) over. Provide (it) to me, so I can include in my brief to destroy (the lies of) Ashcroft. The same for Brother Mustafa. You must force your master to give me a copy of their brief to you or Ramzi.

[REDACTED] Top Mohammed, (supposed) mastermind of the 9/11, has declare that I was not part of (the September 11 plot)—see Moussaoui said not to be part of 9/11 plot, *Washington Post* 28 March and Is Moussaoui Small Fry, CBS News, March 18. Ashcroft fabricated inculpatory statement of Ramzi must be shot out of the court as another (pack of) Ashcroft lies.

This court is well aware that the so-called first law officer has far more than you. You declare that I, Zacarias Moussaoui was the 20th hijacker. There, due to the evidence of the case they intended to sell (to the public) a new 5th plane theory on the understanding that Ramzi and Mohammed [REDACTED STATEMENT] are kept out of the *Show* trial.

(The) Mohammed statements expose Ashcroft no faith in manipulating Ramzi access and statement. Ashcroft wants "Silence," so he can kill Zacarias Moussaoui. The problem, *I am not a lamb, so I will fight.* [REDACTED STATEMENT]

[REDACTED STATEMENT]

Sensured by [REDACTED STATEMENT]

4 April 03

Ashcroft political sensure of the truth

Motion to oppose politically motivated reduction of my motion that exposes Ashcroft manipulation of the case and his attempt to silence Mohammed's statement of Zacarias Moussaoui nonparticipation to the (September 11th attacks) [REDACTED STATEMENT].

[REDACTED]

It was obvious that the SAM [REDACTED STATEMENT] was the means for Ashcroft to sensure politically embarrassing information. Nothing can illustrate more the desperation of Ashcroft when he try to redact a passage on my pleading to get access to (the) Mohammed exculpatory statement. Ashcroft falsely claimed that page three contained statements that are threats against the United States. In fact, Ashcroft should say that they are threat to his political career with a pathetic 20th hijacker theory destroyed by Mohammed and a 5th Plane theory hitting the White House that still has to take off.

The passage in question is as follows [REDACTED PASSAGE]

So as anybody can read there is no threat whatsoever (except of course for Ashcroft's political life; this passage entirely relates to the issue in discussion and must not redact a single word/you can add "e" to Appal if you are touchy)

[REDACTED STATEMENT]

In the Name of God

Sensured by United Sodom of America

April 19, 2003   17 Safar 1423

Slave of God   Slave of Satan
Zacarias Moussaoui   Bush and Ashcroft

5th plane pilot missing on appeal

Emergency strike to force Arch-liar Ashcroft to disclose and unredact
his delirious new 5th plane pilot missing-in-action as briefed to his
Court of Appall.

[REDACTED STATEMENT]

The 5th Plane pilot has gone missing again in the redacted copy of
Ashcroft brief to the Court of Appeal that he sent to Zacarias Moussaoui.

Death Judge Leonie was talking about "inconsistent position regarding
the classifications status of its theory of the case."

Leonie, you don't get the point, its not inconsistent, it is incompetent.

Death Judge, there cannot be any discussion on "substitution" when I
don't know what they want to substitute in the first place. So, you must
send this coupon to Ashcroft

9/11 Lottery Case
20th Hijacker   ❏
5th Plane Pilot Missing in Action   ❏
I, Ashcroft don't know   ❏
Lets kill him anyway   ❏

1st Prize: 1st class seat at Zacarias Moussaoui execution (only joking, it
is not going to happen, [REDACTED STATEMENT])

Slave of God

In the Name of God

Sensured by United Sodom of America

April 13, 03

Slave of God   Slave of Satan
Zacarias Moussaoui   Bush & Ashcroft

Dismiss Ashcroft case

Emergency strike to force Ashcroft to show his ultimate fantasies theory
and to throw out Ashcroft case.

Ashcroft dementia must be stopped. I, Zacarias Moussaoui, must "be
informed of the nature and cause of the accusation" (6th amendment).

I cannot fight an invisible 5th plane.

Nothing in the indictment suggest even remotely the existence of a 5th
plane striking the Dark House (are we still talking about 9/11?).

Everybody knows that Ashcroft wrote this indictment with his 20th
hijacker delirious theory in mind (if he has any of course).

I must know what is the Ashcroft Dementia Theory

Death Judge, you must force Ashcroft to tick the box.

20th Hijacker	❏
5th PLANE to Dark House	❏
I, Ashcroft don't know	❏
Let's just kill him	❏

So again Lieonie I want to know what are the charges and how they are
going to prove it. I know it already. By *lying*? (hearing now a must)

Slave of God

[REDACTED STATEMENT]

Sensured by United (Sodom) of America

April 21, 03

5th plane must land on Moussaoui runway

[REDACTED] at the court of Appall to force *"un-con-petent"* Ashcroft
(English translation incompetent) to disclose the *5th plane pilot missing
in action* briefed to deceive the Court of Appall.

[REDACTED STATEMENT]

The 5th Plane has gone missing again in the redacted briefed of the
Court of Appall given by *in con petent Ashcroft.*

You, [REDACTED] must order your chief officer of the Law to disclose
to Zacarias Moussaoui their 5th plane theory contained in the Appeal
Brief.

Death Judge talked about "inconsistent position regarding the
classifications status of its theory of the case."

In fact, Leonie should talk of incompetent Ashcroft. After the 20th
hijacker, now the 5th plane has gone missing in the Twilight Zone. But
make no mistake Ashcroft will come to understand that 9/11 is
[REDACTED STATEMENT]

In the meantime, I, Zacarias Moussaoui, must be provided with a copy
of the brief to the Court of Appall that retain at least the essence of
Ashcroft persecution dimension theory.

[REDACTED STATEMENT]

[REDACTED STATEMENT]

Sensored [REDACTED] by States.

April 22, 03

Zacarias Moussaoui   vs   Bush and Ashcroft

Lieonie must give due consideration to mastermind 9/11 Sheik Mohammed!!!

[REDACTED] at the court appall to force death judge Leonie Brinkema to give *due reconsideration to* (supposed) *mastermind 9/11 Sheik Mohammed exculpatory statements that were hidden by the delirious Ashcroft at the January 30 hearing on access to Ramzi at trial for Zacarias Moussaoui.*

Oh you! You must order (Death Judge) Brinkema to reconsider entirely the access to Ramzi.

Mastermind 9/11 Mohammed statement that I, Zacarias Moussaoui, was not part of 9/11 Super Operation must be given proper consideration.

In her order, Leonie claim that she has been divested of her authority to reconsider the same issue (April 21, 03) *a lot of nonsense* as she secretly propose to her [REDACTED] government to file a motion of reconsideration if Ashcroft "believe that the substance is sufficiently material to *alter* the courts original ruling" (March 14, 03) Clearly, Leonie was not divested to kill me, indeed, she has vested interest in seeing Zacarias Moussaoui dead. But as I say, [REDACTED STATEMENT].

What is the government trying to hide?

Bibliography

Borchsenius, P. 1963. *The Three Rings. The History of the Spanish Jews.* London: George Allen & Unwin, Ltd.

Bramford, J. 2001. *Body of Secrets.* New York: Random House.

Bremer, L. 1984. *The Iron Wall: Zionist Revisionism from Jabotinsky to Shamir.* London: Zed Books.

Burns, Lt.-Gen. E.L.M. 1962. *Between Arab and Israeli.* Toronto: Clarke, Irwin, & Co.

Byng, E. J. 1944. *The World of the Arabs.* Boston: Little, Brown, & Co.

Clark, R. (ed). 1998. *Challenge to Genocide.* New York: International Action Center.

CNN.com/Transcript. June 23, 2002. Larry King Weekend. Interview with Aicha El-Wafi (regarding Zacharias Moussaoui).

Emerson, G. 1991. *GAZA.* New York: Atlantic Monthly Press.

Garaudy, R. *The Case of Israel: A Study of Political Zionism.*

Glubb, Sir John. 1969. *A Short History of the Arab Peoples.* New York: Dorsett Press.

Golan, Matti. 1976. *The Secret Conversations of Henry Kissinger.* New York Times Book Co.

Hill, W. L. 1961. *The Fall and Rise of Israel*. Grand Rapids, MI: Zondervan Publ.

Hufschmid, E. 2002. *Painful Questions: An Analysis of the September 11th Attack*. Goleta, CA: Endpoint Software.

Hyamson, A. M. (ed). 1971. *The Transformation of Palestine*. Evanston, IL: Northwestern University Press.

Hyamson, A. M. 1942. *Palestine: A Policy*. London: Metheun & Co.

Katz, S.M. 1992. *Soldier Spies*. õvato, CA: Presideo Press

Kayal, A. D. 2002. *The Control of Oil*. London: Kegan-Paul.

Keay, John. 2003. *Sowing the Wind: Seeds of Conflict in the Middle East.* New York: W. W. Norton & Co.

Landau, Rom. 1958. *Islam and the Arabs*. London: George Allen.

Longman, Jere. 2002. *Among the Heroes*. New York: HarperCollins.

Luttwak, E. and D. Horowitz. 1975. *The Israeli Army*. London: Allen Lane.

Manuel, F. E. 1949. *The Realities of American-Palestine Relations.* Washington, D.C: Public Affairs Press.

Muir, Sir William. 1898. *The Caliphate: Its Rise and Fall.* London: Smith, Elder, & Co.

Ovendale, R. 1984. *The Arab-Israeli Wars*. New York: Longman.

Pastor, R. A. 1987. *Condemned to Repetition: The United States and Nicaragua.* New Jersey: Princeton University Press.

Pastore, Albert D. 2005. *Stranger Than Fiction.*

Pollack, E. 2004. The Jewish Shah. In: *Explorations in Nonfiction.* Vol. 6(2): 49-65.

Prouty, F. 1974. *The Secret Team.* New York: Ballentine Books.

Ray, E. and W. H. Schaap (ed). 2003. *Covert Action: The Roots of Terrorism.* Australia: Ocean Press.

Rafizadeh, M. 1987. *Witness: From the Shah to the Secret Arms Deal, an Insider's Account of U.S. Involvement in Iran.* New York: W. M. Morrow & Co.

Reavis, D. J. 1995. *The Ashes of Waco: An Investigation.* New York: Simon & Schuster.

Sachar, A. L. 1967. *A History of the Jews.* New York: A. Knopf.

Saikal, A. 1980. *The Rise and Fall of the Shah.* Princeton, NJ: Princeton Univ. Press.

Schmidt, Dana. 1974. *Armageddon in the Middle East.* New York: John Day & Co.

Schroeder, E. 1955. *Muhammad's People.* Portland, ME: The Bond WheelWright Co.

Shawcross, W. 1988. *The Shah's Last Ride: The Fate of an Ally.* New York: Simon and Schuster.

Shoenman, R. 1988. *The Hidden History of Zionism.* Veritas Press.

Seal, P. 1992. *Gun for Hire.* New York: Random House.

Sutton, A. C. 1976. *Wall Street and the Rise of Hitler.* Seal Beach, CA: '76 Press.

Sykes, Christopher. 1965. *Crossroads to Israel.* London: Collins.

Wright, Robin. 1986. *Sacred Rage.* New York: Touchstone Books

Index